Reported Incidences of Parasitic Infections in Marine Mammals from 1892 to 1978

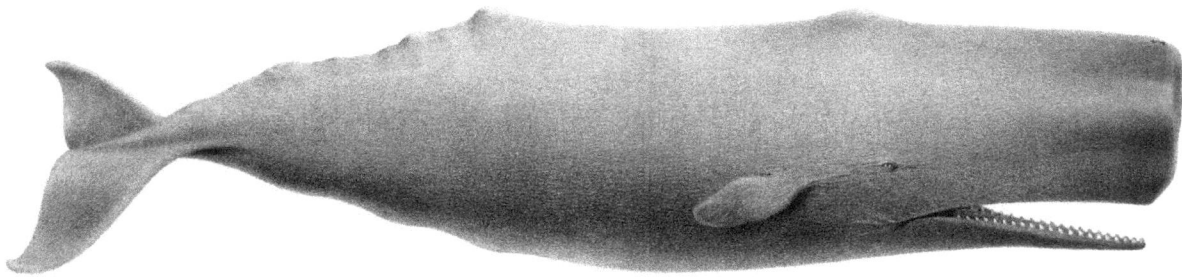

John R. Felix

Zea Books
Lincoln, Nebraska 2013

ISBN 978-1-60962-042-4   paperback
ISBN 978-1-60962-043-1   ebook

Set in Palatino Linotype types.
Design and composition by Paul Royster.

Zea Books are published by the University of Nebraska–Lincoln Libraries

Electronic (pdf) edition available online at
http://digitalcommons.unl.edu/zeabook/

Print edition can be ordered from Lulu.com, at
http://www.lulu.com/spotlight/unllib

Contents

Acknowledgments

I would like to acknowledge my indebtedness to Dr. Sea Rogers Williams VMD, of the National Marine Life Center for providing the descriptive narratives of each of the categories of parasites presented in this bibliography. I also thank Dr. Williams for his valuable comments and suggestions on earlier drafts of this manuscript. I also wish to express my sincere gratitude to Mary Sears of Harvard University's Ernst Mayr Library for her unwavering assistance in helping me track down many of the unwonted reference documents cited in the book. I also would like to thank Dr. Paul Royster and the Office of Scholarly Communication at the University of Nebraska-Lincoln Libraries for format suggestions, cover design, and ultimately agreeing to publish this unorthodox-style reference book. Finally, I would like to thank my wife Gayle for all her support (and patience) during the many years it took to complete this book.

J.R.F.

Introduction

A study of parasites from marine mammals is a fascinating endeavor used to assess animal and environmental heath, as well as document biodiversity, biogeography, marine biology, and basic taxonomic science. A wealth of information can be obtained from understanding the life cycle of marine parasites and their interactions with marine mammals; whose domain include all the seas of the world. The evolutionary history of parasites residing in animals that have returned to oceans is also instructive as to which parasites were carried along with their hosts, and which ones remained in the water and were able to capitalize on the host's return.

All marine mammals are protected by the Marine Mammal Protection Act (MMPA). Consequently when these animals strand or beach themselves they are of interest for either rehabilitation or scientific study. The investigation of parasites from these events can be hindered by a lack of identification, training, or understanding of the parasites encountered by stranding response personnel. The role these parasites play in the health of their host and in stranding events is complicated and has been scrutinized by stranding biologists for decades. Most, if not all, marine mammal will have parasites, but only in select cases will their infestations have played a role in the stranding event, although they will always provide information on the travels and natural history of their host.

In order to separate which parasite infestations influence stranding events or are health concerns, their specific identity must be known. The first step in this endeavor is to review what has been reported in the scientific literature. This data is divided among the primary taxonomic literature from the 1800-1900's, and the basic biology and biomedical literature to the present day. Unfortunately even modern and powerful databases are often skewed to either the basic biology or biomedical literature, and may not index the classical information, and thus a comprehensive search can be time-consuming. In addition, the primary literature can be difficult to obtain and comes in a multitude of languages, much of which has never been translated to English. Previous attempts to review the parasites of marine mammals are instructive but are not complete, in need of updating due to rapid increase in the description of new parasites and improved understanding of the evolutional history of the parasites themselves (Dailey and Brownell, 1972), or limited to particular hosts (Baylis, 1932), (Delyamure, 1955), (Tomilin, 1957), (King, 1964) or parasite taxons (Price, 1932). Using these lists and other published literature to gain a better understanding of infection prevalence and geographical distribution of marine mammal parasites is sometimes difficult since the published lists and literature frequently do not contain detail information about accepted (or suspected) taxonomic synonyms and geographical information about the host and/or parasite.

This document presents an updated and more complete checklist of reported parasites from marine mammals based on literature published between the late 1800's and 1978. Over the past 35 years, published accounts of marine mammal parasitic infections tend to be more readily available and complete.

The format used to present this information is different than previously published checklists. The information presented in the main checklist is supported by appendices denoting the source of information, geographical location of the host/parasite (if known), and possible synonyms the original sources opine for the various parasites. Occasionally, additional information is presented in brief "Remarks". In many cases, the same incident of parasitic infection and/or species synonym is noted by more than one investigator. In such cases, the incident information and/or synonyms are repeated since this may suggest the author agrees (or is at least accepting) the finding or opinion of the original investigator.

With the advent of molecular techniques, global efforts to "barcode" all species, and the addition of newly described species, the state of marine mammal parasitology is in the mist of a flurry of scientific study, but it is from within this cloud that we attempt to provide a resource for stranding response personnel, aquatic animal veterinarians, marine biologists, and professional parasitologists to aid our understanding of these intriguing interactions.

Acanthocephala

Thorny-headed worms or acanthlocephalins are common in seal intestines and found occasionally in dolphins and whales. Their barbed attachment organ, called a proboscis, can penetrate the intestine causing peritonitis and severe disease. There are no known chemotherapeutics that are effective against these parasites. *Corynosoma* from seals, and occasionally dolphins, and *Bolbosoma* from whales are typical examples and, with one exception (*Echinorhynchus*) the only two genera represented in marine mammals.

Their life cycle involves marine invertebrates and often a fish parentic host. Fish eating birds can also be infected, and infections in humans are very rare and likely come from ingestion of intermediate hosts.

Bolbosoma sp.

Hosts and Locality:

From Baylis, 1932 - Found in the whale *Balaenoptera velifera* " [? = *B. physalus* (sic)]". Information regarding the geographical location of hosts was not provided by author.

From Beverley-Burton, 1978 - Found in the Atlantic white-sided dolphin (*Lagenorhynchus acutus*) from Lingley Cove, Edmunds, Maine.

From Margolis and Dailey, 1972 - Found in the sei whale (*Balaenoptera borealis*), the blue whale (*Balaenoptera musculus*), and in the humpback whale (*Megaptera novaengliae*). All hosts were from California.

From Rice, 1963 - Found in the sei whale (*Balaenoptera borealis*), the blue whale (*Balaenoptera musculus*), and in the humpback whale (*Megaptera novaengliae*). All hosts were from the California coast.

Bolbosoma aurantiacum

Synonymy:

From Baylis, 1932 - *Echinorhynchus aurantiacus* Risso, 1826; *Echinorhynchus annulatus* Molin, 1851; *Echinorhynchus bifasciatus* Lühe, 1904; (? sic) *Echinorhynchus pellucidus* Leuckart, 1828; *Echinorhynchus serrani* Linton, 1901; *Bolborhynchus aurantiacus* Porta, 1907.

From Delyamure, 1955 - *Bolbosoma vasculosum*.

Hosts and Locality:

From Baylis, 1932 - Found in the common dolphin (*Delphinus delphis*) and in the Sowerby's whale (*Mesoplodon bidens*). Information regarding the geographical location of hosts was not provided by author.

Bolbosoma balaenae

Synonymy:

From Delyamure, 1955 - *Sipunculus lendix* Phipps, 1774; *Echinorhynchus balaena* Gmelin, 1790; *Echinorhynchus* Rudolphi, 1819; *Bolborhynchus porrigens* Porta, 1906; *Bolbosoma porrigens* Porta, 1908.

From Yamaguti, 1963 - *Echinorhynchus mysticeti* Ben., 1870.

Hosts and Locality:

From Dailey and Brownell, 1972 - Found in the northern bottlenosed whale (*Hyperoodon ampullatus*), the piked whale (*Balaenoptera acutorustrata*), the sei whale (*Balaenoptera borealis*), the fin whale (*Balaenoptera physalus*), the blue whale (*Balaenoptera musculus*), the humpback whale (*Megaptera novaengliae*), and in the Greenland right whale (*Balaena mysticetus*). Information regarding the geographical location of hosts was not provided by authors. See Remarks

From Dailey and Perrin, 1973 - Found in the long beaked dolphins (*Stenella longirostris*)

taken at Lat. 12° 51′ N, Long. 93° 18′ W.; Lat. 7° 11′ N, Long. 90° 32′ W.; Lat. Approx. 8° 51′ N, Long. 107° 18′ W. (eastern Pacific Ocean). Also found in the Eastern Pacific spotted dolphin (*Stenella graffmani*) from the following locations: Lat. 12° 51′ N, Long. 93° 18′ W.; Lat. 7° 11′ N, Long. 90° 32′ W.; and Lat. 14° 30′ N, Long. 99°10′ W.

From Delyamure, 1955 - Found in the sei whale (*Balaenoptera borealis*), the blue whale (*Balaenoptera musculus*), the Greenland whale (*Balaenoptera mysticetus*), the fin whale (*Balaenoptera physalus*), the piked whale (*Balaenoptera acutorustrata*), the humpback whale (*Megaptera nodosa*), and the bottlenosed whale (*Hyperoodon ampullatus*). Geographical distribution includes the Atlantic Ocean (Iceland), and the Tasman Sea (near Sidney, Australia).

From Margolis and Dailey, 1972 - Found in an unidentified whale from Washington.

From Van Cleave, 1953 - Found in an "unidentified whale" from Seattle, Washington in 1918. See Remarks.

Remarks:

The specimen taken from an "unidentified whale" was examined by Van Cleave (1953). It differed slightly from the description of *B. balaenae* accepted by other, including Van Cleave. However, Van Cleave did not feel the difference warranted the naming of a new genus or species.

Dailey and Brownell (1972) listing of this parasite under the Greenland Right Whale (*Balaena mysticetus*) is referenced to Baylis (1932). Baylis identifies this parasite as *Bolbosoma porrigens*.

Bolbosoma bobrovi

Hosts and Locality:

From Dailey and Brownell, 1972 - Found in the Steller sea lion (*Eumetopias jubatus*) and in the northern fur seal (*Callorhinus ursinus*). Information regarding the geographical location of hosts was not provided by authors.

From Delyamure, 1955 - Found in the Steller sea lion (*Eumetopias jubatus*) and the north-

ern fur seal (*Callorhinus ursinus*). Geographical distribution for both hosts includes the Sea of Okhotsk (Tyuleni Island).

From King, 1964 - Found in the northern fur seal (*Callorhinus ursinus*) and in the Steller sea lion (*Eumetopias jubatus*). Information regarding the geographical location of hosts was not provided by author.

Bolbosoma brevicolle

Synonymy:

From Baylis, 1932 - *Echinorhynchus brevicollis* Malm, 1867; *Bolborhynchus brevicollis* Porta, 1908;

From Delyamure, 1955 - *Echinorhynchus brevicollis* Malm, 1867; *Bolborhynchus brevicollis* Porta, 1908; *Bolborhynchus brevicolle* Porta, 1908.

Hosts and Locality:

From Baylis, 1929 - Found in the fin whale (*Balaenoptera physalus*) from Saldanha Bay, and in the blue whale (*Balaenoptera musculus*) from Durban and Saldanha Bay (South Africa and South Georgia).

From Baylis, 1932 - Found in the piked whale (*Balaenoptera acutorustrata*), the sei whale (*Balaenoptera borealis*), the blue whale (*Balaenoptera musculus*), the fin whale (*Balaenoptera physalus*), and in the sperm whale (*Physeter catodon*). Information regarding the geographical location of hosts was not provided by author.

From Dailey and Brownell, 1972 - Found in the sperm whale (*Physeter catodon*), the little piked whale (*Balaenoptera acutorustrata*), the sei whale (*Balaenoptera borealis*), the fin whale (*Balaenoptera physalus*), the blue whale (*Balaenoptera musculus*), and in the black right whale (*Eubalaena glacialis*). Information regarding the geographical location of hosts was not provided by authors.

From Delyamure, 1955 - Found in the sei whale (*Balaenoptera borealis*), the blue whale (*Balaenoptera musculus*), the fin whale (*Balaenoptera physalus*), the piked whale (*Balaenoptera acutorustrata*), the black right whale (*Eubalaena glacialis*), and the sperm whale

(*Physeter catodon*). Geographical distribution includes the North Atlantic Ocean, and the coast of southern Africa and Georgia.

From Edmonds, 1957 - Found in the blue whale (*Balaenoptera musculus*) from Saldanha Bay, South Africa.

Bolbosoma capitatum

Synonymy:

From Baylis, 1932 - *Echinorhynchus capitatus* Linstow, 1880; *Bolborhynchus capitatus* Porta, 1908; (? sic) *Echinorhynchus vasculosus* Rudolphi, 1819.

From Delyamure, 1955 - *Echinorhynchus capitatus* Linstow, 1880; *Bolbosoma capitatum* Porta, 1908.

Hosts and Locality:

From Baylis, 1929 - Found in the slender-beaked dolphin (*Steno bredanensis*) from the west coast of Africa (near Cape Verde).

From Baylis, 1932 - Found in the pilot whale (*Globicephala melaena*), the sperm whale (*Physeter catodon*), the false killer whale (*Pseudorca crassidens*), and in the dolphin (*Steno rostratus*). Information regarding the geographical location of hosts was not provided by author.

From Dailey and Brownell, 1972 - Found in the false killer whale (*Pseudorca crassidens*), the sperm whale (*Physeter catodon*), and in the North Atlantic pilot whale (*Globicephala melaena*). Information regarding the geographical location of host was not provided by authors.

From Delyamure, 1955 - Found in the sperm whale (*Physeter catodon*), the slender-beaked dolphin (*Steno rostratus*) [= *Steno bredanensis*], the false killer whale (*Pseudorca crassidens*), and the pilot whale (*Globicephalus melas*). Geographical distribution includes the Atlantic Ocean and the Mediterranean Sea.

From Yamaguti, 1963 - Found in the pilot whale (*Globicephalus melas*) and the false killer whale (*Pseudorca crassidens*) from the Mediterranean Sea and Atlantic Ocean; the slender-beaked dolphin (*Steno bredanen-*

sis) from Kapverden; the pilot whale (*Globicephalus melas*) from south Australia; and in the pilot whale (*Globicephalus svineval*). See Remarks.

Remarks:

Although Yamaguti (1963) lists the pilot whale (*Globicephalus svineval*) as a host of this parasite, Delyamure (1955) reports *G. svineval* is synonymous with *Globicephalus melas*.

Bolbosoma hamiltoni

Hosts and Locality:

From Baylis, 1929 - Found in the blue whale (*Balaenoptera musculus*) and in the fin whale (*Balaenoptera physalus*) from the Atlantic Ocean (off southern Georgia).

From Baylis, 1932 - Found in the blue whale (*Balaenoptera musculus*) and the fin whale (*Balaenoptera physalus*). Information regarding the geographical location of hosts not was provided by author.

From Dailey and Brownell, 1972 - Found in the fin whale (*Balaenoptera physalus*) and the blue whale (*Balaenoptera musculus*). Information regarding the geographical location of hosts was not provided by authors.

From Yamaguti, 1963 - Found in the blue whale (*Balaenoptera musculus*) and in the fin whale (*Balaenoptera physalus*) from South Georgia and the Ross Sea.

Bolbosoma nipponicum

Hosts and Locality:

From Delyamure, 1955 - Found in the Kurile fur seal (*Callorhynus ursinus curilensis*), the Okhotsk ringed seal (*Phoca hispida okhotensis*), the sei whale (*Balaenoptera borealis*), the piked whale (*Balaenoptera acutorustrata*), and the fin whale (*Balaenoptera physalus*). Geographical distribution includes the Pacific Ocean (near the Kurile Island region and near the coast of Japan), and the Sea of Okhotsk (Tyuleni Island).

From Dailey and Brownell, 1972 - Found in

the ringed seal (*Phoca hispida*), the northern fur seal (*Callorhinus ursinus*), the sei whale (*Balaenoptera borealis*), the fin whale (*Balaenoptera physalus*), and in the little piked whale (*Balaenoptera acutorustrata*). Information regarding the geographical location of hosts was not provided by authors.

From King, 1964 - Found in the ringed seal (*Phoca hispida*) and in the northern fur seal (*Callorhinus ursinus*). Information regarding the geographical location of hosts was not provided by author.

From Yamaguti, 1939 - Found in the piked whale (*Balaenoptera rostrata*) from the "Pacific".

From Yamaguti, 1963 - Found in the piked whale (*Balaenoptera rostrata*) [= *Balaenoptera acutorostrata*] from Japan; the piked whale (*Balaenoptera acutorustrata*), the sei whale (*Balaenoptera borealis*), the fin whale (*Balaenoptera physalus*), the Okhotsk ringed seal (*Phoca hispida okhotensis*), and the Kurile fur seal (*Callorhynus ursinus curilensis*) from the Kurile Island region.

Bolbosoma pellucidum

Synonymy:

From Baylis, 1932- *Echinorhynchus pellucidus* Leuckart, 1828; *Bolborhynchus pellucidus* Porta, 1906.

Hosts and Locality:

From Baylis, 1932 - Found in the common dolphin (*Delphinus delphis*) and in the Sowerby's whale (*Mesoplodon bidens*). Information regarding the geographical location of hosts was not provided by author.

Bolbosoma physeteris

Hosts and Locality:

From Dailey and Brownell, 1972 - Found in the sperm whale (*Physeter catodon*). Information regarding the geographical location of host was not provided by authors.

From Delyamure, 1955 - Found in the sperm whale (*Physeter catodon*) and in the killer whale (*Orca orca*). Geographical distribution

includes the Sea of Okhotsk, and the Pacific Ocean (Kurile Islands region).

Bolbosoma porrigens

Synonymy:

From Delyamure, 1955 - *Echinorhynchus balaena* Gmelin, 1790; *Echinorhynchus porrigens* Rudolphi, 1814; *Bolborhynchus porrigens* Porta, 1906.

Hosts and Locality:

From Baylis, 1932 - Found in the bowhead or arctic right whale (*Balaena mysticetus*), the piked whale (*Balaenoptera acutorustrata*), the sei whale (*Balaenoptera borealis*), the blue whale (*Balaenoptera musculus*), and the humpback whale (*Megaptera nodosa*). Information regarding the geographical location of hosts was not provided by author.

From Delyamure, 1955 - Found in the sei whale (*Balaenoptera borealis*), the blue whale (*Balaenoptera musculus*), the Greenland whale (*Balaenoptera mysticetus*), the fin whale (*Balaenoptera physalus*), the piked whale (*Balaenoptera acutorustrata*), the humpback whale (*Megaptera nodosa*), and the bottlenosed whale (*Hyperoodon ampullatus*). Geographical distribution includes the Atlantic Ocean (Iceland), and the Tasman Sea (near Sidney, Australia).

From Johnston and Deland, 1929 - Found in a whale ("probably" *Megaptera nodosa*) that washed up at Bondi, NSW.

Bolbosoma turbinella

Synonymy:

From Baylis, 1932 - *Echinorhynchus turbinella* Diesing, 1851; *Echinorhynchus ruber* Collett, 1886; *Echinorhynchus porrigens* of Kaiseer, 1893; *Bolborhynchus turbinella* Porta, 1908; *Pomphorhynchus turbinella* Leiper and Atkinson, 1915.

From Delyamure, 1955 - *Echinorhynchus balaenocephalus* Owen, 1803; *Echinorhynchus turbinella* Diesing, 1851; *Echinorhynchus ruber* Collett, 1866; *Bolborhynchus turbinella porrigens* Porta, 1908; *Pomphorhynchus* (Diesing) Porta, by Leiper and Atkinson, 1915. See Remarks.

Hosts and Locality:

From Baylis, 1929 - Found in the sei whale (*Balaenoptera borealis*) from the Antarctic Ocean (Durban, Saldanah Bay, and South Georgia).

From Baylis, 1932 - Found in the the sei whale (*Balaenoptera borealis*), the blue whale (*Balaenoptera musculus*), the humpback whale (*Megaptera nodosa*), and in the bottlenosed whale (*Hyperoodon rostratus*). Information regarding the geographical location of hosts was not provided by author.

From Dailey and Brownell, 1972 - Found in the black right whale (*Eubalaena glacialis*), the sei whale (*Balaenoptera borealis*), the fin whale (Balaenoptera physalus), the blue whale (*Balaenoptera musculus*), the humpback whale (*Megaptera novaengliae*), and in the northern bottlenosed whale (*Hyperoodon ampullatus*). Information regarding the geographical location of hosts was not provided by authors. See Remarks.

From Delyamure, 1955 - Found in the sei whale (*Balaenoptera borealis*), the blue whale (*Balaenoptera musculus*), the true right whale (*Eubalaena glacialis sieboldi*), the fin whale (*Balaenoptera physalus*), the piked whale (*Balaenoptera acutorustrata*), and the humpback whale (*Megaptera novaengliae*). Geographical distribution includes the Atlantic and Pacific Oceans (northern and southern hemispheres); the Sea of Okhotsk; and New Zealand.

From Fukui and Morisita, 1939 - Found in the sei whale (*Balaenoptera borealis*) from Japan. See Remarks.

From Harada, 1931 - Found in the sei whale (*Balaenoptera borealis*) from the northern Pacific (near Japan).

From Margolis and Dailey, 1972 - Found in the sei whale (*Balaenoptera borealis*) from British Columbia.

From Margolis and Pike, 1955 - Found in the sei whale (*Balaenoptera borealis*) from British Columbia.

Remarks:

Yamaguti (1939) believes the specimen identified as *Bolbosoma turbinella* by Fukui and Morisita, 1939, was probably *Bolbosoma nipponcium*.

Unlike Delyamure (1955), Yamaguti (1963) concluded the *Pomphorhynchus turbinella* specimen taken from a humpback whale (*Megaptera novaengliae*) from New Zealand by Leiper and Atkinson (1915) is taxonomically different from *Bolbosoma turbinella*. He references this claim to Meyer (1933).

Dailey and Brownell reference Baylis (1932) in their listing of *Bolbosoma turbinella* in the northern bottlenosed whale (*Hyperoodon ampullatus*). Baylis notes the parasite was found in *Hyperoodon rostratus*. Dailey and Brownell also list *Bolbosoma turbinella* in the black right whale (*Eubalaena glacialis*) and list Delyamure (1955) as a source reference. Delyamure (1955) actually list this parasite under the true right whale (*Eubalaena glacialis sieboldi*).

Bolbosoma vasculosum

Synonymy:

From Delyamure, 1955 - *Echinorhynchus vasculosus* Rudolphi, 1819; *Echinorhynchus aurantiacus* Risso, 1826; *Echinorhynchus pellucidus* Leuckart, 1828; *Echinorhynchus annulatus* Molin, 1851; *Echinorhynchus serrani* Linton, 1888; *Echinorhynchus bifasciatus* Lühe, 1904; *Bolbosoma aurantiacum* (Risso, 1926) Van Cleave, 1924.

From Yamaguti, 1963 - *Bolbosoma thunni* Harada, 1935.

Hosts and Locality:

From Dailey and Brownell, 1972 - Found in the common dolphin (*Delphinus delphis*) and in the Sowerby's beaked whale (*Mesoplodon bidens*). Information regarding the geographical location of hosts was not provided by authors.

From Dailey and Perrin, 1973 - Found in the long beaked dolphins (*Stenella longirostris*) and the Eastern Pacific spotted dolphin (*Stenella graffmani*). Both species of hosts were taken from Lat. 12° 51′ N, Long. 93° 18′ W.; Lat. 7° 11′ N, Long. 90° 32′W.; Lat. Approx. 8° 51′ N, Long. 107° W.

From Delyamure, 1955 - Found in the common dolphin (*Delphinus delphis*) and in the Sowerby's whale (*Mesoplodon bidens*). Geographical distribution includes the Atlantic Ocean and the Mediterranean Sea.

From Van Cleave, 1953 - Found in the Sowerby's beaked whale (*Mesoplodon bidens*) from the Atlantic coast of North America (specific geographical location not provided by the original investigator, Leidy, 1890). Also found in the common dolphin (*Delphinus delphis*) from the Mediterranean Sea. See Remarks.

Remarks:

Van Cleave (1953) suggest that since no sexual mature individuals of this parasite have been discovered since the species was first described over a century ago, the normal definitive host has yet to be determined and *B. vasculosus* may be the immature stage of another species that matures in various whales. However, Yamaguti (1963) reports that adult stages have been found in the common dolphin (*Delphinus delphis*) as well as larval forms in a number of fish species.

Corynosoma sp.

Hosts and Locality:

From Baylis, 1932 - Found in the common dolphin (*Delphinus delphis*). Information regarding the geographical location of host was not provided by author.

From Dailey and Brownell, 1972 - Found in the gray whale (*Eschrichtius gibbosus*), the La Plata or Franciscana dolphin (*Pontoporia blainvillei*), the common dolphin (*Delphinus delphis*), the sea otter (*Enhydra lutris*), and in the northern elephant seal (*Mirounga angustirostris*). Information regarding geographical location of hosts was not provided by authors.

From Delyamure, 1955 - Found in the spotted dolphin (*Delphinus longirostris*) [=? sic *Delphinus delphis*, Rice and Scheffer, 1968] from the Pacific Ocean (Japan). Also found in the common dolphin (*Delphinus delphis*) from South Australia.

From Jellison and Neiland, 1965 - Found in the sea otter (*Enhydra lutris*) from Alaska.

From Johnston and Deland, 1929 - Found in the common dolphin (*Delphinus delphis*) from the Gulf St. Vincent, South Australia. See Remarks.

From Johnston and Edmonds, 1953 - Found in the seal *Otaria forster* (=? *Arctocephalus doriferus*) and in the leopard seal (*Hydrurga leptonyx*) from the Auckland and Cambell Islands regions.

From King, 1964 - Found in the northern elephant seal (*Mirounga angustirostris*), and in the Hawaiian monk seal (*Monachus schauinslandi*). Information regarding geographical location of hosts was not provided by author.

From Margolis and Dailey, 1972 - Found in the ringed seal (*Phoca hispida*) from Alaska.

From Matthews, 1937 - Found in the humpback whale (*Megaptera novaengliae*) [= *Megaptera nodosa*, Rice and Sheffer, 1968] from the Antarctic (Durban).

From Rausch, 1953 - Found in the sea otter (*Enhydra lutris*) from Amchitka (Alaska). See Remarks.

From Rausch and Locker, 1951- Found in the sea otter (*Enhydra lutris*) from Amchitka, Aleutian Islands (Alaska).

From Scheffer and Slipp, 1944 - Found in the harbor seal (*Phoca vitulina*) from Washington.

From Van Cleave, 1953 - Found in the ringed seal (*Phoca hispida*) from Payne Bay, Baffin Island, Clyde River, and Point Barrow (Alaska); the harbor seal (*Phoca vitulina*) from Lake Harbour, and Baffin Island; the Steller sea lion (*Eumetopias jubata*) from St. Paul Island (Alaska); a "spotted seal" from St. Lawrence Island (Alaska); and "unidentified seals" from St. Lawrence Island and Havre St. Pierre, Quebec. See Remarks.

From Young, 1939 - Found in the common dolphin (*Delphinus delphis*) from Australia.

Remarks:

Johnston and Deland (1929) noted the unidentified parasite species found in *Delphinus delphis* "resembl[ed] *C. strumosum*"

The unidentified species of *Corynosoma* that was taken by Rausch (1953) from the sea otter (*Enhydra lutris*) was later identified as *Corynosoma strumosum* by Schiller (1954).

Van Cleave (1953) also lists the sea otter (*Enhydra lutris*) as a host of an unidentified *Corynosoma sp*. However, the parasite was later identified as *Corynosoma enhydri* by Margolis and Dailey (1972).

Corynosoma alaskensis

Hosts and Locality:

From Dailey and Brownell, 1972 - Found in the harbor porpoise (*Phocoena phocoena*). Information regarding the geographical location of host was not provided by authors.

From Golvan, 1959 - Found in the harbor porpoise (*Phocoena phocoena*) from Hooper Bay, Alaska.

From Margolis and Dailey, 1972 - Found in the harbor porpoise (*Phocoena phocoena*) from Alaska.

Corynosoma antarcticum

Synonymy:

From Johnston and Best, 1937 - *Echinorhynchus antarcticum* Rennie 1907; *Corynosoma sipho* Railliet and Henry, 1907; *Corynosoma hamanni* Leiper and Atkinson 1915.

From Yamaguti, 1963 - *Corynosoma hamanni* Linstow, 1892; *Corynosoma sipho* Railliet and Henry, 1907.

Hosts and Locality:

From Dailey and Brownell, 1972 - Found in the Weddell seal (*Leptonychotes weddelli*). Information regarding the geographical location of host was not provided by authors.

From Johnston and Best, 1937 - Found in the Weddell seal (*Leptonychotes weddelli*) from the Antarctic.

From King, 1964 - Found in the Weddell seal (*Leptonychotes weddelli*). Information regarding the geographical location of host was

not provided by author.

From Rennie, J. 1905-1906 - If *Corynosoma antarcticum* = *Echinorhynchus antarcticus*, then found in the Weddell seal (*Leptonychotes weddelli*) from Scotia Bay, South Orkneys.

From Yamaguti, 1963 - Found in the Weddell seal (*Leptonychotes weddelli*), the crab-eating seal (*Lobodon carcinophagus*), and the leopard seal (*Hydrurga leptonyx*). All three host species were from Australia.

Corynosoma australe

Hosts and Locality:

From Dailey and Brownell, 1972 - Found in the South American sea lion (*Otaria byronia*), the leopard seal (*Hydrurga leptonyx*), and the Australian sea lion (*Neophoca cinerea*). Information regarding the geographical location of hosts was not provided by authors.

From Johnston, 1937e - Found in the Australian sea lion (*Neophoca cinerea*) from Pearson Island. See Remarks.

From Johnston and Deland, 1929 - Erroneously reported to be found in the Australian hair seal (*Arctocephalus forsteri*) from Pearson Island, South Australia. See Remarks.

From Johnston and Edmonds, 1953 - Found in the leopard seal (*Hydrurga leptonyx*) and the Hooker's sea lion (*Otaria hookeri*). Both hosts were from the Antarctic (Auckland Islands and Cambell Islands).

From King, 1964 - Found in the leopard seal (*Hydrurga leptonyx*), the Australian fur seal (*Arctocephalus doriferus*), and the Australian sea lion (*Neophoca cinerea*). Information regarding the geographical location of hosts was not provided by author.

Remarks:

The original description of this parasite is found in the Johnston (1937e) paper. Johnston (1937e) originally described this parasite from the South Australian hair seal, incorrectly identified as *Arctocephalus forsteri*. In a later paper (Johnston and Best, 1942), Johnston corrected this mistake and identified the correct host as *Neophoca cinerea*.

Corynosoma bullosum

Synonymy:

From Delyamure, 1955 - *Echinorhynchus bullosum* Linstow, 1892.

Hosts and Locality:

From Baylis, 1929 - Found in the crab-eating seal (*Lobodon carcinophagus*) from Palmer Archipelago (between Anvers Island and Graham's Land).

From Dailey and Brownell, 1972 - Found in the hooded seal (*Cystophora cristata*), the crab-eating seal (*Lobodon carcinophagus*), and in the southern elephant seal (*Mirounga leonina*). Information regarding the geographical location of hosts was not provided by authors.

From Delyamure, 1955 - Found in the crab-eating seal (*Lobodon carcinophagus*), and in the southern elephant seal (*Mirounga leonina*). Geographical distribution includes the Antarctic (Graham's Land, Anvers Land, and other points).

From Edmonds, 1955 - Found in the southern elephant seal (*Mirounga leonina*) from Heard Island and Macquarie Island (Antarctica).

From Edmonds, 1957 - Found in the sea lion (*Mirounga leonina*) from Heard Island and Crozet Islands (Antarctica).

From Johnston and Edmonds, 1953 - Found in the southern elephant seal (*Mirounga leonina*) from the Auckland and Cambell Islands region (Antarctica).

From King, 1964 - Found in the crab-eating seal (*Lobodon carcinophagus*), the hooded seal (*Cystophora cristata*) and in the southern elephant seal (*Mirounga leonina*). Information regarding geographical location of hosts was not provided by author.

From Yamaguti, 1963 - Found in the crab-eating seal (*Lobodon carcinophagus*) from South Georgia and Graham's Islands (Antarctica).

Corynosoma cameroni

Synonymy:

See Remarks

Hosts and Locality:

From Dailey and Brownell, 1972 - Found in the beluga white whale (*Delphinapterus leucas*). Information regarding the geographical location of host was not provided by authors.

From Van Cleave, 1953 - Found in the beluga white whale (*Delphinapterus leucas*) from the Gulf of St. Lawrence, Quebec, Canada.

Remarks:

Van Cleave (1953) re-identified some parasites taken from the white whale (*Delphinapterus leucas*) as *Corynosoma cameroni* that Lyster (1940) had originally identified as *Corynosoma strumosum*.

Corynosoma cetaceum

Synonymy:

From Yamaguti, 1963 - Synonymous with *Corynosoma sp.* of Johnston and Deland, 1929.

Hosts and Locality:

From Dailey and Brownell, 1972 - Found in the bottlenosed dolphin (*Tursiops truncatus*) and in the common dolphin (*Delphinus delphis*). Information regarding the geographical location of hosts was not provided by authors.

From Delyamure, 1955 - Found in the bottlenosed dolphin (*Tursiops truncatus*) and in the common dolphin (*Delphinus delphis*). Geographical distribution of the parasite is Australia.

From Johnston and Best, 1942 - Found in the bottlenosed dolphin (*Tursiops truncatus*) from Port Lincoln (South Australia) and in the common dolphin (*Delphinus delphis*) from St. Vincent Gulf (South Australia).

From Yamaguti, 1963 - Found in the bottlenosed dolphin (*Tursiops truncatus*) and the common dolphin (*Delphinus delphis*). Both host species were from Australia.

Corynosoma clavatum

Synonymy:

From Johnston and Best, 1942 - *Polymorphus clavatus* Goss, 1940.

Hosts and Locality:

From Dailey and Brownell, 1972 - Found in the walrus (*Odobenus rosmarus*) and in the leopard seal (*Hydruga leptonyx*). Information regarding the geographical location of hosts was not provided by authors. See Remarks.

From Johnston and Best, 1942 - Found in the seal *Gypsophoca dorifera* from Yorke Peninsula (Australia). See Remarks.

From King, 1964 - Found in the leopard seal (*Hydruga leptonyx*), and in the walrus (*Odobenus rosmarus*). Information regarding the geographical location of hosts was not provided by author.

Remarks:

Dailey and Brownell (1972) list the leopard seal (*Hydruga leptonyx*) as a host of *C. clavatum* and cite Johnston and Best (1942) as a source reference. However, no mention of this host/parasite relationship could be found in the referenced paper.

Rice and Scheffer (1968) equate *Gypsophoca* with *Arctocephalus* and briefly mention the possible synonymy of *Gypsophoca dorifera* with *Arctocephalus tasmanicus*.

Corynosoma curilensis

Hosts and Locality:

From Dailey and Brownell, 1972 - Found in the sperm whale (*Physeter catodon*). Information regarding the geographical location of host was not provided by authors.

From Delyamure, 1955 - Found in the sperm whale (*Physeter catodon*) from the Sea of Okhotsk (Kurile Island region).

Corynosoma enhydri

Synonymy:

From Margolis and Dailey, 1972 - *Corynosoma macrosomum* Neiland, 1962.

Hosts and Locality:

From Dailey and Brownell, 1972 - Found in the sea otter (*Enhydra lutris*). Information regarding the geographical location of host was not provided by authors.

From Kenyon, 1969 - Found in the sea otter (*Enhydra lutris*) from Alaska.

From Margolis and Dailey, 1972 - Found in the sea otter (*Enhydra lutris*) from Alaska.

From Schiller, 1954 - Found in the sea otter (*Enhydra lutris*) from Komandorskii Islands (Russia).

Corynosoma falcatum

Hosts and Locality:

From Dailey and Brownell, 1972 - Found in the gray seal (*Halichoerus grypus*). Information regarding the geographical location of host was not provided by authors. See Remarks.

From King, 1964 - Found in the gray seal (*Halichoerus grypus*), and in the harbor seal (*Phoca vitulina*). Information regarding the geographical location of hosts was not provided by author.

From Margolis and Dailey, 1972 - Found in the harbor seal (*Phoca vitulina richardi*) from Alaska.

From Van Cleave, 1953 - Found in the gray seal (*Halichoerus grypus*) from Unalaska (Alaska). See Remarks.

Remarks:

Kruidenier (1954) claims the gray seal (*Halichoerus grypus*) does not inhabit the Pacific and the examined hosts were most likely harbor seals (*Phoca vitulina richardi*).

Dailey and Brownell (1972) also list the harbor seal (*Phoca vitulina*) as a host of *Corynosoma falcatum* and cite Van Cleave (1953) as a source reference. However, no mention of this host could be found in Van Cleave's (1953) paper.

Corynosoma hadweni

Synonymy:

From Margolis and Dailey, 1972 - *Corynosoma wegeneri* Heinze, 1934.

Hosts and Locality:

From Dailey and Brownell, 1972 - Found in the ringed seal (*Phoca hispida*), the gray seal (*Ha-*

lichoerus grypus), and in the bearded seal (*Erignathus barbatus*). Information regarding the geographical location of hosts was not provided by authors.

From King, 1964 - Found in the bearded seal (*Erignathus barbatus*), the gray seal (*Halichoerus grypus*), the leopard seal (*Hydrurga leptonyx*), the Weddell seal (*Leptonychotes weddelli*), the crab-eating seal (*Lobodon carcinophagus*), the Ross seal (*Ommatophoca rossi*), and "?" [sic] the South America sea lion (*Otaria byronia*). Information regarding the geographical location of hosts was not provided by author.

From Neiland, 1962 - If *C. hadweni* = *C. wegeneri*, then found in the white whale (*Delphinapterus leucas*) from Alaska.

From Van Cleave, 1953 - Found in the gray seal (*Halichoerus grypus*) from Unalaska (Alaska) [see Remarks]; the ringed seal (*Phoca hispida*) from Alaska (Clyde River, Baffin, Point Barrow, and Kotzebue); the bearded seal (*Erignathus barbatus*) from Alaska (Point Barrow); a "spotted seal" from Alaska (St. Lawrence); unidentified seals from St. Lawrence (Alaska) and seals (*Phoca sp.*) from Alaska (Kotzebue and Unalakeet).

Remarks:

Kruidenier (1954) claims that Van Cleave (1953) erroneously named the gray seal (*Halichoerus grypus*) as a host of this parasite; and it was most likely harbor seals (*Phoca vitulina richardi*) that Van Cleave examined. This claim is supported by Margolis and Dailey (1972).

Corynosoma hamanni

Synonymy:

From Delyamure, 1955 - *Echinorhynchus hamanni* Linstow, 1892; *Echinorhynchus antarcticus* Rennie, 1906; *Corynosoma antarcticus* Leiper and Atkinson, 1914.

From Gower, 1939 - *Corynosoma strumosum*.

From Johnston and Best, 1937 - *Corynosoma antarcticus* Rennie, 1907; *Corynosoma sipho* Railliet and Henry, 1907; *Echinorhynchus antarcticus* Rennie, 1906.

Hosts and Locality:

From Dailey and Brownell, 1972 - Found in the South American sea lion (*Otaria byronia*), the leopard seal (*Hydrurga leptonyx*), the Weddell seal (*Leptonychotes weddelli*), the Ross seal (*Ommatophoca rossi*), and in the crab-eating seal (*Lobodon carcinophagus*). Information regarding the geographical location of hosts was not provided by authors.

From Delyamure, 1955 - Found in the leopard seal (*Hydrurga leptonyx*), the Ross seal (*Ommatophoca rossi*), and the Weddell seal (*Leptonychotes weddelli*). Geographical distribution includes the South Shetlands and South Georgia area (Antarctica). Information regarding specific geographical locations of hosts was not provided by author.

From Edmonds, 1957 - Found in the Weddell seal (*Leptonychotes weddelli*) from Antarctica (Enderby Land).

From Holloway and Bier, 1967 - Found in the Weddell seal (*Leptonychotes weddelli*) from the Antarctic.

From Johnston and Best, 1937 - If *C. hammanni* = *C. antarcticum*, then found in the Weddell seal (*Leptonychotes weddelli*) from the Antarctic (Commonwealth Bay and King George V Land).

From King, 1964 - Found in the South American sea lion (*Otaria bryonia*). Information regarding geographical location of host was not provided by author.

From Leiper and Atkinson, 1915 - Found in the crab-eating seal (*Lobodon carcinophagus*) and the leopard seal (*Hydrurga leptonyx*) from the Antarctic.

From Nikol and Holloway, 1968 - Found in the Weddell seal (*Leptonychotes weddelli*) from McMurdo Sound (Antarctica).

From Yamaguti, 1963 - Found in the leopard seal (*Hydrurga leptonyx*) [= *Ogmorhinus leptonyx*], the crab-eating seal (*Lobodon carcinophagus*), and the Ross seal (*Ommatophoca rossi*). All hosts were from the Antarctic.

Corynosoma macrosomum

Synonymy:

From Margolis and Dailey, 1972 - *Corynosoma enhydri* Morosov, 1940; and *Corynosoma sp.* of Van Cleave, 1953.

See Remarks.

Hosts and Locality:

From Dailey and Brownell, 1972 - Found in the sea otter (*Enhydra lutris*). Information regarding the geographical location of host was not provided by authors.

From Neiland, 1962 - Found in the sea otter (*Enhydra lutris*) from Hinchinbrook Island, Prince William Sound, Alaska, and "apparently" [sic] a single specimen collected from the sea otter (*Enhydra lutris*) by Van Cleave, 1953, from Simeonof Island, Australia.

Remarks:

This parasite was introduced by Neiland (1962). However, according to Margolis and Dailey (1972), Jellison and Neiland (1965) later recognized the parasite as a synonym of *Corynosoma enhydri*.

Corynosoma magdaleni

Hosts and Locality:

From Dailey and Brownell, 1972 - Found in the harbor seal (*Phoca vitulina*) and in the gray seal (*Halichoerus grypus*). Information regarding the geographical location of hosts was not provided by authors.

From King, 1964 - Found in the harbor seal (*Phoca vitulina*) and in the gray seal (*Halichoerus grypus*). Information regarding the geographical location of hosts was not provided by author.

From Montreuil, 1958 - Found in the gray seal (*Halichoerus grypus*) from eastern Canada (Deadman Island, Gulf of St. Lawrence, and Quebec). Also found in the Atlantic harbor seal (*Phoca vitulina concolor*) from eastern Canada. See Remarks.

Remarks:

Montreuil (1958) claims the Atlantic harbor seal (*Phoca vitulina concolor*) is an infrequent accidental host of this parasite. He further notes that intermediate hosts of this parasite include the halibut (*Hippoglossus hippoglossus*) and the shorthorn sculpin (*Myoxocephalus scorpius*).

Corynosoma obtuscens

Hosts and Locality:

From Dailey and Brownell, 1972 - Found in the California sea lion (*Zalophus californianus*). Information regarding the geographical location of host was not provided by authors.

From King, 1964 - Found in the California sea lion (*Zalophus californianus*). Information regarding the geographical location of host was not provided by author.

From Margolis and Dailey, 1972 - Found in the California sea lion (*Zalophus californianus*) from California.

From Van Cleave, 1953 - Found in a California sea lion (*Zalophus californianus*) that died at the San Diego Zoo in 1943. See Remarks.

Remarks:

Van Cleave (1953) claims the intermediate host of this parasite is the leopard grouper (*Mycteroperca pardalis*), which inhabits the west coast of Mexico.

Corynosoma osmeri

Synonymy:

From Delyamure, 1955 - *Corynosoma ambispinigerum* Harada, 1935.

From Van Cleave, 1953 - "appears" to be synonymous with *Corynosoma strumosum* and *Corynosoma ambispinigerum* Harada, 1935.

Hosts and Locality:

From Dailey and Brownell, 1972 - Found in the California sea lion (*Zalophus californianus*). Information regarding the geographical location of host was not provided by authors.

From Delyamure, 1955 - Found in the California sea lion (*Zalophus californianus*) from the northern Pacific Ocean (waters of Japan).

From King, 1964 - Found in the California sea lion (*Zalophus californianus*). Information regarding the geographical location of host was not provided by author.

Remarks:

Van Cleave (1953) claims the identification of this parasite in Japan is erroneous. A brief historical account of this parasite is provided by Delyamure (1955).

Corynosoma rauschi

Hosts and Locality:

From Dailey and Brownell, 1972 - Found in the Hawaiian monk seal (*Monachus schauinslandi*). Information regarding the geographical location of host was not provided by authors.

From Golvan, 1959 - Found in the Hawaiian monk seal (*Monachus schauinslandi*) from Midway Island.

Corynosoma reductum

Synonymy:

From Van Cleave, 1953 - *Echinorhynchas reductus* Linstow, 1905.

Hosts and Locality:

From Dailey and Brownell, 1972 - Found in the ringed seal (*Phoca hispida*). Information regarding the geographical location of host was not provided by authors.

From Delyamure, 1955 - Found in the ringed seal (*Phoca hispida*) from Russia (western Taimyr).

From King, 1964 - Found in the ringed seal (*Phoca hispida*). Information regarding the geographical location of host was not provided by author.

From Van Cleave, 1953 - Found in the gray seal (*Halichoerus grypus*) from Alaska (Baffin Island, Clyde River, and Point Barrow).

Remarks:

Van Cleave (1953) reports this parasite to be rare in occurrence.

Corynosoma semerme

Synonymy:

From Delyamure, 1955 - *Echinorhynchus semerme* Forssell, 1904; *Echinorhynchus strumosum* Rudolphi, 1802 (in part); *Echinorhynchus hystrix* Bremser, 1824 (in part).

From Van Cleave, 1953 - *Echinorhynchus gibber* Olsson, 1893 (in part).

From Yamaguti, 1958 - *Echinorhynchus obovatus* Olsson, 1893 (in part).

Hosts and Locality:

From Codero, 1933 - Found in the South American fur seal (*Arctocephalus australis*) from Uruguay. See Remarks.

From Dailey and Brownell, 1972 - Found in the South American sea lion (*Otaria byronia*), the harbor seal (*Phoca vitulina*), the ringed seal (*Phoca hispida*), the bearded seal (*Erignathus barbatus*), the gray seal (*Halichoerus grypus*), the hooded seal (*Cystophora cristata*), the South American fur seal (*Arctocephalus australis*), the northern fur seal (*Callorhinus ursinus*), and in the harbor porpoise (*Phocoena phocoena*). Information regarding the geographical location of hosts was not provided by authors. See Remarks.

From Delyamure, 1955 - Found in the hooded seal (*Cystophora cristata*), the gray seal (*Halichoerus grypus*), the common seal (*Phoca vitulina*), the ringed seal (*Phoca hispida*), the Okhotsk ringed seal (*Phoca hispida ochotensis*), the walrus (*Odobaenus* (sic) *rosmarus*), and the finned porpoise (*Phocoena phocoena*). Geographical distribution includes Europe, Greenland, Canada, and USSR (Arctic Ocean and Sea of Okhotsk). Information regarding specific geographical location of hosts was not provided by author.

From Fisher, 1952 - Found in the harbor seal (*Phoca vitulina*) from the Fraser River in British Columbia.

From Johnston and Edmonds, 1953 - Found in the New Zealand sea lion (*Neophoca hookeri* [= *Otaria hookeri*]) from the Antarctic (Auckland and Cambell Island region).

From King, 1964 - Found in the bearded seal (*Erignathus barbatus*), the gray seal (*Halichoerus grypus*), the harbor seal (*Phoca vitulina*), the ringed seal (*Phoca hispida*), the hooded seal (*Cystophora cristata*), the northern fur seal (*Callorhinus ursinus*), the South American fur seal (*Arctocephalus australis*), the walrus (*Odobenus rosmarus*), and the South America sea lion (*Otaria byronia*). Information regarding the geographical location of hosts was not provided by author.

From Lyster, 1940 - Found in the bearded seal (*Erignathus barbatus*) from Canada (Lake Harbour). See Remarks.

From Margolis and Dailey, 1972 - Found in the northern fur seal (*Callorhinus ursinus*), the white whale (*Delphinapterus leucas*), the harbor seal (*Phoca vitulina richardi*), and in "unidentified seals". All hosts were from Alaska.

From Neiland, 1962 - Found in the white whale [beluga] (*Delphinapterus leucas*) and in the harbor seal (*Phoca vitulina richardi*). Both hosts were from Alaska.

From Van Cleave, 1953 - Found in the northern fur seal (*Callorhinus ursinus*) from Alaska (Pribilof Islands); the ringed seal (*Phoca hispida*) from Point Barrow (Alaska); unidentified "spotted seals" from St. Lawrence Island (Alaska); America arctic and sub-arctic regions.

Remarks:

Van Cleave (1953), examined the same material as Lyster (1940), and redefined the specimens as *Corynosoma validum*.

Van Cleave (1953) seriously questions Codero's identification and doubts the occurrence of *C. semerme* in the southern hemisphere. However, Johnston (1953) does record the New Zealand sea lion (*Otaria hookeri*) as a host of this parasite.

Dailey and Brownell (1972) also list the walrus (*Odobenus rosmarus*) as a host of *C. semerme* and reference Cameron et al (1940) as a source reference. However, no mention of this host could be found in the Cameron et al (1940) paper.

Corynosoma similis

Hosts and Locality:

From Margolis and Dailey, 1972 - Found in the northern fur seal (*Callorhinus ursinus*), and in the white whale (*Delphinapterus leucas*) from Alaska.

Corynosoma sipho

Synonymy:

From Yamaguti, 1963 - *Corynosoma hamanni* Leiper and Atkinson, 1915; *Corynosoma antarcticum* Johnston and Best, 1937.

Hosts and Locality:

From Dailey and Brownell, 1972 - Found in the Weddell seal (*Leptonychotes weddelli*). Information regarding the geographical location of host was not provided by authors.

From King, 1964 - Found in the Weddell seal (*Leptonychotes weddelli*). Information regarding the geographical location of host was not provided by author.

From Yamaguti, 1963 - Found in the Weddell seal (*Leptonychotes weddelli*) from the Antarctic.

Corynosoma strumosum

Synonymy:

From Delyamure, 1955 - *Echinorhynchus strumosus* Rudolphi, 1802 (in part); *Echinorhynchus hystrix* Bremser, 1842 (in part); *Echinorhynchus ventricosus* Rudolphi, 1809; *Echinorhynchus gibbosus* Rudolphi, 1819; *Echinorhynchus straitus* Villot, 1875; *Echinorhynchus gibber* Olsen, 1894 (in part).

From Margolis and Dailey, 1972 - *Corynosoma osmeri* (Rudolphi, 1802), Lühe, 1904.

See Remarks.

Hosts and Locality:

From Ball, 1930 - Found in the harbour seal (*Phoca vitulina*) from California and Amchitka Island (Alaska).

From Dailey and Brownell, 1972 - Found in the South American sea lion (*Otaria byronia*), the Kerguelen fur seal (*Arctocephalus trop-icalis*), the harbor seal (*Phoca vitulina*), the ringed seal (*Phoca hispida*), the Caspian seal (*Pusa caspica*), the bearded seal (*Erignathus barbatus*), the gray seal (*Halichoerus grypus*), the harp seal (*Pagophilus groenlandicus*), the hooded seal (*Cystophora cristata*), the northern fur seal (*Callorhinus ursinus*), the sea otter (*Enhydra lutris*), the Steller sea lion (*Eumetopias jubata*), the beluga white whale (*Delphinapterus leucas*), and in the harbor porpoise (*Phocoena phocoena*). Information regarding the geographical location of hosts was not provided by authors. See Remarks.

From Delyamure, 1955 - Found in the sea lion (*Eumetopias jubatus*), the walrus (*Odobaenus* (sic) *rosmarus*), the hooded seal (*Cystophora cristata*), the gray seal (*Halichoerus grypus*), the common seal (*Phoca vitulina*), the harbor seal (*Phoca vitulina largha* [= *Phoca richardii*], the ringed seal (*Phoca hispida* [= *Phoca foetida*], the Okhotsk ringed seal (*Phoca hispida ochotensis*), the Caspian seal (*Phoca caspica*), the Greenland seal (*Pagophoca groenlandica*), the bearded seal (*Erignathus barbatus*), the porpoise (*Phocoena phocoena*), and the white whale (*Delphinapterus leucas*). Also found in cats, dogs, and birds. Geographical distribution includes Europe, Atlantic coast, coast of Baltic Sea (Poland), Canada, and California. In USSR found along almost entire coast and northern islands (White Sea, Barents Sea, coast of Novaya Zemyla, Hara Sea, Franz Josef Land, western Taimyr, and other points, Pacific Ocean and Sea of Okhotsk (Kurile Islands, Sakhalin, Tyuleni Island), Caspian Sea, and Lake Ladoga.

From Fisher, 1952 - Found in the harbor seal (*Phoca vitulina*) from the Fraser River in British Columbia.

From King, 1964 - Found in the bearded seal (*Erignathus barbatus*), the gray seal (*Halichoerus grypus*), the harbor seal (*Phoca vitulina*), the ringed seal (*Phoca hispida*), the Caspian seal (*Phoca caspica*), the harp seal (*Pagophilus groenlandicus*), the hooded seal (*Cystophora cristata*), the northern fur seal (*Callorhinus ursinus*), the Kerguelen fur seal (*Arctocephalus tropicalis*), the walrus (*Odobenus rosmarus*), South America sea lion (*Otaria byronia*),

the Steller sea lion (*Eumetopias jubata*), and the California sea lion (*Zalophus californianus*). Information regarding the geographical location of hosts was not provided by author.

From Kurochkin, 1975 - Found in the Caspian seal (*Pusa caspica*) from the Caspian Sea.

From Lyster, 1940 - Found in the bearded seal (*Erignathus barbatus*) from the Canadian region (Cape Smith, Craig Harbor, Clyde River, Pond Inlet); the white whale (*Delphinapterus leucas*) from the Gulf of St. Lawrence; and the ringed seal (*Phoca hispida*) from Cape Smith, Lake Harbour, Payne Bay, Stupart Bay, and Wolstenholme. See Remarks.

From Margolis and Dailey, 1972 - Found in the northern fur seal (*Callorhinus ursinus*), the white whale (*Delphinapterus leucas*), the sea otter (*Enhydra lutris*), the Steller sea lion (*Eumetopias jubatus*), the harbour seal (*Phoca vitulina richardi*), the California sea lion (*Zalophus californianus*), a seal (*Phoca sp.*), and unidentified seals. Geographical distribution includes Alaska, British Columbia, Washington, and California.

From Neiland, 1961 - Found in the northern fur seal (*Callorhinus ursinus*) from Valdez (Alaska).

From Railliet, 1899 - Found in the harbour seal (*Phoca vitulina*) from France (Gulf of Somme).

From Rausch, 1953 - Found in the sea otter (*Enhydra lutris*) from Amchitka Island (Alaska).

From Scheffer and Slipp, 1944 - Found in the harbor seal (*Phoca vitulina*) from Washington.

From Van Cleave, 1953 - Found in the California sea lion (*Zalophus californianus*) from California (Ventura County); the ringed seal (*Phoca hispida*) from Point Barrow (Alaska); the northern fur seal (*Callorhinus ursinus*) from the Pribilof Islands (Alaska); the gray seal (*Halichoerus grypus*) from Unalaska (Alaska); the hooded seal (*Cystophora cristata*) from Europe, the harp seal (*Pagophilus groenlandicus*) from Europe; and "Unidentified seals" from Alaska. See Remarks.

Remarks:

Dailey and Brownell (1972) list the walrus (*Odobenus rosmarus*) as a host of *C. strumosum* and give Van Cleave (1953) as a source reference. However, no mention of this host could be found in the Van Cleave (1953) paper.

Gower (1939) reports *C. strumosum* has been found in ducks from the North Sea.

Kruidenier (1954) points out that Van Cleave (1953) erroneously listed *Halichoerus grypus* as a host of *C. strumosum*, and this host was almost certainly the harbor seal (*Phoca vitulina richardi*).

Van Cleave (1953), examined material which Lyster (1940) identified as *C. strumosum* (taken from the white whale) and renamed the parasite *Corynosoma cameroni*. Similarly, material which Lyster (1940) identified as *C. strumosum* (from the bearded seal), Van Cleave (1953) renamed *Corynosoma hadweni*.

Corynosoma validum

Hosts and Locality:

From Dailey and Brownell, 1972 - Found in the walrus (*Odobenus rosmarus*) and in the bearded seal (*Erignathus barbatus*). Information regarding the geographical location of hosts was not provided by authors.

From Kenyon, 1962 - Found in the walrus (*Odobenus rosmarus divergens*) from Little Diomede Island (Alaska).

From King, 1964 - Found in the bearded seal (*Erignathus barbatus*), and in the walrus (*Odobenus rosmarus*). Information regarding the geographical location of hosts was not provided by author.

From Margolis and Dailey, 1972 - Found in the bearded seal (*Erignathus barbatus*), the walrus (*Odobenus rosmarus*), a seal (*Phoca sp.*) and in an "unidentified seal". All hosts were from Alaska.

From Van Cleave, 1953 - Found in the pacific walrus (*Odobenus divergens*) from Alaska (Wainwright and St. Lawrence Island); the bearded seal (*Erignathus barbatus*) from Alaska (Point Barrow); a "spotted seal"

from St. Lawrence Island; and in a seal (*Phoca sp.*) from Kotzebue (Alaska).

Remarks:

The parasite taken from the bearded seal (*Erignathus barbatus*) and identified by Lyster (1940) as *Corynosoma semerme* was re-identified by Van Cleave (1953) as being *Corynosoma validum*.

Kenyon (1962) notes that the "spotted seal" referred to by Van Cleave (1953) may have been a harbor seal (*Phoca vitulina*). Kenyon further notes the Eskimos on Little Diomede Island commonly refer to *P. vitulina* as "spotted seals".

Corynosoma villosum

Synonymy:

From Margolis and Dailey, 1972 - *Corynosoma sp.* of Rausch and Locker, 1951, and Rausch, 1953.

Hosts and Locality:

From Dailey and Brownell, 1972 - Found in the Steller sea lion (*Eumetopias jubatus*), the sea otter (*Enhydra lutris*), the northern fur seal (*Callorhinus ursinus*), and in the South African fur seal (*Arctocephalus pusillus*). Information regarding the geographical location of hosts was not provided by authors. See Remarks.

From King, 1964 - Found in the northern fur seal (*Callorhinus ursinus*), the Steller sea lion (*Eumetopias jubatus*), and in the South African fur seal (*Arctocephalus pusillus*). Information regarding the geographical location of hosts was not provided by author.

From Margolis, 1956 - Found in the Steller sea lion (*Eumetopias jubatus*). "Most" of the four hosts examined were from Triangle Island (the outermost of the Cape Scott islands that extend westward from the northern tip of Vancouver Island, Canada).

From Margolis and Dailey, 1972 - Found in the northern fur seal (*Callorhinus ursinus*), the sea otter (*Enhydra lutris*), the Steller sea lion (*Eumetopias jubatus*), and in an "unidentified seal". Hosts were from Alaska and British Columbia.

From Van Cleave, 1953 - Found in the Steller sea lion (*Eumetopias jubatus*) from Alaska (St. Lawrence, St. Paul, and the Aleutian Islands); the northern fur seal (*Callorhinus ursinus*) from the Pribilof Islands; and in the sea otter (*Enhydra lutris*) from Amchitka Island (Alaska).

Remarks:

Dailey and Brownell (1972) also list the South African fur seal (*Arctocephalus pusillus*) as a host of *C. villosum* and reference Van Cleave (1953) as a source reference. However, no mention of this host could be found in Van Cleave's (1953) paper.

Corynosoma wegeneri

Synonymy:

From Margolis and Dailey, 1972 - *Corynosoma hadweni* Van Cleave 1953.

Hosts and Locality:

From King, 1964 - Found in the ringed seal (*Phoca hispida*). Information regarding the geographical location of host was not provided by author.

From Margolis and Dailey, 1972 - Found in the white whale (*Delphinapterus leucas*), the harbour seal (*Phoca vitulina richardi*), the ringed seal (*Phoca hispida*), a seal (*Phoca sp.*), and in "unidentified seals". All hosts were from Alaska.

Echinorhynchus sp.

Hosts and Locality:

From Johnston and Deland, 1929 - Found in the dolphin *D. forsteri* ["Probably *D. delphis*"] from the Australian seas.

Acarina

All kinds of surface mites and lice and other marine crustaceans cause various skin and shell infestations of marine mammals and sea turtles. Heavy lice infestations on phocids by *Echinophhirius horridus* has been associated with seal heartworm disease and the lice may be intermediate hosts of that nematode, but experimental evidence has not been conclusive. Whale 'lice' are actually amphipods mostly Cyamids. Nasal Halarachnidae arachnids, as known as mites, are found in phocids where intense infections have caused pathology. The shell and skin of sea turtles is rich in what is referred to as the epibiotia and represents a sub-specialty of sea turtle parasitology that examines barnacles, amphipods, and various crustations, most of which have a more commensal relationship with their host.

Demodex sp.

Hosts and Locality:

From Dailey and Brownell, 1972 - Found in the California sea lion (*Zalophus californianus*). Information regarding the geographical location of host was not provided by authors.

Dermacentor rosmari

Hosts and Locality:

From King, 1964 - Found in the walrus (*Odobenus rosmarus*). Information regarding the geographical location of host was not provided by author.

Halarachne sp.

Hosts and Locality:

From Dailey and Brownell, 1972 - Found in the southern elephant seal (*Mirounga leonia*) and in the Weddell seal (*Leptonychotes weddelli*). Information regarding the geographical location of hosts was not provided by authors.

From Ferris, 1942 - Found in the Steller sea lion (*Eumetopias jubata*) from Pacific Grove, California.

From Fisher, 1952 - Found in the harbor seal (*Phoca vitulina*) from Gibson Islands (at the head of Grenville Channel) in British Columbia.

From King, 1964 - Found in the southern elephant seal (*Mirounga leonia*) and in the Weddell seal (*Leptonychotes weddelli*). Information regarding the geographical location of hosts was not provided by author.

From Margolis and Dailey, 1972 - Found in the Steller sea lion (*Eumetopias jubata*) and in the harbor seal (*Phoca vitulina richardi*) from British Columbia and California.

From Newell, 1947 - Found in the Weddell seal (*Leptonychotes weddelli*) from Antarctica (South Orkney Islands, Orcades du Sud [61° S, 46° W]) and in the harbor seal (*Phoca vitulina richardi*) from the west coast of North America.

Remarks:

Newell (1947) noted that the distribution of the *Halarachne* is the North Atlantic, Pacific coast of North America, South Orkneys "?" [sic]; and "probably as widely distributed as Pinnipedia or at least Phocidae."

Halarachne americana

Hosts and Locality:

From Dailey and Brownell, 1972 - Found in the Caribbean monk seal (*Monachus tropicalis*). Information regarding the geographical location of host was not provided by authors.

From King, 1964 - Found in the Caribbean

monk seal (*Monachus tropicalis*). Information regarding the geographical location of host was not provided by author.

From Newell, 1947 - Found in the Caribbean monk seal (*Monachus tropicalis*) from an unidentified zoo.

Remarks:

Finnegan (1934) doubts this parasite could have the same geographical distribution as the Caribbean monk seal (West Indies, Coast of Yucatan to Florida and the Bahamas). However, Newell (1947) feels the geographical distribution of both the host and parasite could coincide.

Newell (1947) discusses the possible taxonomic relationship between this parasite and *Halarachne miroungae*.

Halarachne halichoeri

Synonymy:

From Margolis and Dailey, 1972 - *Halarachne otariae* Ferris, 1925 (in part).

Hosts and Locality:

From King, 1964 - Found in the gray seal (*Halichoerus grypus*). Information regarding the geographical location of host was not provided by author.

From Margolis and Dailey, 1972 - Found in the harbor seal (*Phoca vitulina richardi*) from Washington and California.

From Newell, 1947 - Found in the gray seal (*Halichoerus grypus*) from Ireland to the Baltic Sea.

From Scheffer and Slipp, 1944 - Found in the harbor seal (*Phoca vitulina richardi*) from the state of Washington.

Remarks:

Newell (1947) discusses the possible taxonomic relationship between this parasite and *Halarachne miroungae*.

Halarachne miroungae

Synonymy:

From Newell, 1947 - "Possibly" *Halarachne halichoeri* Scheffer and Slipp, 1944.

Hosts and Locality:

From Dailey and Brownell, 1972 - Found in the northern elephant seal (*Mirounga angustirostris*) and in the sea otter (*Enhydra lutris*). Information regarding the geographical location of hosts was not provided by authors.

From Doetschman, 1941 - Found in the California harbor seal (*Phoca richardi*) and in the northern elephant seal (*Mirounga angustirostris*) from the San Diego Zoo.

From Kenyon et al, 1965 - Found in the sea otter (*Enhydra lutris*) from Alaska (Amchitka Island) and the Seattle Zoo in Washington.

From King, 1964 - Found in the common seal (*Phoca vitulina*) and in the northern elephant seal (*Mirounga angustirostris*). Information regarding the geographical location of hosts was not provided by author.

From Margolis and Dailey, 1972 - Found in the northern elephant seal (*Mirounga angustirostris*), the sea otter (*Enhydra lutris*) and in the harbor seal (*Phoca vitulina richardi*) from Alaska, California (San Diego Zoo), and Baja California.

From Newell, 1947 - Found in the northern elephant seal (*Mirounga angustirostris*) from Guadalupe Island, off Baja California (29° N, 118° W), and in the harbor seal (*Phoca vitulina richardi*) from California (Pacific Grove (36° 28' N, 122° W) and Washington (47° 15' N, 122° 30' W).

Remarks:

Newell (1947) discusses the possible taxonomic relationship of this parasite with *Halarachne halichoeri* and *Halarachne americana*.

Halarachne reflexa

Synonymy:

See Remarks.

Hosts and Locality:

From Tubb, 1937 - Found in the Tasmanian sea bear (*Arctocephalus tasmanicus*) from Lady

Julia Percy Island in South Australia.

Remarks:

In their listing of parasites of the Tasmanian fur seal (*Arctocephalus tasmanicus*), Dailey and Brownell (1972) refer to this parasite as "*Orthohalarachne reflexa*" and cite Tubb (1937) as a source reference. However, Tubb (1937) uses the genus "*Halarachne*" rather than "*Orthohalarachne*".

Lorryia leptonychotes

Hosts and Locality:

From Johnston, 1937d - Found among cestodes from a Weddell seal (*Leptonychotes weddelli*) from Commonwealth Bay, King George V Land (Antarctica)

Orthohalarchne attenuata

Synonymy:

From Margolis and Dailey, 1972 - *Halarachne attenuata* Banks, 1910.

From Newell, 1947 - *Halarachne attenuata* Banks, 1910.

Hosts and Locality:

From Dailey and Brownell, 1972 - Found in the Steller sea lion (*Eumetopias jubata*). Information regarding the geographical location of host was not provided by authors. See Remarks.

From Dailey and Hill, 1970 - Found in the northern fur seal (*Callorhinus ursinus*) and the California sea lion (*Zalophus californianus*) from southern California (Alamitos Bay to Ãno Nuevo Island).

From Keyes, 1965 - Found in the northern fur seal (*Callorhinus ursinus*) from the Pribilof Islands, Alaska.

From King, 1964 - Found in the Steller sea lion (*Eumetopias jubata*), the South African fur seal (*Arctocephalus pusillus*), and in the northern fur seal (*Callorhinus ursinus*). Information regarding the geographical location of hosts was not provided by author.

From Margolis and Dailey, 1972 - Found in the Steller sea lion (*Eumetopias jubata*), the northern fur seal (*Callorhinus ursinus*), and in the California sea lion (*Zalophus californianus*) from Alaska, Oregon, and California.

From Newell, 1947 - Found in the Steller sea lion (*Eumetopias jubata*) from the Bering Sea and in the northern fur seal (*Callorhinus ursinus cynocephalus*) [= *Callorhinus ursinus*] from the Bering Sea and Oregon. Geographical distribution includes the Pribilof Islands in the Bering Sea (57° 5' N, 170°25' W) to Depoe Bay, Oregon (44° 50' N, 124° 5' W).

Remarks:

Dailey and Brownell (1972) also list the South African fur seal (*Arctocephalus pusillus*) as a host to this parasite and give Newell (1947) as a source reference. Although no mention of this host could be found in the Newell (1947) paper, King (1964) does list *Arctocephalus pusillus* as a host of *Orthohalarchne attenuate*.

Oudemans (1926) noted a specimen of this parasite was taken from a seal pup from St. Paul Island. However, Newell (1947) points out that Oudemans incorrectly assumed the island to be located in the Indian Ocean instead of the Bering Sea.

Orthohalarchne diminuata

Synonymy:

From Margolis and Dailey, 1972 - *Halarachne diminuata* Doetschman, 1944.

From Newell, 1947 - *Halarachne diminuata* Doetschman, 1944.

Hosts and Locality:

From Dailey and Brownell, 1972 - Found in the California sea lion (*Zalophus californianus*). Information regarding the geographical location of host was not provided by authors. See Remarks.

From Dailey and Hill, 1970 - Found in the California sea lion (*Zalophus californianus*) and in the Steller sea lion (*Eumetopias jubata*). Both hosts were taken from locations in southern to central California (Alamitos Bay to Nuevo Island).

From Doetschman, 1944a - Found in the California sea lion (*Zalophus californianus*) from the California coast.

From Keyes, 1965 - Found in the northern fur seal (*Callorhinus ursinus*) from the Pribilof Islands.

From King, 1964 - Found in the California sea lion (*Zalophus californianus*), the South African fur seal (*Arctocephalus pusillus*) and in the northern fur seal (*Callorhinus ursinus*). Information regarding the geographical location of hosts was not provided by author.

From Margolis and Dailey, 1972 - Found in the Steller sea lion (*Eumetopias jubata*), the northern fur seal (*Callorhinus ursinus*) and in the California sea lion (*Zalophus californianus*) from Alaska, British Columbia, and California.

From Newell, 1947 - Found in the California sea lion (*Zalophus californianus*) from California and the northern fur seal (*Callorhinus ursinus*) from St. Paul Island in the Bering Sea (57° 5' N, 170° 25' W).

Remarks:

Dailey and Brownell (1972) also list the South African fur seal (*Arctocephalus pusillus*) as a host to this parasite and give Newell (1947) as a source reference. However, no mention of this host could be found in the Newell (1947) paper.

Orthohalarchne megellanica

Synonymy:

From Newell, 1947 - *Halarachne megellanica* Finnegan, 1934.

Hosts and Locality:

From Dailey and Brownell, 1972 - Found in the South American sea lion (*Otaria byronia*) and in the South American fur seal (*Arctocephalus australis*). Information regarding the geographical location of hosts was not provided by authors.

From King, 1964 - Found in the South American fur seal (*Arctocephalus australis*), and in the South American sea lion (*Otaria byronia*). Information regarding the geograph-

ical location of hosts was not provided by author.

From Newell, 1947 - Found in the South American sea lion (*Otaria byronia*) from the Falkland Islands (52° S, 60° W).

Orthohalarchne reflexa

Hosts and Locality:

From Dailey and Brownell, 1972 - Found in the Tasmanian fur seal (*Arctocephalus tasmanicus*). Information regarding the geographical location of host was not provided by authors.

From King, 1964 - Found in the Tasmanian fur seal (*Arctocephalus tasmanicus*). Information regarding the geographical location of host was not provided by author.

Orthohalarchne rosmari

Synonymy:

From Newell, 1947 - *Halarachne rosmari*.

Hosts and Locality:

From Newell, 1947 - The specimen, taken from a walrus (*Odobenus rosmarus*), was examined at the Hamburg Zoo seven years after capture in Franz-Joseph Land (81° N, 60° E).

Remarks:

Newell (1947) feels the validity of this species depends on the accuracy of the original description provided by Oudemans (1916).

Orthohalarchne zalophi

Synonymy:

From Margolis and Dailey, 1972 - *Halarachne zalophi* Oudemanss, 1916; *Halarachne otariae* Steding, 1923.

From Newell, 1947 - *Halarachne zalophi* Oudemanss, 1916; *Halarachne otariae* Steding, 1923.

Hosts and Locality:

From Dailey and Brownell, 1972 - Found in the Steller sea lion (*Eumetopias jubata*). Information regarding the geographical location of host was not provided by authors.

From Doetschman, 1941- If *Orthohalarchne zalophi* = *Halarachne zalophi*, then found in 70% of the 74 California sea lions (*Zalophus californianus*), Steller sea lion (*Eumetopias jubata*), California harbor seals (*Phoca richardi*) and elephant seals (*Mirounga angustirostris*) that were examined from the San Diego Zoo.

From King, 1964 - Found the California sea lion (*Zalophus californianus*) and in a captive (zoo) Steller sea lion (*Eumetopias jubata*). Information regarding the geographical location of hosts was not provided by author.

From Margolis and Dailey, 1972 - Found the Steller sea lion (*Eumetopias jubata*) and in the California sea lion (*Zalophus californianus*) from California and the Göttinggen Zoo in Germany.

From Newell, 1947 - Found in the Steller sea lion (*Eumetopias jubata*) from St. Paul Island (Alaska, Bering Sea) and the San Diego Zoo. Also found in the California sea lion (*Zalophus californianus*) from Pacific Grove, California (36° 36′ N, 122° W).

Raphignathus johnstoni

Hosts and Locality:

From Womersley, 1937 - Found in the Weddell seal (*Leptonychotes weddelli*) from Commonwealth Bay and King George V Land.

Anoplura

Anoplura or sucking lice (as opposed to chewing lice) are blood-feeding ectoparasites of mammals. The species of the family Echinophthiriidae are medium-to-large lice and are parasites of aquatic carnivores in the Pinnipedia (seals, walruses, and sea lions) and Mustelidae (river otters).

Antarctophthirius callorhini

Synonymy:

From Margolis and Dailey, 1972 - *Haematopinus callorhini* Osborn, 1899; *Antarctophthirus monachus* Kellogg and Ferris, 1915.

Hosts and Locality:

From King, 1964 - Found on the northern fur seal (*Callorhinus ursinus*). Information regarding the geographical location of host was not provided by author.

From Margolis and Dailey, 1972 - Found on the northern fur seal (*Callorhinus ursinus*) from Alaska.

Antarctophthirius lobodontis

Hosts and Locality:

From Dailey and Brownell, 1972 - Found on the crab-eating seal (*Lobodon carcinophagus*). Information regarding the geographical location of host was not provided by authors.

From King, 1964 - Found on the crab-eating seal (*Lobodon carcinophagus*). Information regarding the geographical location of host was not provided by author.

From Murray et al, 1965 - Found on the crab-eating seal (*Lobodon carcinophagus*) from Antarctica.

Antarctophthirius mawsoni

Hosts and Locality:

From Dailey and Brownell, 1972 - Found on the Ross seal (*Ommatophoca rossi*). Information regarding the geographical location of host was not provided by authors.

From King, 1964 - Found on the Ross seal (*Ommatophoca rossi*). Information regarding the geographical location of host was not provided by author.

Antarctophthirius microchir

Hosts and Locality:

From Dailey and Brownell, 1972 - Found on the South American sea lion (*Otaria byronia*), the California sea lion (*Zalophus californianus*), the Australian sea lion (*Neophoca cinerea*), the New Zealand sea lion (*Phocarctos hookeri*), and on the Steller's sea lion (*Eumetopias jubata*). Information regarding the geographical location of hosts was not provided by authors.

From Doetschman, 1944b - Found on the California sea lion (*Zalophus californianus*), the Steller's sea lion (*Eumetopias jubata*) and the harbor seal (*Phoca vitulina richardii*). All hosts were from the San Diego Zoological Hospital.

From Enderlein, 1906 - Found on the New Zealand sea lion (*Neophoca hookeri*) [= *Phocarctos hookeri*] from the Auckland Islands.

From Ferris, 1916 - Found on the Steller sea lion (*Eumetopias jubata*) from the west coast of North America (California to Alaska), and on the California sea lion (*Zalophus californianus*) from the California coast.

From Jellison, 1952 - Found on the Steller sea lion (*Eumetopias jubata*) from St. Paul Island (Pribilof), Alaska.

From King, 1964 - Found on the California sea lion (*Zalophus californianus*), the Steller sea lion (*Eumetopias jubata*), the South American sea lion (*Otaria byronia*), the Australian sea lion (*Neophoca cinerea*) and the New Zealand sea lion (*Phocarctos hookeri*). Information regarding the geographical location of hosts was not provided by author.

From Margolis and Dailey, 1972 - Found on the Steller's sea lion (*Eumetopias jubata*), the harbour seal (*Phoca vitulina richardii*), and the California sea lion (*Zalophus californianus*) in Alaska, British Columbia and California (wild and captive animals).

Remarks:

Dailey and Brownell (1972) also list the South American sea lion (*Otaria byronia*) and the Australian sea lion (*Neophoca cinerea*) as host of *A. microchir* and cite Enderlein (1906) as a source reference. However, no mention of these hosts could be found in the Enderlein (1906) paper.

Antarctophthirius ogmorhini

Hosts and Locality:

From Dailey and Brownell, 1972 - Found on the leopard seal (*Hydrurga leptonyx*) and the Weddell seal (*Leptonychotes weddelli*). Information regarding the geographical location of hosts was not provided by authors.

From Enderlein, 1906 - Found on the leopard seal (*Hydrurga leptonyx*) from Victorialand (Antarctica).

From King, 1964 - Found on the leopard seal (*Hydrurga leptonyx*), and on the Weddell seal (*Leptonychotes weddelli*). Information regarding the geographical location of hosts was not provided by author.

From Murray et al, 1965 - Found on the Weddell seal (*Leptonychotes weddelli*) from the Antarctic.

Antarctophthirius trichechi

Hosts and Locality:

From King, 1964 - Found on the walrus (*Odobenus rosmarus*). Information regarding the geographical location of hosts was not provided by author.

From Margolis and Dailey, 1972 - Found on

the walrus (*Odobenus rosmarus*) from St. Lawrence Island (Bering Sea).

From Weber, 1950 - Found on the walrus (*Odobenus rosmarus*) from Alaska (Point Barrow). See Remarks.

Remarks:

Weber (1950) notes this parasite has also been found on walruses (*Odobenus rosmarus*) from Greenland and Spitzbergen.

Echinophthiriidae sp.

Hosts and Locality:

From Fisher, 1952 - Found on the harbor seal (*Phoca vitulina*) from the Skeena River area of British Columbia (Ecstall River and Gibson Islands).

Echinophthirius fluctus

Synonymy:

From Margolis and Dailey, 1972 - *Proechinophthirius fluctus*

Hosts and Locality:

From Barabash-Nikiforov, 1935 - Found on the sea otter (*Enhydra lutris*) from the Commander Islands.

Echinophthirius horridus

Hosts and Locality:

From Ass, 1935 - Found on the Baikal seal (*Pusa sibirica*) from Lake Baikal.

From Dailey and Brownell, 1972 - Found on the harbor seal (*Phoca vitulina*), the Baikal seal (*Pusa sibirica*), the bearded seal (*Erignathus barbatus*), the gray seal (*Halichoerus grypus*), the harp seal (*Phoca groenlandica*), the hooded seal (*Cystophora cristata*), and the ringed seal (*Pusa hispida*). Information regarding the geographical location of hosts was not provided by authors.

From King, 1964 - Found on the common seal (*Phoca vitulina*), the Baikal seal (*Pusa sibirica*), the bearded seal (*Erignathus barbatus*), the gray seal (*Halichoerus grypus*), the harp seal (*Phoca groenlandica*), the hooded seal (*Cystophora cristata*), and on the ringed seal (*Pusa hispida*). Information regarding the geographical location of the hosts was not provided by author.

From Kurochkin, 1975 - Found on the bearded seal (*Erignathus barbatus*) from the Bering Sea.

From Margolis and Dailey, 1972 - Found on the harbor seal (*Phoca vitulina richardi*) and the ringed seal (*Pusa hispida*) from Alaska, British Columbia, and California (wild and captive animals).

From Weber, 1950 - Found on the bearded seal (*Phoca hispida*) from Alaska (Beaufort Sea). See Remarks.

Remarks:

Weber (1950) notes this parasite also has been found on *Phoca sp.* from Europe, Greenland, Alaska and California.

Haematopinus trichechi

Hosts and Locality:

From King, 1964 - Found on the walrus (*Odobenus rosmarus*). Information regarding the geographical location of the host was not provided by author.

Lepidophthirius macrorhini

Hosts and Locality:

From Dailey and Brownell, 1972 - Found on the southern elephant seal (*Mirounga leonia*). Information regarding the geographical location of the host was not provided by authors.

From King, 1964 - Found on the southern elephant seal (*Mirounga leonia*). Information regarding the geographical location of the host was not provided by author.

From Murray and Nicholls, 1965 - Found on the southern elephant seal (*Mirounga leonia*) from Macquarie Island (Antarctica).

Proechinophthirius fluctus

Synonymy:

From Margolis and Dailey, 1972 - *Echinophthirius fluctus* Ferris, 1916.

Hosts and Locality:

From King, 1964 - Found on the northern fur seal (*Callorhinus ursinus*). Information regarding the geographical location of the host was not provided by author.

From Margolis and Dailey, 1972 - Found on the northern fur seal (*Callorhinus ursinus*) and on the Steller's sea lion (*Eumetopias jubata*) from Alaska and California (Stanford Museum specimen).

Proechinopthirius zumpti

Hosts and Locality:

From Dailey and Brownell, 1972 - Found on the South African fur seal (*Arctocephalus pusillus*). Information regarding the geographical location of the host was not provided by authors.

From King, 1964 - Found on the South African fur seal (*Arctocephalus pusillus*). Information regarding the geographical location of the host was not provided by author.

Cestoda

The adult cestode is known as a tapeworm for their long ribbon-like appearance, and are common in the intestines of marine mammals. Care must be taken to collect the entire worm including the head or attachment organ called the scolex. Without a scolex identification may require molecular techniques. Several worms in the small intestine together can cause a complete obstruction leading to death in dolphins, but most adult tapeworms cause little acute pathology. Tapeworms can however rob their hosts of essential nutrients over their long lives. As with human infections, small numbers of adult tapeworms cause minimal disease while the larval forms can be very damaging.

Adult Diphyllobothriidae are particularly well represented in marine mammals. Larval cestodes are also very common in the blubber and in the body cavity of dolphins, particularly '*Phyllobothrium delphini*' and '*Monorygma grimaldii*', but since cestodes are properly named for the adult form, which have not been described for either specimen, these names can not be valid. Recent molecular work assigns them close affinity with *Clistobothrium*. Very small and potentially pathogenic cestode larva can also be found in the body cavity, attached to the serosal surface of organs, and embedded in muscle tissue in sea turtles. Most larval forms belong to the Tetraphyllidea, who live as adults in sharks, thus the marine mammal or sea turtle would have to be consumed by a shark for the parasite to complete its life-cycle.

Abothrium gadi

Hosts and Locality:

From Margolis and Dailey, 1972 - Found in the Steller's sea lion (*Eumetopias jubata*) from British Columbia. See Remarks.

Remarks:

Margolis and Dailey (1972) regard this as a "pseudoparasite" of the Steller's sea lion. Since the parasite is commonly found in fishes of the family Gadidae, the authors speculate the host probably ingested a gadid just prior to examination.

Adenocephalus pacificus

Synonymy:

From Margolis, 1956 - *Diphyllobothrium pacificum* Nybelin, 1931; *Bothriocephalus sp.* Stiles and Hassall, 1899; *Adenocephalus septentrionalis* Nybelin, 1929; "Species #2" of Stunkard, 1848; and *Diphyllobothrium glaciale* Markowski 1952.

From Yamaguti, 1959 - *Diphyllobothrium glaciale* Cholodkowsky, 1915; *Adenocephalus septentrionalis* Nybelin, 1929; *Cordicephalus arctocephalinus* (Johnston, 1937) [= *arctocephali*] Drummond, 1937.

Hosts and Locality:

From Dailey and Brownell, 1972 - Found in the Steller's sea lion (*Eumatopias jubata*) and the South American fur seal (*Arctocephalus australis*). Information regarding the geographical location of hosts was not provided by authors.

From Delyamure, 1955 - Found in the south fur seal (*Arctocephalus australis*) from Antarctica.

From King, 1964 - Found in the Steller's sea lion (*Eumatopias jubata*) and the South American fur seal (*Arctocephalus australis*). Information regarding the geographical location of hosts was not provided by author.

From Margolis, 1956 - If *Diphyllobothrium pacificum* = *Adenocephalus pacificum*, then found in the northern fur seal (*Callorhinus ursinus*), the Steller's sea lion (*Eumatopias jubata*), and the California sea lion (*Zalophus californianus*). Geographical distribution includes Alaska, British Columbia, and California.

From Markowski, 1952b - If *Diphyllobothrium glaciale* = *Diphyllobothrium pacificum*, then found in the northern fur seal (*Callorhinus ursinus*) from Alaska (Pribilof Islands and St. George Island), and in the Australian sea lion (*Neophoca cinerea*) from Masatierra (San Fernandez Islands).

From Yamaguti, 1959 - If *Diphyllobothrium glaciale* = *Diphyllobothrium pacificum*, then found in the northern fur seal (*Callorhinus ursinus*), the New Zealand fur seal (*Arctocephalus forsteri*), the Tasmanian fur seal (*Arctocephalus tasmanicus),* the South American fur seal (*Arctocephalus australis*), and the Australian sea lion (*Neophoca cinerea*). Author states the geographical location of the parasite as the Pacific.

Adenocephalus septentrionalis

Synonymy:

From Margolis, 1956 - *Diphyllobothrium pacificum* Nybelin, 1931; *Bothriocephalus sp.* Stiles and Hassall, 1899; "Species #2" of Stunkard, 1848; and *Diphyllobothrium glaciale* Markowski, 1952.

From Yamaguti, 1959 - *Diphyllobothrium glaciale* Cholodkowsky, 1915; *Adenocephalus septentrionalis* Nybelin, 1929; *Cordicephalus arctocephalinus* Drummond, 1937.

Hosts and Locality:

From Dailey and Brownell, 1972 - Found in the northern fur seal (*Callorhinus ursinus*). Information regarding the geographical location of host was not provided by authors.

From Delyamure, 1955 - Found in the northern fur seal (*Callorhinus ursinus*) from the Bering Sea (Commander Islands).

From King, 1964 - Found in the northern fur seal (*Callorhinus ursinus*). Information regarding the geographical location of host was not provided by author.

Remarks:

The number of host species and geograph-

ical distribution of this parasite will greatly increase if *A. septentrionalis* is determined to be synonymous with *Diphyllobothrium glaciale* and/or *Diphyllobothrium pacificum*.

Anophryocephala sp.

Hosts and Locality:

From Dailey and Brownell, 1972 - Found in the short-fin pilot whale (*Globicephala macrorhyncha*). Information regarding the geographical location of host was not provided by authors.

Anophryocephalus anophrys

Synonymy:

From Delyamure, 1955 - *Tetrabothrium albertinii* Brighety, 1931.

Hosts and Locality:

From Dailey and Brownell, 1972 - Found in the ringed seal (*Phoca hispida*). Information regarding the geographical location of host was not provided by authors.

From Delyamure, 1955 - Found in the ringed seal (*Phoca hispida*) from Spitzbergen and Iceland.

From King, 1964 - Found in the ringed seal (*Phoca hispida*). Information regarding the geographical location of host was not provided by author.

Anophryocephalus ochotensis

Hosts and Locality:

From Dailey and Brownell, 1972 - Found in the Steller's sea lion (*Eumatopias jubata*). Information regarding the geographical location of host was not provided by authors.

From Delyamure, 1955 - Found in the Steller's sea lion (*Eumatopias jubata*) from Tyulent Island (Sea of Okhotsk).

From King, 1964 - Found in the Steller's sea lion (*Eumatopias jubata*). Information regarding the geographical location of host was not provided by author.

Baylissia baylisi

Hosts and Locality:

From Dailey and Brownell, 1972 - Found in the crab-eating seal (*Lobodon carcinophagus*). Information regarding the geographical location of host was not provided by authors.

From King, 1964 - Found in the crab-eating seal (*Lobodon carcinophagus*) Information regarding the geographical location of host was not provided by author.

From King, 1983 - Found in the crab-eating seal (*Lobodon sp.*). Information regarding the geographical location of host was not provided by author.

From Markowski, 1952a - Found in the crab-eating seal (*Lobodon carcinophagus*) from the Antarctic (Deception Island and Debenham Island).

Remarks:

This genus was introduced by Markowski (1952a).

Baylisiella tecta

Synonymy:

From Markowski, 1952a - *Bothriocephalus tectus* Linstow, 1892; *Dobothriocephalus tectus* Zschokke, 1903; *Diphyllobothrium tectum* Meggitt, 1924; *Cordicephalus tectus* Wardle, McLoed and Stewart, 1947.

Hosts and Locality:

From King, 1964 - Found in the southern elephant seal (*Mirounga leonina*). Information regarding the geographical location of host was not provided by author.

From King, 1983 - Found in the southern elephant seal (*Mirounga leonina*). Information regarding the geographical location of host was not provided by author.

From Markowski, 1952a - Found in the southern elephant seal (*Mirounga leonina*) from the Antacrtic (Bay of Isles, South Georgia).

Remarks:

Delyamure (1955) does not mention *B. tecta* but recognizes *Diphyllobothrium tecta* instead. The genus *Baylisiella* was introduced by Markowski (1952a).

Bothriocephalus sp.

Hosts and Locality:

From Dailey and Brownell, 1972 - Found in the Mediterranean monk seal (*Monachus monachus*). Information regarding the geographical location of host was not provided by authors.

From King, 1964 - Found in the common seal (*Phoca vitulina*), and in the Mediterranean monk seal (*Monachus monachus*). Information regarding the geographical location of hosts was not provided by author.

Clestobothrium glaciale

Hosts and Locality:

From Delyamure, 1955 - Found in the fur seal (*Callorhinus ursinus*) from Kamchatka.

Remarks:

This species was listed by Delyamure (1955) under "Species of Cestodes of uncertain taxonomic position".

Cysticercus cellulosae

Hosts and Locality:

From Dailey and Brownell, 1972 - Found in the Mediterranean monk seal (*Monachus monachus*). Information regarding the geographical location of host was not provided by authors.

From King, 1964 - Found in the Mediterranean monk seal (*Monachus monachus*). Information regarding geographical location of host was not provided by author.

Remarks:

This parasite is not listed by Delyamure (1955) or Yamaguti (1959).

Diphyllobothrium sp.

Hosts and Locality:

From Cowan, 1966 - Found in the North Atlantic pilot whale (*Globicephala melaena*) from eastern Newfoundland. See Remarks.

From Dailey and Brownell, 1972 - Found in the Kerguelen fur seal (*Arctocephalus tropicalis*), the North Atlantic pilot whale (*Globicephala melaena*), the giant bottlenosed whale (*Berardius bairdi*), the sei whale (*Balaenoptera borealis*) and in the bottlenosed dolphin (*Tursiops truncatus*). Information regarding the geographical location of hosts was not provided by authors. See Remarks.

From Delyamure, 1955 - Found in the bottlenosed dolphin (*Tursiops truncatus*). Information regarding the geographical location of host was not provided by author. Also found immature parasites in the sei whale (*Balaenoptera borealis*) from the Pacific Ocean (Commander Island region). See Remarks.

From Kenyon, 1962 - Found in the bearded seal (*Erignathus barbatus*) from Little Diomede Island (Alaska). Author states the parasites were probably *D. cordatum* and *D. lanceolatum*.

From King, 1964 - Found in the Kerguelen fur seal (*Arctocephalus tropicalis*). Information regarding the geographical location of the host not provide by author.

From Lyster, 1940 - Found in the harp seal (*Pagophilus groenlandicus*) from Lake Harbour, Clyde River and Baffin Island. Also found in the bearded seal (*Erignathus barbatus*) from Cape Smith, N.W.T., Cape Dorset, Baffin Island and Wolstenholme (Quebec).

From Margolis and Dailey, 1972 - Found in the sei whale (*Balaenoptera borealis*) and in the bearded seal (*Erignathus barbatus*) from Alaska and California.

From Markowski, 1952a - Found in the crab-eating seal (*Lobodon carcinophagus*) from South Sandwich.

From McEwin, 1957 - Found in the sea elephant (*Mirounga leonina*) from Antarctica (American Bay, Possession Is., Crozets).

From Rice, 1963 - Found in the sei whale (*Balaenoptera borealis*) from California.

Remarks:

Johnston (1937b) notes the range for this parasite extends from the Ross Sea and Graham Lands-South Orkneys region to Macquarie Island.

Infection was reported by Cowan (1967). Location was reported by Cowan (1966).

Rice (1963) questions the identification of this parasite as referenced in the Delyamure (1955) paper.

Dailey and Brownell cite Delyamure (1955) in their listing the giant bottlenosed whale (*Berardius bairdi*) as a host of *Diphyllobothrium sp.* Delyamure lists the bottlenosed whale (*Hyperoodon ampullatus*) as a host of *Diphyllobothrium sp.*; there is no mention of the giant bottlenosed whale (*Berardius bairdi*).

Diphyllobothrium alascense

Hosts and Locality:

From Margolis and Dailey, 1972 - Found in the harbour seal (*Phoca vitulina richardi*) from Alaska.

Diphyllobothrium antarcticus

Synonymy:

From Markowski, 1952a - *Glandicephalus antarcticus* Baird, 1853; *Bothriocephalus antarcticus* Baird, 1853; *Dibothrium antarcticum* Diesing, 1863; *Diplogonoporus antarcticus* Lühe, 1899; *Dibothriocephalus antarcticus* Shipley, 1907; *Glandicephalus antarcticus* Fuhrmann, 1920.

Hosts and Locality:

From Markowski, 1952a - Found in the Ross seal (*Ommatophoca rossi*) from the Antarctic.

Remarks:

Markowski (1952a) and Yamaguti (1959) referred to this parasite as *Glandicephalus antarcticus*, and used *D. antarcticus* as a synonym. However, Delyamure (1955) retains *D. antarcticus*.

Diphyllobothrium archeri

Synonymy:

From Delyamure, 1955 - *Dibothriocephalus archeri* Leiper and Atkinson, 1914.

From Markowski, 1952a - *Diphyllobothrium lashleyi* Leiper and Atkinson, 1914; *Dibothriocephalus lashleyi* Leiper and Atkinson, 1914.

From Yamaguti, 1959 - *Diphyllobothrium mobilis* Leiper and Atkinson, 1914; *Dibothriocephalus scotti* Shipley, 1907; *Dibothriocephalum wilsoni* Shipley, 1907.

See Remarks.

Hosts and Locality:

From Dailey and Brownell, 1972 - Found in and the Weddell seal (*Leptonyhcotes weddelli*). Information regarding the geographical location of host was not provided by authors.

From Delyamure, 1955 - Found in the Weddell seal (*Leptonyhcotes weddelli*) from an unknown location in the Antarctic.

From King, 1964 - Found in the Weddell seal (*Leptonyhcotes weddelli*). Information regarding the geographical location of host was not provided by author.

From Markowski, 1952a - If *D. archeri* = *D. lashleyi*, then found in the Weddell seal (*Leptonyhcotes weddelli*) from the Antarctic (Debenham Islands, Deception Island, and Melchior Archipelago).

From Yamaguti, 1959 - If *D. archeri* = *D. wilsoni*, then found in the Weddell seal (*Leptonyhcotes weddelli*), the Ross seal (*Ommatophoca rossi*), and the sea leopard (*Hydrurga leptonyx*) [= *Ogmorhynus leptonyx*] from the Antarctic.

Remarks:

Delyamure (1955) questions the original description and classification in his brief historical summary of this parasite.

Diphyllobothrium arctocephali

Hosts and Locality:

From Drummond, 1937 - Found in the Tas-

manian sea bear (*Arctocephalus tasmanicus*) from Lady Julia Percy Island in South Australia.

Diphyllobothrium arctocephalinum

Synonymy:

From Markowski, 1952b - *Dibothriocephalus scoticum* Rennie and Reid, 1912; *Diphyllobothrium arctocephali* Drummond, 1937; *Dibothriocephalus pygoscelis* Rennie and Reid, 1912; *Cordicephalus arctocephalinus* Wardle, McLeod and Stewart, 1947.

Hosts and Locality:

From Dailey and Brownell, 1972 - Found in the Australian sea lion (*Neophoca cinerea*) and Australian fur seal (*Arctocephalus doriferus*). Information regarding the geographical location of host was not provided by authors. See Remarks.

From King, 1964 - Found in the South African fur seal (*Arctocephalus pusillus*), the Tasmanian fur seal (*Arctocephalus tasmanicus*), and in the Australian sea lion (*Neophoca cinerea*). Information regarding the geographical location of hosts was not provided by author.

From Johnston, 1937e - Erronaneously reported to be found in the Australian hair seal (*Arctocephalus forsteri*) from Pearson Island (South Australia). See Remarks.

From Rand, 1959 - Found in the South African fur seal (*Arctocephalus pusillus*) from the southwest coast of Cape Providence.

Remarks:

In his original paper, Johnston (1937e) lists *Arctocephalus forsteri* as a host of this parasite. However, in a later paper (Johnston and Mawson, 1941), he clarifies that the host was actually an Australian sea lion (*Neophoca cinerea*).

Dailey and Brownell (1972) also list the South African fur seal (*Arctocephalus pusillus*) and Tasmanian fur seal (*Arctocephalus tasmanicus*) as hosts of *D. arctocephalinum* and cite "Johnston, 1937" as a source reference. However, there is no "Johnston, 1937" in their bibliography. Johnston did publish a paper in 1937 that describes cestodes found during the Australasian Antarctic Expedition of 1911-1914 (Johnston, 1937b); however no mention of these pinniped species as being hosts of *D. arctocephalinum* could be found.

Diphyllobothrium cameroni

Hosts and Locality:

From Dailey and Brownell, 1972 - Found in the Hawaiian monk seal (*Monachus schauinslandi*). Information regarding the geographical location of host was not provided by authors.

From Rausch, 1969 - Found in the Hawaiian monk seal (*Monachus schauinslandi*) from the Midway Atoll and Leeward Islands.

Remarks:

This species was first proposed by Rausch in 1969.

Diphyllobothrium coniceps

Synonymy:

From Delyamure, 1955 - *Bothriophalus lanceolatus* Germanos, 1895.

From Markowski, 1952b - *Dibothriocephalum cordatum* Leuckart, 1863; *Bothriocephalus cordatus* Leuckart, 1863; *Dibothrium cordatum* Diesing, 1863; *Dibothriocephalus cordatus* Lühe, 1899; *Bothriocephalum schistochilus* Germanos, 1895; *Dibothriocephalum schistochilus* Meggitt, 1924; *Dibothriocephalus romeri* Zschokke, 1903; *Dibothriocephalum romeri* Meggitt, 1924; *Bothriocephalus coniceps* Linstow, 1905; *Bothriocephalum macrophallus* Linstow, 1905; *Dibothriocephalum macrophallus* Meggitt, 1924.

Hosts and Locality:

From Dailey and Brownell, 1972 - Found in the Mediterranean monk seal (*Monachus monachus*). Information regarding the geographical location of host was not provided by authors.

From Delyamure, 1955 - If *D. coniceps* = *D. schistochilus*, then found in the bearded seal (*Erignathus barbatus*), the Greenland seal (*Pagophoca groenlandica*), and in the common seal (*Phoca vitulina*). Geographical distribution includes Spitzbergen (Krasnaya Bay, Zhenevra Bay, and "other places along coast"), Russia (Nokuev Island, Kanin Point, Novaya Zemlya [Russkaya gavan], the coast of west Taimyr, and Kotel'nyi Island. Specific locations of hosts were not provided by author.

From King, 1964 - Found in the Mediterranean monk seal (*Monachus monachus*). Information regarding geographical location of this host was not provided by author.

From Markowski, 1952b - If *D. coniceps* = *D. cordatum*, then found in the walrus (*Odobenus rosmarus*) from Godhavn (Greenland); the bearded seal (*Erignathus barbatus*) from the Hinlopen Straits (Spitzbergen); and in the Greenland or harp seal (*Phoca groenlandica*) from Ginevra Bay (Spitzbergen).

Diphyllobothrium cordatum

Synonymy:

From Markowski, 1952b - *Bothriocephalus cordatus* Leuckart, 1863; *Dibothrium cordatum* Diesing, 1863; *Dibothriocephalus cordatus* Lühe, 1899; *Bothriocephalus schistochilus* Germanos, 1895; *Dibothriocephalus schistochilus* Lühe, 1899; *Diphyllobothrium schistochilus* Meggitt, 1924; *Dibothriocephalus romeri* Zschokke, 1903; *Diphyllobothrium romeri* Meggitt, 1924; *Bothriocephalus coniceps* Linstow, 1905; *Diphyllobothrium coniceps* Meggitt, 1924; *Bothriocephalus macrophallus* Linstow, 1905; *Diphyllobothrium macrophallus* Meggitt, 1924.

From Wardle et al, 1947 - *Cordicephalus auctorum*.

Hosts and Locality:

From Dailey and Brownell, 1972 - Found in the walrus (*Odobenus romarus*), the bearded seal (*Erignathus barbatus*), the harp seal (*Pagophilus groenlandicus*), and the harbor seal (*Phoca vitulina*). Information regarding the geographical location of hosts was not provided by authors.

From Delyamure, 1955 - Found in the bearded seal (*Erignathus barbatus*), harbor seal (*Phoca vitulina*) and Greenland seal (*Phoca groenlandica*). Geographical distribution includes the Arctic Ocean and North Sea (Greenland, Iceland, Siberia, Polar Canada); Pacific Ocean (Bering Sea "?" [sic], Japan); and Russia (Bering Sea and Kaluchin [Siberia]). The author does not specify which hosts were found in which specific location.

From Hilliard, 1960 - Found in the bearded seal (*Erignathus barbatus*) from Alaska.

From King, 1964 - Found in the walrus (*Odobenus romarus*), the bearded seal (*Erignathus barbatus*), the harp seal (*Pagophilus groenlandicus*), and the harbor seal (*Phoca vitulina*). Information regarding the geographical location of hosts was not provided by author.

From Margolis and Dailey, 1972 - Found in the bearded seal (*Erignathus barbatus*) from Alaska.

From Markowski, 1952b - Found in the walrus (*Odobenus romarus*) from Godhavn (Greenland), the bearded seal (*Erignathus barbatus*) from Hinlopen Straits (Spitzbergen), and the harp seal (*Phoca groenlandica*) from Ginevra Bay (Spitzbergen).

From Railliet, 1899 - Found in the harbor seal (*Phoca vitulina*) from the Gulf of Somme (France).

From Yamaguti, 1959 - Found in the walrus (*Odobenus romarus*), the bearded seal (*Erignathus barbatus*), and the harp seal (*Phoca groenlandica*) from Greenland and Spitzbergen. The author does not specify which hosts were found in which specific location.

Diphyllobothrium elegans

Synonymy:

From Markowski, 1952b - *Bothriocephalus elegans* Krabbe, 1865; *Dibothriocephalus elegans* Zschokke, 1903.

See Remarks.

Hosts and Locality:

From Dailey and Brownell, 1972 - Found in the Mediterranean monk seal (*Monachus mona-*

chus). Information regarding the geographical location of host was not provided by authors.

From Delyamure, 1955 - If *D. elegans* = *D. tetrapterus*, then found in the monk seal (*Monachus monachus*), the bearded seal (*Erignathus barbatus*), the common seal (*Phoca vitulina*), and the hooded seal (*Cystophora cristata*). All hosts were from northern Europe (specific locations not provided by author).

From King, 1964 - Found in the common seal (*Phoca vitulina*), the Mediterranean monk seal (*Monachus monachus*), and the hooded seal *Cystophora cristata*). Information regarding the geographical location of hosts was not provided by author.

From Markowski, 1952b - Found in the monk seal (*Monachus monachus*) from Senegal, and in the common seal (*Phoca vitulina*) from an unknown location.

From Yamaguti, 1959 - Found in *Phoca cristata*, the common seal (*Phoca vitulina*), and the Steller's sea lion (*Eumetopias jubata*) from unspecified locations in Denmark and Greenland.

Remarks:

Delyamure (1955) presents an historic account of *D. tetrapterus*, but does not mention *D. elegans*. Although Delyamure does not list *Diphyllobothrium elegans*, he does present *Bothriocephalus elegans* (Krabbe, 1865) as a synonym of *Diphyllobothrium tetraspterus*. *B. elegans* is listed as a synonym *D. elegans* by Markowski (1952a). Delyamure also lists *Krabbe tetrapterus* (Siebold, 1848) and *Diplogonoporus tetrapterus* (Siebold, 1848) as being synonymous with *D. tetrapterus*.

Margolis (1956) does not lists *D. elegans*, but does list *Diplogonoporus tetrapterus*. Delyamure (1955) listed *D. tetrapterus* as synonymous with *B. elegans*, which Markowki (1952b) lists as synonymous with *D. elegans*.

Diphyllobothrium fasciatus

Hosts and Locality:

From King, 1964 - Found in the ringed seal (*Phoca hispida*). Information regarding the geographical location of host was not provided by author.

Diphyllobothrium fuhrmanni

Synonymy:

From Delyamure, 1955 - *Diphyllobothrium stemmacephalum* Yamaguti, 1935 nec *D. stemmacephalum* Cobbold, 1858.

Hosts and Locality:

From Dailey and Brownell, 1972 - Found in the long beaked dolphin (*Stenella longirostris*) and in the black finless porpoise (*Neophocoena phocoenoides*). Information regarding the geographical location of hosts was not provided by authors.

From Delyamure, 1955 - Found in the finless porpoise (*Neomeris phocaenoides*) and the spotted dolphin (*Prodelphis longirostris* [= *Delphinus dussumieri*]) from the Pacific Ocean (off coast of Japan and China).

From Yamaguti, 1959 - Found in *Delphinus dussumieri* [= *Prodelphinus longirostris*] and *Neomeris phocaenoides* from the South China Sea.

Diphyllobothrium glaciale

Synonymy:

From Margolis and Dailey, 1972 - *Cordicephalus arctocephalinus* Johnston, 1937; *Diphyllobothrium pacificum* Nyberlin, 1931; "Species No. 2" of Stunkard, 1948; *Diphyllobothrium krotovi* Delyamure, 1955.

From Markowski, 1952b - *Bothriocephalus sp.* Stiles and Hassall, 1899; *Clestobothrium glaciale* Cholodkovsky, 1915; *Adenocephalus pacificus* Nyberlin, 1931.

From Wardle et al, 1947 - *Diphyllobothrium arctocephali* Drummond, 1937; *Diphyllobothrium grandis* Blanchard, 1894.

Hosts and Locality:

From Dailey and Brownell, 1972 - Found in the South American fur seal (*Arctocephalus australis*), and in the northern fur seal (*Callorhinus ursinus*). Information regarding the

geographical location of hosts was not provided by authors.

From King, 1964 - Found in the South American fur seal (*Arctocephalus australis*), and in the northern fur seal (*Callorhinus ursinus*). Information regarding the geographical location of hosts was not provided by author.

From Markowski, 1952b - Found in the South American fur seal (*Arctocephalus australis*) from Masatierra Juan, Fernandez Islands; and in the northern fur seal (*Callorhinus ursinus*) from the Pribylov Islands and St. George Island.

Remarks:

A brief historical account of *D. glaciale* is provided by Delyamure (1955) and Margolis (1954).

Diphyllobothrium hians

Synonymy:

From Markowski, 1952b - *Dibothrium hians* Diesing, 1850; *Bothriocephalus hians* Leuckart, 1863; *Dibothriocephalus hians* Lühe, 1899; *Diphyllobothrium hians* Meggitt, 1924; *Dibothriocephalus polycalceolus* Ariola, 1896; *Diphyllobothrium polycalceolum* Meggitt, 1924; *Bothriocephalus sp.* Chapin, 1925; *Diphyllobothrium variabile* (Krabbe, 1865) Guiart, 1935.

Hosts and Locality:

From Dailey and Brownell, 1972 - Found in the harbor seal (*Phoca vitulina*), the bearded seal (*Erignathus barbatus*), the Mediterranean monk seal (*Monachus monachus*), the Hawaiian monk seal (*Monachus schauinslandi*), and in the ringed seal (*Phoca hispida*). Information regarding the geographical location of hosts was not provided by authors.

From King, 1964 - Found in the harbor seal (*Phoca vitulina*), the bearded seal (*Erignathus barbatus*), the Mediterranean monk seal (*Monachus monachus*), the Hawaiian monk seal (*Monachus schauinslandi*), and in the ringed seal (*Phoca hispida*). Information regarding the geographical location of hosts was not provided by author.

From Markowski, 1952b - Found in the Hawaiian monk seal (*Monachus schauinslandi*) from Laysan Island, Hawaii; and in a "seal, probably the common seal (*Phoca vitulina*)" from the London Zoological Gardens.

Diphyllobothrium krooyi

Hosts and Locality:

From Dailey and Brownell, 1972 - Found in the northern fur seal (*Callorhinus ursinus*). Information regarding the geographical location of hosts was not provided by authors. See Remarks.

Remarks:

Dailey and Brownell (1972) cite Delyamure (1955) as a source reference for this claim. However, no mention of this parasite was found in the Delyamure paper. Dailey and Brownell's listing may be a translation or typographic misspelling of *Diphyllobothrium krotovi*.

Diphyllobothrium krotovi

Synonymy:

From Delyamure, 1955 - *Bothriocephalus sp.* Stiles and Hassall, 1899.

From Margolis and Dailey, 1972 - *Diphyllobothrium pacificum* Nyberlin, 1931; *Adenocephalus septentrionalis* Nyberlin, 1931; *Cordicephalus arctocephalinus* Johnston, 1937; *Diphyllobothrium glaciale* Cholodkovsky, 1915.

Hosts and Locality:

From Delyamure, 1955 - Found in the Kurile fur seal (*Callorhinus ursinus curilensis*), and in the Alaskan fur seal (*Callorhinus ursinus alascanus*). Geographical distribution includes the Pacific Ocean (St. Paul Island, Alaska), and Russia (Sea of Okhotsk [Tyuleni Island]).

From King, 1964 - Found in the northern fur seal (*Callorhinus ursinus*). Information regarding specific geographical location of host was not provided by author.

From Margolis and Dailey, 1972 - Found in the northern fur seal (*Callorhinus ursinus*), the

Steller's sea lion (*Eumetopias jubata*), and the California sea lion (*Zalophus californianus*). Geographical distribution includes Alaska, British Columbia, and California. The author does not specify which hosts were found in which specific location.

Remarks:

Delyamure (1955) provides a brief historical account of this parasite.

Dailey and Brownell (1972) list a parasite under *C. ursinus* as "*Diphyllobothrium krooyi*" and reference it to Delyamure (1955). This is probably a translation or typographic misspelling of *Diphyllobothrium krotovi*.

Diphyllobothrium lanceolatum

Synonymy:

From Delyamure, 1955 - *Bothriocephalus lanceolatus* Krabbe, 1865; *Dibothriocephalus lanceolatus* Krabbe, 1865; *Cordiocephalus lanceolatus* (Krabbe, 1865) Wardle, McLeob and Stewart, 1948.

From Markowski, 1952b - "Species No.1" of Stunkard, 1948.

From Stunkard and Schoenborn, 1936 - *Diphyllobothrium schistochilus* and *Diphyllobothrium coniceps*.

From Wardle et al, 1947 - *Cordicephalus phocarus*.

From Yamaguti, 1959 - *Diphyllobothrium coniceps* Linstow, 1905.

Hosts and Locality:

From Dailey and Brownell, 1972 - Found in the ringed seal (*Phoca hispida*), the bearded seal (*Erignathus barbatus*), the Mediterranean monk seal (*Monachus monachus*), the harp seal (*Pagophilus groenlandicus*), the white whale (*Delphinapterus leucas*), and the harbor porpoise (*Phocoena phocoena*). Information regarding the geographical location of hosts was not provided by authors.

From Delyamure, 1955 - Found in the bearded seal (*Phoca barbatus*), the ringed seal (*Phoca hispida*), the Okhotsk ringed seal (*Phoca hispida ochotensis*), *Phoca sp*, monk seal ["?" sic]

(*Monachus monachus*), and the finned porpoise (*Phocoena phocoena*). Geographical distribution includes various points in the Arctic Ocean, North Sea, Barents Sea, Kara Sea, Bering Sea, Okhotsk Sea, Baltic Sea, Greenland, Spitzbergen, Jan Mayen Island, Hooker Island, Alaska, St. Lawrence Island, and in Russia (Novaya Zembya, Hooker Island, western Taimyr, Kotel'nyi Island, and Sakhalin). Specific locations of where the hosts were found are mentioned for a bearded seal (*Phoca barbatus*) from Greenland (Baffin Bay and Godhavn), a bearded seal (*Phoca barbatus*) from the coast of Greenland, a bearded seal (*Phoca barbatus*) from the Kara Sea, a bearded seal (*Phoca barbatus*) from Russkaya Gavan' (Hooker Island), Karrskie Vorot, and Loginov Island. A ringed seal (*Phoca hispida*) was from Russkaya Gavan' and another from the west coast Novaya Zembya; a bearded seal (*Phoca barbatus*) was from Alaska (St. Lawrence Island); and a porpoise (*Phocoena phocoena*) from the Baltic Sea.

From Delyamure and Kleinenberg, 1958 - Found in the white whale (*Delphinapterus leucas*). Information regarding the geographical location of host was not provided by authors.

From Joyeux and Baer, 1936 - Found in the monk seal (*Monachus monachus*). Information regarding the geographical location of host was not provided by authors.

From King, 1964 - Found in the bearded seal (*Erignathus barbatus*), the ringed seal (*Phoca hispida*), the harp seal (*Pagophilus groenlandicus*), and in the monk seal (*Monachus monachus*). Information regarding specific geographical location of hosts was not provided by author.

From Margolis and Dailey, 1972 - Found in the harbor seal (*Phoca vitulina richardi*) and in a bearded seal (*Erignathus barbatus*) from Alaska. See Remarks.

From Markowski, 1952b - Found in the bearded seal (*Erignathus barbatus*) from Godhavn (Greenland), Hinlopen Straits, Ginevra Bay, Spitzbergen (80° 06' N, 15° 40'E), and Ungava (Canada).

From Yamaguti, 1959 - Found in the bearded seal (*Erignathus barbatus*) from Godhavn, Spitzbergen, Ungava, and St. Lawrence Island, Alaska.

Remarks:

Delyamure (1955) provides a historical account and detailed description of this parasite.

Margolis and Dailey (1972) provide a brief summary of the taxonomic history of this parasite.

Diphyllobothrium lashleyi

Synonymy:

From Delyamure, 1955 - *Dibothriocephalum tectus*, Linstow, 1892; *Bothriocephalus tectus* Linstow, 1892; *Dibothriocephalum clavatum* Railliet and Henry, 1912; *Dibothriocephalum scoticum* Railliet and Henry, 1912.

From Johnston, 1937b - *Dibothriocephalus lashleyi* Leiper and Atkinson, 1914.

From Markowski, 1952a - *Dibothriocephalus lashleyi* Leiper and Atkinson, 1914; *Dibothriocephalus archeri* Leiper and Atkinson, 1914; *Diphyllobothrium archeri* Meggitt, 1924.

From McEwin, 1957 - *Dibothriocephalus lashleyi* Leiper and Atkinson, *Diphyllobothrium lashleyi* Meggitt, 1924.

Hosts and Locality:

From Dailey and Brownell, 1972 - Found in and the Weddell seal (*Leptonyhcotes weddelli*). Information regarding the geographical location of host was not provided by authors.

From Delyamure, 1955 - If *D. lashleyi* = *D. tectus*, then found in the Weddell seal (*Leptonyhcotes weddelli*), the leopard seal (*Hydrurga leptonyx*), and the southern elephant seal (*Mirounga leonina*) from Antarctica (Peterman Island) and Georgia.

From Johnston, 1937b - Found in the Weddell seal (*Leptonyhcotes weddelli*) from the Antarctic (Commonwealth Bay).

From King, 1964 - Found in and the Weddell seal (*Leptonyhcotes weddelli*). Information regarding the geographical location of host was not provided by author.

From Markowski, 1952a - Found in the Weddell seal (*Leptonyhcotes weddelli*) from the Antarctic (Debenham Islands, Deception Island, and Melchior Archipelago).

From McEwin, 1957 - Found in the Weddell seal (*Leptonyhcotes weddelli*) from the Antarctic (Enderby Island [65° 50′ S, 54° 23′ E], Commonwealth Bay, Cape Denison, and King George V Land).

Remarks:

D. lashleyi has been redescribed by McEwin (1957).

Diphyllobothrium latum

Synonymy:

From Delyamure, 1955 - *Taenia lata* Linnaeus, 1758; *Taenia grisea* Pellas, 1761; *Taenia acephala* Vogel, 1772; *Taenia membranocea* Pellas, 1781; *Taenia lata hominus* Bloch, 1782; *Taenia dentata* Batsch, 1786; *Taenia lata candida* Fischer, 1789; *Taenia inerme humina* Brera, 1802; *Halisis membranocea* (Pallas, 1761) Zeder, 1803; *Taenia humana inermis* Rudolphi, 1810; *Bothriocephalus hominis* Lamark, 1816; *Bothriocephalus latus* (Linnearus, 1758) Bremser, 1819; *Dibothrium latum* (Linnearus, 1758) Diesing, 1850; *Taenia vertebrata* Leuckart, 1866; *Bothriocephalus balticus* Kuchermeister, 1886; *Dibothriocephalus latus* (Linnearus, 1758) Lühe, 1899.

From Yamaguti, 1959 - *Dibothrium serratum* Diesing, 1850; *Diphyllobothrium americanus* Hall and Wigdor, 1918.

Hosts and Locality:

From Dailey and Brownell, 1972 - Found in the walrus (*Odobenus romarus*), the ringed seal (*Phoca hispida*), the bearded seal (*Erignathus barbatus*), the hooded seal (*Cystophora cristata*), the Mediterranean monk seal (*Monachus monachus*), the harbor seal (*Phoca vitulina*) and the harbor porpoise (*Phocoena phocoena*). Information regarding the geographical location of hosts was not provided by authors.

From Delyamure, 1955 - Found in the walrus (*Odobenus romarus*), the bearded seal (*Erignathus barbatus*), the hooded seal (*Cystophora cristata*), the ringed seal (*Phoca hispida*), the common seal (*Phoca vitulina*), the monk seal ["?" sic] (*Monachus monachus*), and the finned poipoise (*Phocoena phocoena*). Geographical distribution for pinnipeds includes northern Europe, northeast and North Atlantic, and the Arctic Ocean (European-Greenland part). Geographical distribution for cetaceans includes the Baltic Sea and the North Atlantic.

From King, 1964 - Found in the walrus (*Odobenus romarus*), the ringed seal (*Phoca hispida*), the bearded seal (*Erignathus barbatus*), the hooded seal (*Cystophora cristata*), the Mediterranean monk seal (*Monachus monachus*), and in the harbor seal (*Phoca vitulina*). Information regarding the geographical location of hosts was not provided by author.

From Schmidt-Ries, 1939 - Found in the harbor porpoise (*Phocoena phocoena*) from the Baltic Sea.

Remarks:

Delyamure (1955) lists a number of other definite hosts including man, domestic cat and dog, and numerous terrestrial carnivorus mammals belonging to the families of *Canidae, Fekidae, Viverridae, Mustelidae,* and *Ursidae*. In addition, Delyamure lists a number of intermediate hosts, including Crustaceans (Copepoda)- cyclops (*Cyclops strenuous*, etc.) and diaptomus (*Diaptomus gracilis* and *Diaptomus graciloides*). Supplementary hosts in various species of fish (*Esox lucius, Perca fluviatilus, Acerica cernua, Lota vulgaris, Salmo lacustris, Salmo salar, Coregonus lavaretus, Coregonus albula, Osmerus eperlanus, Lucioperca lucioperca, Gottus gobio,* and *Pygosteus pungitius*). Delyamure (1955) also provides a brief historical summary of *D. latum*.

Eguchi (1934) discusses the salmon (*Oncorhynchus*) as a carrier of *D. latum*.

Markowski (1952b) questions the accuracy of the identification of this parasite in pinnipeds that were made by earlier investigators.

A review of the morphological characteristics and occurrence of *D. latum* in the Alaska region is provided by Rausch and Hilliard (1970).

Diphyllobothrium macrocephalus

Synonymy:

From Delyamure, 1955 - *Diphyllobothrium macrocephalus* Linstow, 1905.

From Markowski, 1952b - *Diphyllobothrium cordatum* Leuckart, 1863; *Bothriocephalus cordatus* Leuckart, 1863; *Dibothrium cordatum* Diesing, 1863; *Dibothriocephalus cordatus* Lühe, 1899; *Bothriocephalus schistochilus* Germanos, 1895; *Dibothriocephalus schistochilus* Lühe 1899; *Diphyllobothrium schistochilus* Meggitt, 1924; *Dibothriocephalus romeri* Zschokke, 1903; *Diphyllobothrium romeri* Meggith, 1924; *Bothriocephalus coniceps* Linstow, 1905; *Diphyllobothrium coniceps* Meggitt, 1924; *Bothriocephalus macrocephalus* Linstow, 1905.

Hosts and Locality:

From Dailey and Brownell, 1972 - Found in the northern fur seal (*Callorinus ursinus*) and the bearded seal (*Erignathus barbatus*). Information regarding the geographical location of hosts was not provided by authors.

From Delyamure, 1955 - Found in the northern fur seal (*Callorinus ursinus*) and the bearded seal (*Erignathus barbatus*) from the North Sea and eastern seas.

From King, 1964 - Found in the bearded seal (*Erignathus barbatus*). Information regarding the geographical location of host was not provided by author.

From Markowski, 1952b - If *D. macrocephalus* = *D. cordatum*, then found in the walrus (*Odobenus romarus*) from Godhavn (Greenland); the bearded seal (*Erignathus barbatus*) from Hinlopen Straits (Spitzbergen); and the Greenland harp seal (*Phoca groenlandica*) from Ginevra Bay (Spitzbergen).

From Wardle et al, 1947 - If *D. macrocephalus* = *C. auctorum*, then found in "seals" from northern Atlantic waters.

Diphyllobothrium macrophallos

Hosts and Locality:

From King, 1964 - Found in the northern fur seal (*Callorinus ursinus*). Information regarding the geographical location of host was not provided by author.

Diphyllobothrium mobile

Synonymy:

From Johnston, 1937b - *Dibothriocephalus mobilis* Rennie and Reid, 1912; *Dibothriocephalum wilsoni* Railliet and Henry, 1912; *Dibothriocephalus coatsi* Leiper and Atkinson, 1914; *Diphyllobothrium mobilis* Meggitt, 1924.

From Markowski, 1952a - *Dibothriocephalus mobilis* Rennie and Reid, 1912; *Dibothriocephalum wilsoni* Railliet and Henry, 1912; *Dibothriocephalus coatsi* Leiper and Atkinson, 1914 (nec Rennie and Reid, 1912).

From McEwin, 1957 - *Dibothriocephalus mobilis* Rennie and Reid, 1912; *Dibothriocephalus mobilis* Fuhrmann 1921; *Diphyllobothrium mobile* (Rennie and Reid) Meggitt, 1924.

Hosts and Locality:

From Dailey and Brownell, 1972 - Found in the Ross seal (*Ommatophoca rossi*). Information regarding the geographical location of host was not provided by authors.

From Johnston, 1937b - Found in the Weddell seal (*Leptonyhcotes weddelli*) and in the Ross seal (*Ommatophoca rossi*) from the Antarctic (Queen Mary Land).

From King, 1964 - Found in the Weddell seal (*Leptonyhcotes weddelli*) and in the Ross seal (*Ommatophoca rossi*). Information regarding geographical location of hosts was not provided by author.

From Markowski, 1952a - Found in the Weddell seal (*Leptonyhcotes weddelli*) from Debenham Islands (Antarctica).

From McEwin, 1957 - Found in the Weddell

seal (*Leptonyhcotes weddelli*) off Enderby Island (65° 50′ S, 54° 23′ E).

From Yamaguti, 1959 - Found in the Weddell seal (*Leptonyhcotes weddelli*) from Antarctica.

Remarks:

Some authors suggest the *D. mobile* is synonymous with *D. mobilis*. Delyamure (1955) lists *D. mobilis* (Rennie and Reid, 1912), along with other synonyms, under *D. quadratum*. These other synonyms include *Dibothriocephalus coatsi*, which Markowski considers synonymous with *D. mobile*. Yamaguti (1959) recognizes both *D. mobile* and *D. mobilis*, the latter being synonymous with *D. wilsoni*. As noted above, Markowski (1952a) list *Dibothriocephalus mobilis* and *Dibothriocephalum wilsoni* as synonyms of *D. mobilis*.

If *D. mobile* is the same as *D. mobilis* and *D. wilsoni*, other hosts listed by Yamaguti (1959), include the Ross seal (*Ommatophoca rossi*), the Weddell seal (*Leptonychotes weddelli*), and *Ogmorhinus leptonyx*; all from the Antarctic.

Diphyllobothrium osmeri

Hosts and Locality:

From Dailey and Brownell, 1972 - Found in the harbor seal (*Phoca vitulina*). Information regarding the geographical location of host was not provided by authors.

From Margolis and Dailey, 1972 - Found in the harbor seal (*Phoca vitulina richardi*) from Alaska.

From Neiland, 1962 - Found in the harbour seal (*Phoca vitulina richardi*) from Alaska.

Remarks:

Neiland (1962) notes that *D. osmeri* has been found in the rainbow smelt (*Osmerus dentex*) from Alaska.

Diphyllobothrium pacificum

Synonymy:

From Margolis, 1956 - *Adenocephalus pacifi-*

cus Nybelin, 1931; "Species #2" of Stunkard, 1948.

From Margolis and Dailey, 1972 - *Bothriocephalus sp.* Stiles and Hassall, 1899; *Adenocephalus septentrionalis* Nybelin, 1931; *Cordicephalus arctophalinus* Johnston, 1937, and Wardle, McLeod and Stewart, 1947; *Diphyllobothrium glaciale* Cholodkovsky, 1915 and Markowski 1952; *Diphyllobothrium krotovi* Delyamure, 1955.

Hosts and Locality:

From Baer, 1969 - Found in the South American sea lion (*Otaria byronia*) from the Guanape Islands (Peru).

From Dailey, 1975 - Found in the California sea lion (*Zalophus californianus*) from the Galapagos Islands.

From Dailey and Brownell, 1972 - Found in the California sea lion (*Zalophus californianus*), the northern fur seal (*Callorhinus ursinus*), and the Steller's sea lion (*Eumatopias jubata*). Information regarding the geographical location of hosts was not provided by authors.

From Delyamure, 1955 - Found in the southern fur seal *Arctocephalus australis* from Antarctica.

From Keyes, 1965 - Found in the northern fur seal (*Callorhinus ursinus*) from the Pribilof Islands (Alaska).

From Margolis, 1956 - Found in the Steller's sea lion (*Eumatopias jubata*) from Quatsino Sound, Vancouver Island, and British Columbia; and in the northern fur seal (*Callorhinus ursinus*) from the north Pacific.

From Margolis and Dailey, 1972 - Found in the northern fur seal (*Callorhinus ursinus*), the Steller's sea lion (*Eumetopias jubata*), and in the California sea lion (*Zalophus californianus*) from Alaska, British Columbia, and California.

From Nybelin, 1931 - Found in the fur seal (*Arctocephalus australis*) from Juan Fernandez Islands. See Remarks.

Remarks:

Markowski (1952b) considers *Arctocephalus australis* to be synonymous with *Neophoca ci-*

nerea. Sivertsen (1954) disagrees and claims these are distinct species. Siversten further claims that the *A. australis* referred to by Nyberlin was actually the fur seal *Arctophoca philippi.* For a review of the taxonomic history of *D. pacificum,* see Margolis (1954), Margolis (1956), and Baer et al (1967).

Diphyllobothrium perfoliatum

Synonymy:

From Johnston, 1937b - *Diphyllobothrium clavatum* Railliet and Henry, 1912; *Dibothriocephalus perfoliatum* Fuhrmann, 1924.

From Markowski, 1952a - *Diphyllobothrium clavatum* Railliet and Henry, 1912; *Glandicephalus perfoliatus* Railliet and Henry, 1912; *Dibothriocephalus perfoliatum* Fuhrmann, 1920; *Diphyllobothrium rufum* Leiper and Atkinson, 1914.

From Yamaguti, 1959 - *Glandicephalus perfoliatus* Railliet and Henry, 1912; *Cordicephalus tectus* Wardel, McLoed and Stewart, 1947.

See Remarks.

Hosts and Locality:

From Dailey and Brownell, 1972 - Found in and the Weddell seal (*Leptonyhcotes weddelli*). Information regarding the geographical location of host was not provided by authors.

From Delyamure, 1955 - Found in the Weddell seal (*Leptonyhcotes weddelli*) from the Antarctic.

From Johnston, 1937b - Found in the Weddell seal (*Leptonyhcotes weddelli*) from Antarctic (Commonwealth Bay).

From King, 1964 - Found in and the Weddell seal (*Leptonyhcotes weddelli*). Information regarding the geographical location of host was not provided by author.

From Markowski, 1952a - If *D. perfoliatum* = *Glandicephalus perfoliatus,* then found in the Weddell seal (*Leptonyhcotes weddelli*) from the Antarctic. Specific locations include Debenham Islands, Stella Creek, Deception Island, Argentine Islands (Galindez Island and Winter Island), Beascochea Bay; Gra-

ham Land (Hut Cove and Hope Bay), and Palmer Archipelago (Port Lockroy and Wiencke Island).

From Yamaguti, 1959 - If *D. perfoliatum* = *Glandicephalus perfoliatus,* then found in the Weddell seal (*Leptonyhcotes weddelli*) from the Antarctic.

Remarks:

Delyamure (1955) does not give any synonyms for this parasite. The synonym *D. refum* described by Markowski (1952a) was later redescribed by McEwin (1957) as a variety of *Glandicephalus perfoliatus.*

Diphyllobothrium polycalceolum

Hosts and Locality:

From King, 1964 - Found in the common seal (*Phoca vitulina*). Information regarding the geographical location of host was not provided by author.

Diphyllobothrium quadratum

Synonymy:

From Delyamure, 1955 - *Dibothriocephalum mobilis* Rennie and Reid, 1912.

From Johnston, 1937b - *Bothriocephalus quadratus* Linstow, 1892; *Dibothriocephalus quadratus* Zschokke, 1903; *Dibothriocephalus coatsi* Rennie and Reid, 1912; *Diphyllobothrium resimum* Fuhrmann, 1921; *Diphyllobothrium coatsi* Meggitt, 1924.

From Markowski, 1952a - *Bothriocephalus quadratus* Linstow, 1892; *Dibothriocephalus quadratus* Zschokke, 1903; *Cordicephalus quadratus* Wardle, McLeob and Stewart, 1947; *Dibothriocephalus coatsi* Rennie and Reid, 1912; *Bothriocephalus coatsi* Fuhrmann, 1920; *Dibothriocephalus resimum* Railliet and Henry, 1912.

From McEwin, 1957 - *Bothriocephalus quadratus* Linstow, 1892; *Dibothriocephalus quadratus* Zschokke, 1903; *Dibothriocephalum quadratus* Railliet and Henry, 1912; *Dibothriocephalus coatsi* Rennie and Reid, 1912; *Bothriocephalus coatsi* Fuhrmann, 1921; *Diphyllobothrium coatsi* Meggitt, 1924.

Hosts and Locality:

From Dailey and Brownell, 1972 - Found in the leopard seal (*Hydrurga leptonyx*) and the Weddell seal (*Leptonyhcotes weddelli*). Information regarding the geographical location of hosts was not provided by authors.

From Delyamure, 1955 - Found in the sea leopard (*Hydrurga leptonyx*) and the Weddell seal (*Leptonyhcotes weddelli*) from Antarctica (near Peterman Island), South Georgia, and from a leopard seal (*Hydrurga leptonyx*) that died in the Moscow Zoo.

From Johnston, 1937b - Found in the leopard seal (*Hydrurga leptonyx*) from the Antarctic (South Georgia).

From King, 1964 - Found in the leopard seal (*Hydrurga leptonyx*) and the Weddell seal (*Leptonyhcotes weddelli*). Information regarding the geographical location of hosts was not provided by author.

From Markowski, 1952a - Found in leopard seals (*Hydrurga leptonyx*) from Antarctica (Galindez Island, Argentine Islands, Debenham Islands, Horseshoe Island, Sandefjord Harbour, and Coronation Island).

From McEwin, 1957 - Found in leopard seals (*Hydrurga leptonyx*) from Heard Island (Antarctica).

Remarks:

D. quadratus has been redescribed by McEwin (1957).

Diphyllobothrium romeri

Synonymy:

From Markowski, 1952b - *Diphyllobothrium cordatum* Leuckart, 1863; *Dibothrium cordatum* Diesing, 1863; *Dibothriocephalus cordatus* Lühe, 1899; *Bothriocephalus schistochilus* Germanos, 1895; *Dibothriocephalus schistochilus* Lühe, 1899; *Diphyllobothrium schistochilus* Meggitt, 1924; *Dibothriocephalus romeri* Zschokke, 1903; *Bothriocephalus coniceps* Linstow, 1905; *Diphyllobothrium coniceps* Meggitt, 1924; *Bothriocephalus macrophallus* Linstow, 1905; *Diphyllobothrium macrophallus* Meggitt, 1924.

Hosts and Locality:

From Dailey and Brownell, 1972 - Found in the walrus (*Odobenus romarus*). Information regarding the geographical location of host was not provided by authors.

From Delyamure, 1955 - Found in the walrus (*Odobenus romarus*) from the Arctic and from the White Sea (point of exit).

From King, 1964 - Found in the walrus (*Odobenus romarus*). Information regarding the geographical location of host was not provided by author.

From Markowski, 1952b - If *D. romeri* = *D. cordatum*, then found in the walrus (*Odobenus romarus*) from Godhavn (Greenland), the bearded seal (*Erignathus barbatus*) from Hinlopen Straits (Spitzbergen), and in the harp seal (*Phoca groenlandica*) from Ginevra Bay (Spitzbergen).

Remarks:

Markowski (1952b) provides a brief historical account of this parasite and discusses problems with identifying the *D. romeri* (= *D. cordatum*) species.

Diphyllobothrium rufum

Synonymy:

From Markowski, 1952a - *Glandicephalus perfoliatus* Railliet and Henry, 1912; *Diphyllobothrium perfoliatum* Railliet and Henry, 1912; *Dibothriocephalus perfoliatum* Fuhrmann, 1920; *Diphyllobothrium clavatum* Railliet and Henry, 1912.

From Yamaguti, 1959 - *Cordicephalus tectus* Wardel, McLoed and Stewart, 1947.

See Remarks.

Hosts and Locality:

From Dailey and Brownell, 1972 - Found in and the Weddell seal (*Leptonyhcotes weddelli*). Information regarding the geographical location of host was not provided by authors.

From Delyamure, 1955 - Found in the Weddell seal (*Leptonyhcotes weddelli*) from an unspecified location in the Antarctic.

From Johnston, 1937b- Found in the Weddell seal (*Leptonyhcotes weddelli*) from the Antarctic (Commonwealth Bay).

From King, 1964 - Found in and the Weddell seal (*Leptonyhcotes weddelli*). Information regarding the geographical location of host was not provided by author.

From Markowski, 1952a - If *D. rufum* = *Glandicephalus perfoliatus*, then found in the Weddell seal (*Leptonyhcotes weddelli*) from the Antarctic. Specific locations include the Debenham Islands, Stella Creek, Deception Island, Argentine Islands (Galindez Island and Winter Island), Beascochea Bay, Graham Land (Hut Cove and Hope Bay), and Palmer Archipelago (Port Lockroy and Wiencke Island).

From Yamaguti, 1959 - If *D. rufum* = *Glandicephalus perfoliatus*, then found in the Weddell seal (*Leptonyhcotes weddelli*) from the Antarctic.

Remarks:

D. rufum was redescribed as a variety of *D. perfoliatus* by McEwin (1957).

Diphyllobothrium schistochilus

Synonymy:

From Markowski, 1952b - *Diphyllobothrium cordatum* Leuckart, 1863; *Bothriocephalus cordatus* Leuckart, 1863; *Dibothrium cordatum* Diesing, 1863; *Dibothriocephalus schistochilus* Lühe, 1899; *Diphyllobothrium romeri* Meggitt, 1924; *Dibothriocephalus romeri* Zschokke, 1903; *Bothriocephalus coniceps* Linstow, 1905; *Diphyllobothrium coniceps* Meggitt, 1924; *Bothriocephalus macrophallus* Linstow, 1905; *Diphyllobothrium macrophallus* Meggitt, 1924.

Hosts and Locality:

From Dailey and Brownell, 1972 - Found in the harbor seal (*Phoca vitulina*), the harp seal (*Pagophilus groenlandicus*), and in the bearded seal (*Erignathus barbatus*). Information regarding the geographical location of hosts was not provided by authors.

From Delyamure, 1955 - Found in the bearded seal (*Erignathus barbatus*), the Greenland seal (*Phoca groenlandica*), and in the common seal (*Phoca vitulina*). Geographical distribution includes Spitzbergen (Krusnaya Bay, Zhenevra Bay, and other places along the coast), and Russia (Nokuev Island, Kanin Point, Novaya Zembya [Russkaya gavan'], coast of western Taimyr, and Kotel'nyi Island). The author does not specify which hosts were found in which specific location.

From Johnson et al, 1966 - Found in the bearded seal (*Erignathus barbatus*) from Alaska.

From King, 1964 - Found in the harbor seal (*Phoca vitulina*), the harp seal (*Pagophilus groenlandicus*), and in the bearded seal (*Erignathus barbatus*). Information regarding the geographical location of hosts was not provided by author.

From Margolis and Dailey, 1972 - Found in the bearded seal (*Erignathus barbatus*) from Alaska.

From Markowski, 1952b - If *D. schistochilus* = *D. cordatum*, then found in the walrus (*Odobenus romarus*) from Godhavn; the bearded seal (*Erignathus barbatus*) from Hinlopen Straits (Spitzbergen); and the Greenland seal (*Phoca groenlandica*) from Ginevra Bay (Spitzbergen).

Remarks:

Delyamure (1955) provides a brief historical account of this parasite.

Diphyllobothrium scoticum

Synonymy:

From Delyamure, 1955 - *Bothriocephalus tectus* Linstow, 1892; *Diphyllobothrium tectus* Linstow, 1892; *Dibothriocephalus lashleyi* Leiper and Atkinson, 1914.

From Johnston, 1937b - *Dibothriocephalus pygoscelis* Rennie and Reid, 1912.

From Markowski, 1952b - *Dibothriocephalus scoticum* Rennie and Reid, 1912; Railliet and Henry, 1912; *Dibothriocephalum scoti-*

cum Meggitt, 1924; *Dibothriocephalus pygosce-lis* Rennie and Reid, 1912; *Diphyllobothrium arctocephalinum* Johnston, 1937; *Diphyllobothrium arctocephali* Drummond, 1937; *Cordicephalus arctocephalinus* Wardle, McLeod and Stewart, 1947.

From McEwin, 1957 - *Dibothriocephalus scoticum* Rennie and Reid, 1912; *Diphyllobothrium scoticum* Rennie and Reid, Meggit, 1924; *Dibothriocephalus pygoscelis* Rennie and Reid, 1912

See Remarks.

Hosts and Locality:

From Dailey and Brownell, 1972 - Found in the South American sea lion (*Otaria byronia*) and the leopard seal (*Hydrurga leptonyx*). Information regarding the geographical location of hosts was not provided by authors.

From Delyamure, 1955 - Found in the Weddell seal (*Leptonyhcotes weddelli*), the elephant seal (*Mirounga leonina*), and in the sea leopard (*Hydrurga leptonyx*) from Antarctica (Peterman Island) and Georgia.

From Johnston, 1937b - Found in the leopard seal (*Hydrurga leptonyx*) from the Antarctic (Macquarie Island).

From King, 1964 - Found in the South American sea lion (*Otaria byronia*) and the leopard seal (*Hydrurga leptonyx*). Information regarding the geographical location of hosts was not provided by author.

From Markowski, 1952a - Found in the leopard seal (*Hydrurga leptonyx*) from Debenham Islands.

From McEwin, 1957 - Found in the leopard seal (*Hydrurga leptonyx*) from Antarctica (Heard Island).

Remarks:

Margolis (1954) states *Diphyllobothrium glacial* is synonymous with *Cordicephalus arctocephalinus* Wardle, 1947. *Cordicephalus arctocephalinus* is considered to be synonymous with *D. scoticum* by Markowski (1952b). *D. glacial* was taken from a northern fur seal (*Callorhinus ursinus*) in the Pribilof Islands (Alaska). Margolis and Dailey (1972) consider *C. arctocephalinus* to be synonymous

with *Diphyllobothrium pacificum*. This parasite was found in the northern fur seal (*Callorhinus ursinus*), Steller's sea lion (*Eumetopias jubata*), and California sea lion (*Zalophus californianus*) from Alaska, British Columbia and California (Margolis and Dailey do not specify which hosts were taken from which locations). Reviews of *D. pacificum* are provided by Margolis (1956), and Baer et al (1967).

Diphyllobothrium scotti

Synonymy:

From Delyamure, 1955 - *Dibothriocephalus scotti* Shipley, 1907.

From Markowski, 1952a - *Dibothriocephalum wilsoni* Shipley, 1907; *Dibothriocephalus wilsoni* Shipley, 1907; *Dibothriocephalum scotti* Shipley, 1907; *Dibothriocephalum mobilis* Leiper and Atkinson, 1915 (nec Rennie and Reid, 1912).

From Yamaguti, 1959 - *Dibothriocephalum wilsoni* Shipley, 1907; *Dibothriocephalum mobilis* Leiper and Atkinson, 1915 (nec Rennie and Reid).

Hosts and Locality:

From Dailey and Brownell, 1972 - Found in the Ross seal (*Ommatophoca rossi*). Information regarding the geographical location of host was not provided by authors.

From Delyamure, 1955 - Found in the Ross seal (*Ommatophoca rossi*) from Antarctica.

From Johnston, 1937b - Found in the Ross seal (*Ommatophoca rossi*) from the Antarctic (Queen Mary Land).

From King, 1964 - Found in the Ross seal (*Ommatophoca rossi*). Information regarding the geographical location of host was not provided by author.

From Markowski, 1952a - If *D. scotti* = *D. wilsoni*, then found in the Weddell seal (*Leptonyhcotes weddelli*) and in the leopard seal (*Hydrurga leptonyx*) from Deception Island, Beascochea Bay, Debenham Islands, Melchior Archipelago, Argentine Islands (Galindez Island), and South Sandwich.

From Yamaguti, 1959 - If *D. scotti* = *D. wilsoni*, then found in the sea leopard (*Hydrurga leptonyx*) and the Weddell seal (*Leptonyhcotes weddelli*) from Antarctica.

Diphyllobothrium stemmacephalum

Synonymy:

From Baylis, 1932 - *Dibothrium stemmacephalum* Diesing, 1863; *Bothriocephalus stemmacephalum* Braun, 1883.

From Delyamure, 1955 - *Dibothrium stemmacephalum* Cobbold, 1858.

Hosts and Locality:

From Baylis, 1932 - Found in the common dolphin (*Delphinus delphis*) and in the harbor porpoise (*Phocoena phocoena*). Information regarding the geographical location of hosts was not provided by author.

From Dailey and Brownell, 1972 - Found in the common dolphin (*Delphinus delphis*) and in the harbor porpoise (*Phocoena phocoena*). Information regarding the geographical location of hosts was not provided by authors.

From Delyamure, 1955 - Found in the finned porpoise (*Phocoena phocoena*) from the North Atlantic (coast of England and other points); North Sea; and Black Sea (off the coast of Romania). Delyamure notes this parasite is not found in USSR.

From Yamaguti, 1959 - Found in the finned porpoise (*Phocoena phocoena*) from the Firth of Forth, and in the dolphin *Delphinus dussumieri* (= *Delphinus longirostris*) from the Pacific.

Remarks:

A brief historical synopsis is provided by Delyamure (1955).

Diphyllobothrium tectum

Synonymy:

From Delyamure, 1955 - *Diphyllobothrium clavatum* Railliet and Henry, 1912; *Dibothriocephalum scoticum* Railliet and Henry, 1912; *Dibothriocephalus lashleyi* Leiper and Atkinson, 1914.

From Johnston, 1937b - *Bothriocephalus tectus* Linstow, 1892.

From Markowski, 1952a - *Baylisiella tecta* Linstow, 1892; *Bothriocephalus tectus* Linstow, 1892; *Dibothriocephalus tectus* Zschokke, 1903; *Cordicephalus tectus* Wardle, McLeod and Stewart, 1947.

Hosts and Locality:

From Dailey and Brownell, 1972 - Found in the southern elephant seal (*Mirounga leonina*), the Weddell seal (*Leptonyhcotes weddelli*), and in the leopard seal (*Hydrurga leptonyx*). Information regarding the geographical location of hosts was not provided by authors.

From Delyamure, 1955 - Found in the Weddell seal (*Leptonyhcotes weddelli*), the elephant seal (*Mirounga leonina*), and in the sea leopard (*Hydrurga leptonyx*) from Antarctica (Peterman Island) and Georgia.

From Johnston, 1937b - Found in the elephant seal (*Mirounga leonina*) from the Antarctic (Macquaire Island).

From Markowski, 1952a - Found in the elephant seal (*Mirounga leonina*) from the Bay of Isles, South Georgia.

From Rennie and Reid, 1912 - Found in the leopard seal (*Hydrurga leptonyx*) from Antarctica.

Remarks:

Delyamure (1955) and Yamaguti (1959) refer to *D. tectum* as *D. tectus*. Markowski (1952a) list *D. tectum* with other synonyms that are also listed by Delyamure (1955) under *D. tectus*.

Diphyllobothrium tetrapterus

Synonymy:

From Delyamure, 1955 - *Diplogonoporus tetrapterus* Siebold, 1848; *Bothriocephalus tetrapterus* Siebold, 1948; *Bothriocephalus variabile* Krabbe, 1894; *Bothriocephalus elegans* Krabbe, 1865; *Krabbea tetrapterus* Siebold, 1848.

Hosts and Locality:

From Dailey and Brownell, 1972 - Found in the

Mediterranean monk seal (*Monachus mona-chus*). Information regarding the geograph-ical location of host was not provided by authors.

From Delyamure, 1955 - Found in the monk seal (*Monachus monachus*), the common seal (*Phoca vitulina*), the ringed seal (*Phoca his-pida*), the bearded seal (*Erignathus barba-tus*), and in the hooded seal (*Cystophora cris-tata*). Geographical distribution is northern Europe.

Diphyllobothrium ventropapillatum

Hosts and Locality:

From Dailey and Brownell, 1972 - Found in the leopard seal (*Hydrurga leptonyx*). Informa-tion regarding the geographical location of host was not provided by authors.

From Delyamure, 1955 - Found in the leopard seal (*Hydrurga leptonyx*) from the Moscow Zoo. See Remarks.

From King, 1964 - Found in the leopard seal (*Hydrurga leptonyx*). Information regarding the geographical location of host was not provided by author.

Remarks:

The leopard seal (*Hydrurga leptonyx*) died at the Moscow Zoo two weeks after arriving from Antarctica. Delyamure (1955) believed the animal was infected prior to reaching Moscow. The host contained approximately 100 fully matured parasites.

Diphyllobothrium wilsoni

Synonymy:

From Johnston, 1937b - *Dibothriocephalus mobi-lis* Leiper and Atkinson, 1915.

From Markowski, 1952a - *Dibothriocephalus wil-soni* Shipley, 1907; *Dibothriocephalus scotti* Shipley, 1907; *Dibothriocephalum scotti* Megg-itt, 1924; *Dibothriocephalus mobilis* Leiper and Atkinson, 1915.

From Yamaguti, 1959 - *Dibothriocephalum archeri*.

Hosts and Locality:

From Dailey and Brownell, 1972 - Found in the leopard seal (*Hydrurga leptonyx*), the Ross seal (*Ommatophoca rossi*), and in the Weddell seal (*Leptonyhcotes weddelli*). Information re-garding the geographical location of hosts was not provided by authors.

From Delyamure, 1955 - Found in the Ross seal (*Ommatophoca rossi*) and the Weddell seal (*Leptonyhcotes weddelli*) from Antarctica (near Peterman Island).

From Johnston, 1937b - Found in the Weddell seal (*Leptonyhcotes weddelli*) and the Ross seal (*Ommatophoca rossi*) from the Antarc-tic (Queen Mary Land, Commonwealth Bay, and Graham's Land).

From King, 1964 - Found in the leopard seal (*Hydrurga leptonyx*), the Ross seal (*Omma-tophoca rossi*), and in the Weddell seal (*Lep-tonyhcotes weddelli*). Information regarding the geographical location of hosts was not provided by author.

From Markowski, 1952a - Found in the Wed-dell seal (*Leptonyhcotes weddelli*) and in the leopard seal (*Hydrurga leptonyx*) from Ant-arctica. Specific locations include Deception Island, Beascochea Bay; Debenham Islands, Melchior Archipelago, Argentine Islands (Galindez Island), and South Sandwich.

Remarks:

Markowski (1952a) discusses and compares *D. wilsoni* with *D. scotti*.

Diplogonoporus sp.

Hosts and Locality:

From Dailey and Brownell, 1972 - Found in the sperm whale (*Physeter catodon*). Information regarding the geographical location of host was not provided by authors.

From Delyamure, 1955 - Found in the sperm whale (*Physeter catodon*) from the Sea of Ok-hotsk (Kurile Islands region).

From Margolis and Dailey, 1972 - Found in the northern fur seal (*Callorhinus ursinus*) from Alaska.

Diplogonoporus balaenopterae

Synonymy:

From Delyamure, 1955 - *Bothriocephalus balaenopterae* Lönnberg, 1891.

Hosts and Locality:

From Baylis, 1932 - Found in the sei whale (*Balaenoptera borealis*). Information regarding the geographical location of host was not provided by author.

From Dailey and Brownell, 1972 - Found in the sei whale (*Balaenoptera borealis*), the humpback whale (*Megaptera novaengliae*), and in the fin whale (*Balaenoptera physalus*). Information regarding the geographical location of hosts was not provided by authors.

From Delyamure, 1955 - Found in the sei whale (*Balaenoptera borealis*) and the fin whale (*Balaenoptera physalus*). Geographical distribution includes the Arctic Ocean (coast of Norway), and Russia (Kurile Islands and Sea of Okhotsk).

From Margolis and Dailey, 1972 - Found in the humpback whale (*Megaptera novaengliae*) and in an unidentified whale from Washington and California.

From Markowski, 1955 - Found in the blue whale (*Balaenoptera musculus*), the fin whale (*Balaenoptera physalus*), and the sei whale (*Balaenoptera borealis*). All hosts were from the Antarctic (South Georgia).

From Rausch, 1964 - Found in the humpback whale (*Megaptera novaengliae*) from San Francisco, California.

From Rice, 1963 - Found in the humpback whale (*Megaptera novaengliae*) from California.

From Yamaguti, 1959 - Found in the sei whale (*Balaenoptera borealis*) from Scandinavia and Japan.

Diplogonporus fasciatus

Synonymy:

From Delyamure, 1955 - *Diphyllobothrium fasciatus* Krabbe, 1865.

From Margolis and Dailey, 1972 - *Diplogonporus sp.* Stunkard, 1848.

From Markowski, 1952b - *Bothriocephalus fasciatus* Krabbe, 1865; *Krabbea fasciata* Blanchard, 1894; "Species #4" of Stunkard, 1848.

Hosts and Locality:

From Dailey and Brownell, 1972 - Found in the Steller's sea lion (*Eumatopias jubata*) and the ringed seal (*Phoca hispida*). Information regarding the geographical location of hosts was not provided by authors.

From Delyamure, 1955 - Found in the ringed seal (*Phoca hispida*) from the Arctic Ocean (coast of Norway).

From King, 1964 - Found in the Steller's sea lion (*Eumatopias jubata*). Information regarding the geographical location of host was not provided by author.

From Margolis, 1954 - Found in the Steller's sea lion (*Eumatopias jubata*) from St. Paul Island (Alaska).

From Margolis and Dailey, 1972 - Found in the Steller's sea lion (*Eumetopias jubata*) from Alaska.

Remarks:

Delyamure (1955) claimed the internal structure of this organism has not been sufficiently studied to justify placing this species under *Diplogonopous* and not *Diphyllobothrium.*

Diplogonoporus tetrapterus

Synonymy:

From Delyamure, 1955 - *Bothriocephalus tetrapterus* Siebold, 1848; *Bothriocephalus variabile* Krabbe, 1865; *Krabbea tetrapterus* (Siebold, 1865) Blanchard, 1894; *Bothriocephalus elegans* Krabbe, 1865; *Diphyllobothrium tetrapterus* Siebold, 1848.

From Margolis and Dailey, 1972 - *Diplogonporus sp.* Stunkard, 1848.

From Markowski, 1952b - *Diplogonoporus variabilis* Meggitt, 1924; *Diphyllobothrium variabilis* Baer, 1925; *Diplogonoporus septentrionalis*

Cholodkovsky, 1915; and "Species No. 3" of Stunkard, 1948.

Hosts and Locality:

From Dailey and Brownell, 1972 - Found in the Steller's sea lion (*Eumatopias jubata*), the common seal (*Phoca vitulina*), the ringed seal (*Phoca hispida*), the bearded seal (*Erignathus barbatus*), the hooded seal (*Cystophora cristata*), the sea otter (*Enhydra lutris*) and in the northern fur seal (*Callorhinus ursinus*). Information regarding the geographical location of hosts was not provided by authors.

From Delyamure, 1955 - Found in the monk seal (*Monachus monachus*), the bearded seal (*Erignathus barbatus*), the common seal (*Phoca vitulina*), the ringed seal (*Phoca hispida*), and in the hooded seal (*Cystophora cristata*). Geographical distribution is northern Europe.

From Johnson et al, 1966 - Found in the bearded seal (*Erignathus barbatus*) from Alaska.

From King, 1964 - Found in the bearded seal (*Erignathus barbatus*), the common seal (*Phoca vitulina*), the ringed seal (*Phoca hispida*), the monk seal (*Monachus monachus*), the hooded seal (*Cystophora cristata*), the northern fur seal (*Callorhinus ursinus*), and in the Steller's sea lion (*Eumatopias jubata*). Information regarding the geographical location of hosts was not provided by author.

From Margolis and Dailey, 1972 - Found in the northern fur seal (*Callorhinus ursinus*), the sea otter (*Enhydra lutris*), and the Steller's sea lion (*Eumetopias jubata*). All hosts were from Alaska and British Columbia.

From Rausch, 1964 - Found in the sea otter (*Enhydra lutris*) from Alaska.

From Stunkard, 1948 - Found in the Steller's sea lion (*Eumetopias jubata*) and the northern fur seal (*Callorhinus ursinus*). Both hosts were from St. Paul Island (Alaska).

Remarks:

A brief historical summary of this parasite is provided by Delyamure (1955).

Glandicephalus antarcticus

Synonymy:

From Johnston, 1937b - *Bothriocephalus antarcticus* Baird, 1853; *Dibothrium antarcticum* Ariola 1900; *Diplogonoporus antarcticus* Lühe, 1899; *Dibothriocephalus antarcticus* Shipley, 1907; *Diphyllobothrium antarcticum* Railliett and Henry 1912; *Krabbea antarctica* Blanchard 1894; *Bothriocephalus tectus* Linstow 1902.

Hosts and Locality:

From Johnston, 1937b - Found in the Ross seal (*Ommatophoca rossi*) from the Antarctic.

From King, 1964 - Found in the Ross seal (*Ommatophoca rossi*). Information regarding the geographical location of host was not provided by author.

Glandicephalus perfoliatus

Synonymy:

From McEwin, 1957 - *Diphyllobothrium perfoliatum* Railliett and Reid 1912; *Diphyllobothrium clavatum* Railliett and Reid 1912; *Dibothriocephalus perfoliatus* Fuhrmann 1937; *Diphyllobothrium rufum* Johnston 1937.

Hosts and Locality:

From McEwin, 1957 - Found in the Weddell seal (*Leptonyhcotes weddelli*) from the Antarctic (Enderby Island [65° 50' S, 54° 23' E], Commonwealth Bay, Cape Denison, King George V Land).

Glandicephalus perfoliatus var. *rufus*

Synonymy:

From McEwin, 1957 - *Diphyllobothrium rufum* Leiper and Atkinson 1914.

Hosts and Locality:

From McEwin, 1957 - Found in the Weddell seal (*Leptonyhcotes weddelli*) from Enderby Island [65° 50' S, 54° 23' E] in the Antarctic.

Hexagonoporus physeteris

Hosts and Locality:

From Dailey and Brownell, 1972 - Found in the sperm whale (*Physeter catodon*). Information regarding the geographical location of host was not provided by authors.

From Delyamure, 1955 - Found in the sperm whale (*Physeter catodon*) from the Sea of Okhotsk (Kurile Islands region).

Ligula sp.

Hosts and Locality:

From King, 1964 - Found in the gray seal (*Halichoerus grypus*). Information regarding the geographical location of host was not provided by author.

Monorygma sp.

Hosts and Locality:

From Dailey and Brownell, 1972 - Found in the long beaked dolphin (*Stenella longirostris*), the Hawaiian spinner dolphin (*Stenella roseiventris*), the narrow-snouted dolphin (*Stenella attenuata*), the striped dolphin (*Stenella caeruleoalba*), the eastern Pacific spotted dolphin (*Stenella graffmani*), the broad-beaked dolphin (*Peoponocephalus electra*) and in the short-finned pilot whale (*Globicephala macrorhyncha*). Information regarding the geographical location of hosts was not provided by authors.

Monorygma chamissonii

Synonymy:

From Baylis, 1932 - "Possibly identical to *Monortgma grimaldii, vide infra*"; *Taenia chamissonii* Linton, 1905; (?sic) *Cysticercus delphini* Rudolphi, 1819, nec1810.

From Southwell and Walker, 1936 - *Taenia chamissonii*.

From Williams, 1968 - *Phyllobothrium chamissoni*.

Hosts and Locality:

From Baylis, 1932 - Found in the Atlantic white-sided dolphin (*Lagenorhynchus acutus*). Information regarding the geographical location of host was not provided by author.

From Dailey and Brownell, 1972 - Found in the Atlantic white-sided dolphin (*Lagenorhynchus acutus*). Information regarding the geographical location of host was not provided by authors.

From Williams, 1968 – Baylis (1932) described this parasite from an Atlantic white-sided dolphin (*Lagenorhynchus acutus*), probably the same host referenced by Linton (1905) that was taken off Massachusetts (Vineyard Sound).

Remarks:

A taxonomic review of this genus was provided by Delyamure (1955), and Williams (1968).

Monorygma delphini

Synonymy:

From Baylis, 1932 - *Stenotaenia delphini* Gervais, 1870.

See Remarks.

Hosts and Locality:

From Baylis, 1932 - Found in the common dolphin (*Delphinus delphis*). Information regarding the geographical location of host was not provided by author.

From Dailey and Brownell, 1972 - Found in the bottlenosed dolphin (*Tursiops truncatus*) and the common dolphin (*Delphinus delphis*). Information regarding the geographical location of hosts was not provided by authors.

From Williams, 1968 (in describing material identified by Baylis, 1932) - Found in the bottlenosed dolphin (*Tursiops truncatus*), and in the common dolphin (*Delphinus delphis*). Both hosts were taken from the Falkland Islands.

Remarks:

The taxonomic status and historical account of this parasite is very involved. Reviews are provided by Delyamure (1955) and Williams (1968). A brief account was presented by Dailey and Brownell (1972). Williams, in his review, suggests *Monorygma* may be synonymous with the *Phyllobothrium* genus.

Monorygma grimaldii

Synonymy:

From Baylis, 1932 - *Taenia grimaldii* Moniez, 1889; *Cysticercus Taenia grimaldii* Moniez, 1889; *Cysticercus grimaldii* Braum, 1898.

From Delyamure, 1955 - Kutes vermineux de la cavite' abdominate d'um *Douphin* Redi, 1684; *Dubium delphini* Rudolphi, 1810; *Cysticercus delphini* (species *dubia*) Rudolphi, 1819; *Cephalocotyleum delphini delphis* Diesing, 1850; *Phyllobothrium sp.* Ed. van Beneden, 1868; *P. delphini* P. v. Beneden 1870; Cysticerque de *Taenia grimaldii* Moniez, 1889; *Cysticercus Taenia grimaldii* Braum, 1898; *Taenia schamissoni* Linton, 1905; Cysticerque du groupe *grimaldii* Baer, 1932.

See Remarks.

Hosts and Locality:

From Baylis, 1932 - Found in the white-sided dolphin (*Langenorhynchus acutus*), the common dolphin (? [sic] *Delphinus delphis*), and the pygmy sperm whale (*Kogia breviceps*). Information regarding the geographical location of hosts was not provided by author.

From Dailey and Brownell, 1972 - Found in the bottlenosed dolphin (*Tursiops truncatus*), the Atlantic white-sided dolphin (*Langenorhynchus acutus*), the North Atlantic pilot whale (*Globicephala melaena*), the pygmy sperm whale (*Kogia breviceps*), and in a dolphin (*Delphinus sp.*) Information regarding the geographical location of hosts was not provided by authors.

From Dailey and Perrin, 1973 - Found in the Eastern Pacific spotted dolphin (*Stenella graffmini*) captured at Lat. 12° 51′ N, Long. 93° 18′ W; Lat. 7° 11′ N, Long. 90° 32′ W.; Lat. approx. 8° 11′ N, Long. 107°W.

From Delyamure, 1955 - Found in the bottlenosed dolphin (*Tursiops truncatus*), the Atlantic white-sided dolphin (*Langenorhynchus*

acutus), the North Atlantic pilot whale (*Globicephala melaena*), and in a dolphin (*Delphinus sp.*). Geographical distribution includes various points in the Atlantic Ocean and in the Mediterranean Sea (off the coasts of Spain, Finland and Corsica).

Remarks:

Delyamure (1955) gives an historical account of this parasite. He also lists marine mammals as "reservoir hosts" and sharks (probably of the genus *Scyllium*) as the definitive host of this parasite.

Williams (1968) reviewed the *Monorygma* genus and questions the overall validity of the genus and the dearth of accurate information needed to distinguish *Monorygma grimaldii* from *Phyllobothrium delphini*.

Phyllobothrium sp.

Hosts and Locality:

From Baylis, 1932 - Found in the bottlenose dolphin (*Tursiops truncatus*) and in the white-sided dolphin (*Lagenorhynchus acutus*). Information regarding the geographical location of hosts was not provided by author.

From Baylis and Hamilton, 1934 - Found in the South American sea lion (*Otaria byronia*) from the Falkland Islands.

From Dailey and Brownell, 1972 - Found in the Pacific striped dolphin (*Lagenorhynchus obliquidens*), the long-beaked dolphin (*Stenella longirostris*), the Hawaiian spinner dolphin (*Stenella roseiventris*), the narrow-snouted dolphin (*Stenella attenuata*), the eastern pacific spotted dolphin (*Stenella graffmani*), the northern right whale dolphin (*Lissodelphis borealis*), the killer whale (*Orcinus orca*), the short-finned pilot whale (*Globicephala macrorhyncha*), the Dall porpoise (*Phocoenoides dalli*), the dwarf sperm whale (*Kogia simus*), the Atlantic white-sided dolphin (*Lagenorhynchus acutus*), the dwarf sperm whale (*Kogia simus*), the goose beaked whale (*Ziphius cavirostris*), and in the striped dolphin (*Stenella caeruleoalba*). Information regarding the geographical location of hosts was not provided by authors.

From Johnston, 1937b, - Found in the Southern elephant seal (*Mirounga leonina*) from the Antarctic (Macquaire Island).

From King, 1964 - Found in the Southern elephant seal (*Mirounga leonina*). Information regarding the geographical location of host was not provided by author.

From Markowski, 1952b - Citing "Baylis in (sic) Hamilton, 1934", found in the South American sea lion (*Otaria byronia*) from the "Arctic and other regions".

From Markowski, 1955 - Larvae found in the sperm whale (*Physeter catodon*) and the dusky dolphin (*Lagenorhynchus obscurus*) from Durban, Simon's Town, South Africa, and South Georgia.

From Rennie and Reid, 1912 - Larval specimen found in the Weddell seal (*Leptonychotes weddelli*) from the Antarctic.

From Williams, 1968 - Found in the bottlenose dolphin (*Tursiops truncatus*) from the Falkland Islands, and in the Atlantic whitesided dolphin (*Lagenorhynchus acutus*) from Woods Hole (Massachusetts) and the Falkland Islands. Also mentioned are the dusky dolphin (*Lagenorhynchus obscurus*), the sperm whale (*Physeter catodon*), and the Weddell seal (*Leptonychotes* [= *Ogmorhynchus*] *weddelli*). The author did not provide information regarding the geographical location of the hosts (see Markowski, 1955).

Phyllobothrium delphini

Synonymy:

From Baylis, 1932 - *Hydatis delphini* Bosc, 1802; *Cysticercus delphini* Laennec, 1804; *Cysticercus delphini* Rudolphi, 1810; *sp. Vermis delphini delphis* Rud, 1810; *Cephalocotyleum delphini delphis* Diesing, 1850; ? (sic) *Cysticercus physeteris* Diesing, 1863; (*vide Phyllobothrium physeteris, infra*).

From Delyamure, 1955 - *Hydatis delphini* Bosc, 1802; *Cysticercus delphini* Laennec, 1804; *Cysticercus sp.* Bennett, 1937; *Cysticercus - mysticeti* Diesing, 1850; *Cysticercus physeteris* Diesing, 1863; larva *Phyllbothrium sp.* Ed. van Beneden, 1868; *Phyllobothrium inchoatum*

Leidy, 1891; *Scolex delphini* Stossich, 1897; Plerocercoids of group *delphini* Baer, 1932; *Phyllobothrium sp.* Carnot, 1822 and Rennie and Reid, 1912.

From Williams, 1968 - *Phyllobothrium tumidum* Linton, 1922.

Hosts and Locality:

From Baylis, 1932 - Found in the common dolphin (*Delphinus delphis*), the Risso dolphin (*Grampus griseus*), and in the bottlenose dolphin (*Tursiops truncatus*). Information regarding the geographical location of hosts was not provided by author.

From Dailey and Brownell, 1972 - Found in the South American sea lion (*Otaria byronia*), the leopard seal (*Hydrurga leptonyx*), the Weddell seal (*Leptonychotes weddelli*), the South American fur seal (*Arctocephalus australis*), the Risso dolphin (*Grampus griseus*), the North Atlantic pilot whale (*Globicephala melaena*), the sperm whale (*Physeter catodon*), the pigmy sperm whale (*Kogia breviceps*), the Sowerby beaked whale (*Mesoplodon bidens*), the giant bottlenosed whale (*Berardius bairdi*), the bowhead or Greenland right whale (*Balaena mysticetus*), the fin whale (*Balaenoptera physalus*), and in the bottlenose dolphin (*Tursiops truncatus*). Information regarding the geographical location of hosts was not provided by authors.

From Dailey and Perrin, 1973 - Found in the eastern Pacific spotted dolphin (*Stenella graffmani*) and the long-beaked dolphin (*Stenella longirostris*). Both hosts taken from the following locations:
1) Lat. 12° 51' N, Long. 93° 18' W.
2) Lat. 7° 11' N, Long. 90° 32' W.
3) Lat. approx. 8° 11' N, Long. 107°W.

From Delyamure, 1955 - Author states the definitive, intermediate and supplementary hosts are not known. Author lists as "reservoir hosts" the following: the bowhead whale (*Balaena mysticetus*), the sowerby dolphin (*Mesopodon bidens*), the sperm whale (*Physeter catodon*), the pigmy sperm whale (*Kogia brevicepa*), the Risso dolphin (*Grampus griseus*), the common dolphin (*Delphinus delphis*), the bottlenosed dolphin (*Tursiops tursio*), the pilot whale (*Globicephalus melas*), and the Weddell seal (*Leptonychotes wedelli*). Geographical distribution is the Atlantic Ocean (Azore Islands); Cape Finisterre and other points; the Mediterranean Sea (Gibraltar, Corsica); Australia; Antarctica; and the Pacific Ocean (Commander Island region).

From Guiart, 1935 - Found in the North Atlantic pilot whale (*Globicephala melaena*) from the Mediterranean Sea.

From King, 1964 - Found in the Weddell seal (*Leptonychotes weddelli*), the South American sea lion (*Otaria byronia*), the South American fur seal (*Arctocephalus australis*), the South African fur seal (*Arctocephalus pusillus*), the Kerguelen fur seal (*Arctocephalus tropicalis*), and in the leopard seal (*Hydrurga leptonyx*). Information regarding the geographical location of hosts was not provided by author.

From Margolis and Dailey, 1972 - Found in the fin whale (*Balaenoptera physalus*), the north Pacific giant bottlenosed whale (*Berardius bairdi*), the common dolphin (*Delphinus delphis*), the pacific white-sided dolphin (*Lagenorhynchus obliquidens*), and in the sperm whale (*Physeter catodon*). Geographical distribution includes British Columbia and California (specific host locations not provided by authors).

From Markowski, 1952b - Found in the South American sea lion (*Otaria byronia*) and the South American fur seal (*Arctocephalus australis*) from the "Arctic and other regions".

From Rice, 1963 - Found in the giant bottlenosed dolphin (*Berardius bairdi*) and the sperm whale (*Physeter catodon*). Both hosts were from California.

From Southwell and Walker, 1936 - Found in the South American fur seal (*Arctocephalus australis*), the South American sea lion (*Otaria byronia*), and the leopard seal (*Hydrurga leptonyx*). All hosts were from the Falkland Islands.

From Williams, 1968 - Found in the Sowerby beaked whale (*Mesoplodon bidens*) from Belgium; the common dolphin (*Delphinus delphis*) from Belgium and the Falkland Islands; the Risso dolphin (*Grampus griseus*) from the Falkland Islands; the bottlenose dolphin (*Tursiops truncatus*) from the Falkland Islands; the North Atlantic pilot whale (*Globicephala melaena*) from Britian; the sperm whale (*Physeter catodon*) from the Falkland Islands; the pigmy sperm whale (*Kogia breviceps*) from South Australia; and the South American fur seal (*Arctocephalus australis*) from the Falkland Islands.

See Remarks.

Remarks:

There has been considerable confusion regarding the identification and classification of *D. delphini*. Historical surveys and reviews are provided by Delyamure (1955) and Williams (1968). Williams (1968), does not believe *P. physeteris* to be a valid species or identical with *P. delphini* and questions the identification and conclusions reached by Southwell and Walker (1936).

Dailey and Brownell (1972) list the Greenland right whale (*Balaena mysticetus*) as a host to *P. delphini* and cite Baylis (1932) as a source reference. Actually, Baylis lists the host with *P. physeteris* and states that *P. delphini* and *P. physeteris* may be identical. Baylis does not provide information regarding the geographical location of the hosts.

Dailey and Brownell (1972), also list the South African fur seal (*Arctocephalus pusillus*) and the Kerguelen fur seal (*Arctocephalus tropicalis*) as hosts of *P. delphini*. For both cases they reference Markowski (1952b) as a source reference. However, no mention of these hosts could be found in either of Markowski's papers published in 1952 (Markowski, 1952a, Markowski, 1952b). However, both these host species are listed by King (1964). Markowski (1952b) does list the South American sea lion (*Otaria byronia*) and the South American fur seal (*Arctocephalus australis*) as hosts of *Phyllobothrium delphini*. In reference to the giant bottlenosed whale (*Berardius bairdi*), Dailey and Brownell (1972) list this parasite under the spelling "*Trigonocotyle sp.*"

Phyllobothrium hians

Synonymy:

From Delyamure, 1955 - *Bothriocephalus phocaefoetidae* Creplin, 1825.

From Markowski, 1952b - *Bothriocephalus hians* Leuckart, 1863; *Dibothriocephalus hians* Lühe, 1899; *Dibothriocephalus polycalceolus* Ariola, 1896; *Diphyllobothrium polycalceolum* Meggitt, 1924; *Bothriocephalus sp.* Chapin, 1925; *Diphyllobothrium variabile* Krabbe, 1865.

From Yamaguti, 1959 - *Cordicephalus phocarus* Wardle, McLeod and Stewart, 1947.

Hosts and Locality:

From Delyamure, 1955 - Found in the ringed seal (*Phoca hispida*) from Europe and Iceland.

From Markowski, 1952b - Found in the Hawaiian monk seak (*Monachus schauinslandi*) from Laysan Island (Hawaii), and in a harbor seal (*Phoca vitulina*) from an unspecified location. Also found in a seal from the London Zoological Gardens that Markowski states was probably a harbor seal (*Phoca vitulina*) from an unknown location.

From Stiles and Hassall, 1899 - Found in the bearded seal (*Erignathus barbatus*), and the harbor seal (*Phoca vitulina*). Hosts were mentioned as being from an unknown location in the north Pacific Ocean.

From Yamaguti, 1959 - Found in the monk seal (*Phoca monachus*), the ringed seal (*Phoca hispida*), the bearded seal (*Phoca barbatus*), and in the northern fur seal (*Callorhinus ursinus curilensis*). All hosts were from the North Atlantic Ocean (specific geographical locations of hosts not specified by author).

Remarks:

Markowski (1952b) provides a brief historical account of this parasite.

Phyllobothrium inchoatum

Synonymy:

From Baylis, 1932 - "Possibly identical with *P. lactuca* v. Beneden, 1850."

Hosts and Locality:

From Baylis, 1932 - Found in the Sowerby's whale (*Mesoplodon bidens*). Information regarding the geographical location of host was not provided by author.

Phyllobothrium physeteris

Synonymy:

From Baylis, 1932 - "possibly identical to *P. delphini* (Bosc)".

Hosts and Locality:

From Baylis, 1932 - Found in the bowhead whale (*Balaena mysticetus*) and the sperm whale (*Physeter catodon*). Information regarding geographical location of hosts was not provided by author.

Remarks:

Dailey and Brownell (1972) list the host reference by Baylis under *Phyllobothrium delphini*.

Plicobothrium globicephalae

Hosts and Locality:

From Rausch and Margolis, 1969 - Found in the North Atlantic pilot whale (*Globicephala melaena*) from Trinity Bay (Newfoundland).

From Dailey and Brownell, 1972 - Found in the North Atlantic pilot whale (*Globicephala melaena*). Information regarding the geographical location of host was not provided by authors.

Remarks:

This genus and species was introduced by Rausch and Margolis (1969).

Polypocephalus tortus

Synonymy:

From Markowski, 1952b - *Pyramicocephalus phocarum* Fabricius, 1780; *Taenia phocarum* Fabricius, 1780; *Alyselminthus phocarum* de Blainville, 1828; *Bothriocephalus phocarum* Krabbe, 1865; *Pyramicocephalus phocarum* Braun, 1900; *Pyramicocephalus phocarum* Guiat, 1935; *Cordicephalus phocarum* Wardle, McLeod and Stewart, 1947; *Taenia phocae* Fabricius, 1793; *Alyselminthus lanceolata-anthocephala* Rudolphi, 1810; *Tetrabothrium anthocephalus* Diesing, 1850; *Bothrocephalus* anthocephalus Baird, 1853; *Pyramiococephalus anthocephalus* Monticelli, 1890; *Anthobothrium tortum* Linstow, 1904.

Hosts and Locality:

From Dailey and Brownell, 1972 - Found in the bearded seal (*Erignathus barbatus*). Information regarding geographical location of host was not provided by authors.

From King, 1964 - Found in the bearded seal (*Erignathus barbatus*) and in the ringed seal (*Phoca hispida*). Information regarding geographical location of hosts was not provided by author.

From Markowski, 1952b - If *Polypocephalus tortus* = *Pyramicocephalus phocarum*, then found in the bearded seal (*Erignathus barbatus*) from Hinlopen Straits, Spitzbergen, and Baffin Bay.

Remarks:

Delyamure (1955) gives *Polypocephalus tortus* "Uncertain taxonomic" status.

Priapocephalus sp.

Synonymy:

From Dailey and Brownell, 1972 - *Tetrabothius sp.* See Remarks.

Hosts and Locality:

From Dailey and Brownell, 1972 - Found in the gray whale (*Eschrichtius gibbosus = robustus*). Information regarding geographical location of host was not provided by authors. See Remarks.

From Rice and Wolman, 1971 - Found in the gray whale (*Eschrichtius robustus*) from California (between Half Moon Bay [Lat. 37° 30′ N] and Point Reyes [Lat. 38° 00′ N]).

Remarks:

Dailey and Brownell (1972) list the gray whale (*Eschrichtius gibbosus* [= *Eschrichtius robustus*]) as a host of unidentified *Priapocephalus*. In a footnote they mention that through "personal communication" with Rice, the parasite is synonymous with *Tetrabothrius sp.*, which was reported by Rice (1963) to be a parasite found in *E. gibbosus* from California (San Francisco Bay).

Priapocephalus eschrichtii

Hosts and Locality:

From Murav'eva and Treskchev, 1970 - Found in the gray whale (*Eschrichtius gibbosus*) from the Chuckchee Sea.

Priapocephalus grandis

Hosts and Locality:

From Baylis, 1932 - Found in the sei whale (*Balaenoptera borealis*), the blue whale (*Balaenoptera musculus*), and in the whale "*Balaena antarctica*, [? *B. australis*]" (sic). Information regarding the geographical location of hosts was not provided by author.

From Clark, 1956 - Found in the sperm whale (*Physeter catodon*) from the Azore Islands.

From Dailey and Brownell, 1972 - Found in the sperm whale (*Physeter catodon*), the sei whale (*Balaenoptera borealis*), the fin whale (*Balaenoptera physalus*), the blue whale (*Balaenoptera musculus*) and in the black right whale (*Eubalaena glacialis)*. Information regarding the geographical location of hosts was not provided by authors.

From Delyamure, 1955 - Found in the sei whale (*Balaenoptera borealis*), the blue whale (*Balaenoptera musculus*), the fin whale (*Balaenoptera physalus*), and in the black right whale (*Eubalaena glacialis*). Geographical distribution includes the south Arctic Ocean, South Africa, South Shetlands, South Georgia, and small islands south of 50° S latitude.

From Markowski, 1955 - Found in the sei whale (*Balaenoptera borealis*), the blue whale (*Balaenoptera musculus*), the fin whale (*Balaenoptera physalus*) and in the sperm whale (*Physeter catodon*). Hosts geographical localities include Saldanha Bay and Durban (South Africa), South Georgia, Southern Ocean (56° 40′ 32″ S, 24° 33″ W); Porto Pim; and the Azores.

From Prudhoe, 1969 - Found in the blue whale (*Balaenoptera musculus*) from the Antarctic (65° 41′ S, 178°29′ 30″ E).

Priapocephalus minor

Hosts and Locality:

From Baylis, 1932 - Found in the sei whale (*Balaenoptera borealis*). Information regarding the geographical location of host was not provided by author.

From Dailey and Brownell, 1972 - Found in the fin whale (*Balaenoptera physalus*). Information regarding the geographical location of host was not provided by authors.

From Delyamure, 1955 - Found in the sei whale (*Balaenoptera borealis*) and the fin whale (*Balaenoptera physalus*). Geographical distribution includes the Atlantic Ocean (west coast of Norway) and the Sea of Okhotsk (Kurile Island region).

From Yamaguti, 1959 - Found in the fin whale (*Balaenoptera physalus*) and the sei whale (*Balaenoptera borealis*) from Sweden and France.

Pseudophyllidae sp.

Hosts and Locality:

From Dailey and Brownell, 1972 - Found in the gray whale (*Eschrichtius gibbosus*). Information regarding the geographical location of host was not provided by authors.

From Tomilin, 1967 - Unidentified species found in the gray whale (*Eschrichtius gibbosus*) from the Chuckchee Sea.

Pyramicocephalus phocarum

Synonymy:

From Markowski, 1952b - *Taenia phocarum* Fabricius, 1780; *Alyselminthus phocarum* de Blainville, 1828; *Bothriocephalus phocarum* Krabbe, 1865; *Cordicephalus phocarum* Wardle, McLeod and Stewart, 1947; *Taenia phocae* Fabricius, 1793; *Alyselminthus lanceolata-lobata* Zeder, 1800; *Halysis lanceolata-lobata* Zeder, 1803; *Taenia anthocephala* Rudolphi, 1810; *Tetrabothrium anthocephalus* Diesing, 1850; *Bothrocephalus anthocephalus* Baird, 1853; *Pyramiocephalus anthocephalus* Monticelli, 1890; *Anthobothrium tortum* Linstow, 1904; *Polypocephalus tortus* Meggitt, 1924.

Hosts and Locality:

From Dailey and Brownell, 1972 - Found in the Steller's sea lion (*Eumatopias jubata*), the bearded seal (*Erignathus barbatus*), the hooded seal (*Cystophora cristata*), the sea otter (*Enhydra lutris*) and in the ringed seal (*Phoca hispida*). Information regarding the geographical location of hosts was not provided by authors.

From Delyamure, 1955 - Found in the Steller's sea lion (*Eumetopias jubata*), the bearded seal (*Erignathus barbatus*), the hooded seal (*Cystophora cristata*), the ringed seal (*Phoca hispida*) and in the Okhotsk ringed seal (*Phoca hispida okhotensis*). Geographical distribution covers the Arctic Ocean (Iceland, Greenland, Spitzbergen, northern Canada, and Alaska), and Russia (White Sea, Nokuev Island, Kotel'nyi Island, Novaya Zemlya, Barents Sea, and Sea of Okhotsk [Aniva Chaiskii Gulfs]).

From Hilliard, 1960 - Found in the bearded seal (*Erignathus barbatus*) from St. Lawrence Island (Alaska).

From Kenyon, 1962 - Found in the bearded seal (*Erignathus barbatus*) from Little Diomede Island (Alaska).

From King, 1964 - Found in the bearded seal (*Erignathus barbatus*), the ringed seal (*Phoca hispida*), the hooded seal (*Cystophora cristata*), and in the Steller's sea lion (*Eumatopias jubata*). Information regarding the geographical location of hosts was not provided by author.

From Margolis and Dailey, 1972 - Found in the sea otter (*Enhydra lutris*), the bearded seal (*Erignathus barbatus*), the harbour porpoise (*Phocoena phocoena*), and in a seal (*Phoca sp.*). All hosts were from Alaska.

From Markowski, 1952b - Found in the bearded seal (*Erignathus barbatus*) from Hinlopen Straits, Spitzbergen, and Baffin Bay.

From Rausch, 1953 - Found in the sea otter (*Enhydra lutris*) from the Arctic coast of Alaska.

From Rausch and Hilliard, 1970 - Found free plerocercoids in the stomach of a common porpoise (*Phocoena phocoena*) from Hooper Bay (Alaska).

Remarks:

The cod (*Gadus*) is thought to play an important role in the life cycle of this parasite [see Delyamure (1955); Hilliard (1960); and Rauch and Hilliard, (1970)].

Schistocephalus solidus

Hosts and Locality:

From Dailey and Brownell, 1972 - Found in the harbor seal (*Phoca vitulina*) and the ringed seal (*Pusa hispida*). Information regarding geographical location of hosts was not provided by authors.

From Delyamure, 1955 - Larval parasites found in the harbor seal (*Phoca vitulina*) and the ringed seal (*Pusa hispida*). Information regarding geographical location of hosts was not provided by author.

From King, 1964 - Found in the gray seal (*Halichoerus grypus*), and the common seal (*Phoca vitulina*). Information regarding geographical location of hosts was not provided by author.

Remarks:

Yamaguti (1959) lists species of fish, frogs and birds as hosts of this parasite but give no mention of any marine mammals being hosts. Markowski (1952b) categorizes this parasite as "incerte sedis" and does not list any host species nor provide any additional information. Hilliard (1960) does not list any marine mammals as host of this parasite in samples taken in Alaska.

Dailey and Brownell (1972) note that the parasite specimen taken from the ringed seal was in the larval stage.

Scolex delphini

Hosts and Locality:

From Baylis, 1932 - Found in the Risso's dolphin (*Grampus griseus*). Information regarding the geographical location of host was not provided by author.

Strobilocephalus sp.

Hosts and Locality:

From Dailey and Brownell, 1972 - Found in the Eastern Pacific spotted dolphin (*Stenella graffmani*). Information regarding the geographical location of host was not provided by authors.

Strobilocephalus triangularis

Synonymy:

From Baylis, 1932 - *Tetrabothrium triangulare* Diesing, 1850; *Prothecocotyle triangulare* Fuhrmann, 1899; *Tetrabothrius triangularis* Fuhrmann, 1903.

From Delyamure, 1955 - *Tetrabothrium triangulare* Diesing, 1850; *Prothecocotyle triangulare* Fuhrmann, 1899; *Tetrabothrius triangularis* Fuhrmann, 1904.

Hosts and Locality:

From Baylis, 1932 - Found in the bottlenosed whale (*Hyperoodon rostratus*), the dolphin (*Delphinus sp.*), and in the white-sided dolphin (*Lagenorhynchus acutus*). Information regarding the geographical location of hosts was not provided by author.

From Dailey and Brownell, 1972 - Found in the rough-toothed dolphin (*Steno bredanensis*), the Atlantic white-sided dolphin (*Lagenorhynchus acutus*), the Sowerby beaked whale (*Mesoplodon bidens*), the northern bottlenosed whale (*Hyperoodon ampullatus*), and in a dolphin (*Delphinus sp*). Information regarding the geographical location of hosts was not provided by authors.

From Dailey and Perrin, 1973 - Found in the eastern Pacific spotted dolphin (*Stenella graffmani*) taken at Lat. 12° 51' N, Long. 93° 18' W.

From Delyamure, 1955 - Found in the northern bottlenosed whale (*Hyperoodon ampullatus*), the Sowerby beaked whale (*Mesoplodon bidens*), the Atlantic white-sided dolphin (*Lagenorhynchus acutus*), the rough-toothed dolphin (*Steno bredanensis*) [= *steno rostratus*], and in a dolphin (*Delphinus sp.*). Geographical distribution includes the Atlantic Ocean (near Lisbon and off the coast of Brazil).

From Yamaguti, 1959 - Found in the rough-toothed dolphin (*Steno bredanensis*), the northern bottlenosed whale (*Hyperoodon ampullatus*), the Atlantic white-sided dolphin (*Lagenorhynchus acutus*), and in a dolphin (*Delphinus sp.*). Geographical distribution is the Atlantic and Pacific Oceans. Material described by the author was taken from the Marshall Islands.

Remarks:

A brief historical account of this genus is provided by Delyamure (1955).

Tetrabothrium sp.

Hosts and Locality:

From Margolis and Dailey, 1972 - Found in the sei whale (*Balaenoptera borealis*) and the gray whale (*Eschrichtius gibbosus*). Both hosts were from California.

From Rice, 1963 - Found in the sei whale (*Balaenoptera borealis*) and the gray whale (*Eschrichtius gibbosus*). Both hosts were from California.

Tetrabothrium albertini

Synonymy:

From Delyamure, 1955 - *Anophryocephalus anophrys* Baylis, 1922.

Hosts and Locality:

From Markowski, 1952b - Found in the seal *Phoca vitulina* [= *P. maculata*]. Information regarding the geographical location of host was not provided by author.

See Remarks.

Remarks:

From Delyamure (1955) - If *Tetrabothrium albertini* is synonymous with *Anophryocephalus anophrys*, then this parasite also was found in a ringed seal (*Phoca hispida* [= *Phoca maculata*]) from Spitzbergen Island.

Markowski (1952b) equates *P. maculate* with the harbor seal (*Phoca vitulina*), while Delyamure (1955) equates *Phoca maculata* with the ringed seal *Phoca hispida*.

Tetrabothrium arsenyevi

Hosts and Locality:

From Dailey and Brownell, 1972 - Found in the sei whale (*Balaenoptera borealis*). Information regarding the geographical location of host was not provided by authors. See Remarks.

From Delyamure, 1955 - Found in the sei whale (*Balaenoptera borealis*) from the Antarctic.

Remarks:

This species was first introduced by Delyamure (1955). Dailey and Brownell (1972) list this as a parasite of the sei whale under the spelling "*Tetrobathrius arsenyevi*".

Tetrabothrium curilensis

Hosts and Locality:

From Dailey and Brownell, 1972 - Found in the sperm whale (*Physeter catodon*). Information regarding the geographical location of host was not provided by authors.

From Delyamure, 1955 - Found in the sperm whale (*Physeter catodon*) from the Sea of Okhotsk and the Pacific Ocean (Kurile Islands).

Tetrabothrius affinis

Synonymy:

From Baylis, 1932 - *Diplobothrium affine* Lönnberg, 1891; *Tetrabothrium (Diplobothrium) affine* Lönnberg, 1892.

From Delyamure, 1955 - *Orians wilsoni* Leiper and Atkinson, 1914; *Tetrabothrium wilsoni* (Leiper and Atkinson, 1914) Baylis, 1926.

From Markowski, 1955 - *Diplobothrium affine* Lönnberg (in Jägerskiöld, 1891); *Tetrabothrium (Diplobothrium) affine* Lönnberg, 1892.

Hosts and Locality:

From Baylis, 1932 - Found in the sei whale (*Balaenoptera borealis*) and the blue whale (*Balaenoptera musculus*). Information regarding geographical location of hosts was not provided by author.

From Dailey and Brownell, 1972 - Found in the fin whale (*Balaenoptera physalus*), the blue whale (*Balaenoptera musculus*) and in the sei whale (*Balaenoptera borealis*). Information regarding geographical location of hosts was not provided by authors.

From Delyamure, 1955 - Found in the sei whale (*Balaenoptera borealis*), the blue whale (*Balaenoptera musculus*), and in the fin whale (*Balaenoptera physalus*). Geographical distribution is Europe (coast of Norway), South Africa (Cape Town), New Zealand, and Antarctica (South Shetlands Islands).

From Markowski, 1955 - Found in the blue whale (*Balaenoptera musculus*) and the sperm whale (*Physeter catodon*) from Saldanha Bay; South Africa (Durban); South Georgia; and at location Lat. 58° 32' S, Long. 34° 52' E.

From Prudhoe, 1969 - Found in the blue whale (*Balaenoptera musculus*) from the Antarctic (65° 41' S, 178° 29' 30"E).

Remarks:

Brief historical data of *T. affinis* is provided by Delyamure (1955).

Tetrabothrius forsteri

Synonymy:

From Baylis, 1932 - *Taenia forsteri* Krefft, 1871; *Prosthecocotyle forsteri* Monticelli, 1892; *Tetrabothrium triangulare* Leidy, 1892 nec Diesing, 1850.

From Delyamure, 1955 - *Taenia forsteri* Krefft, 1871; *Prosthecocotyle forsteri* (Krefft, 1871) Monticelli, 1892; *Tetrabothrium triangulare* Leidy, 1892 (nec Diesing, 1850); *Prosthecocotyle diplosoma* Guiart, 1935; *Prosthecocotyle pachysoma* Guiart, 1935.

Hosts and Locality:

From Baylis, 1932 - Found in the common dolphin (*Delphinus delphis*), the Sowerby's whale (*Mesoplodon bidens*) and in the dolphin (*Steno rostratus*). Information regarding the geographical location of hosts was not provided by author.

From Beverley-Burton, 1978 - Found in the Atlantic white-sided dolphin (*Lagenorhyn-

chus acutus*) from Lingley Cove, Edmunds, Maine.

From Dailey and Brownell, 1972 - Found in the rough-toothed dolphin (*Steno bredanensis*) and the common dolphin (*Delphinus delphis*). Information regarding the geographical location of host was not provided by authors. See Remarks.

From Dailey and Perrin, 1973 - Found in the spotted porpoise (*Stenella graffmani*) captured at Lat.12° 51' N, Long. 93° N18' W; and at Lat. 7° 11' N, Long. 90° N32' W (eastern tropical pacific). Also found in the spinner porpoise (*Stenella longirostris*) captured at Lat. 12° 51' N, Long 93° N 18' W; Lat 70°11' N, Long 90° N32' W, and at Lat. approx. 8 ° N, Long 107° W (eastern tropical pacific).

From Delyamure, 1955 - Found in the common dolphin (*Delphinus delphis*) from the New Zealand coast (Port Jackson), Naples Harbor, and the Medirerranean Sea. Also found in the Sowerby's whale (*Mesoplodon bidens*) and the dolphin (*Steno rostratus*) {= *S. frontatus*}. Geographical distribution of the parasite includes the Mediterranean Sea (Bay of Naples, coasts of Sardinia and Spain), and the southern part of the Pacific Ocean (New Zealand region).

From Yamaguti, 1959 - Found in the common dolphin (*Delphinus delphis*) from Australia and the Medirerranean Sea. Also found in *Steno frontatus* and the Sowerby whale (*Mesoplodon bidens*). Information regarding the geographical location of the later two hosts was not provided by author.

Remarks:

Historic taxonomic information of this parasite is provided by Delyamure (1955).

Baylis (1932) reported this parasite was found in *Steno rostraus* rather than *Steno bredanensis*.

Tetrabothrium ruudi

Hosts and Locality:

From Baylis 1932 - Found in the fin whale (*Balaenoptera physalus*). Information regarding the geographical location of host was not provided by author.

From Dailey and Brownell, 1972 - Found in the fin whale (*Balaenoptera physalus*). Information regarding the geographical location of host was not provided by authors.

From Delyamure, 1955 - Found in the fin whale (*Balaenoptera physalus*) from the west coast of Norway, waters of France, and Russia (Kronotskii Gulf [Pacific Ocean]).

From Markowski, 1955 - Found in the fin whale (*Balaenoptera physalus*) from the Antarctic (South Georgia).

Tetrabothrius schaeferi

Synonymy:

From Markowski, 1955 - *Tetrabothrius affine* Baylis, 1926; *Tetrabothrius sp.* Rees, 1953.

Hosts and Locality:

From Markowski, 1955 - Found in the blue whale (*Balaenoptera musculus*) from South Georgia and Southern Ocean.

Tetrabothrius wilsoni

Synonymy:

From Baylis, 1932 - *Oriana wilsoni* Leiper and Atkinson, 1914.

From Delyamure, 1955 - *Tetrabothrium affinis* Lönnberg, 1892; *Tetrabothrium* (*Diplobothrium*) *affine* Lönnberg 1892; *Orians wilsoni* Leiper and Atkinson, 1914; *Diplobothrium affine* Lönnberg, 1891.

Hosts and Locality:

From Baylis, 1932 - Found in the sei whale (*Balaenoptera borealis*). Information regarding the geographical location of host was not provided by author.

From Dailey and Brownell, 1972 - Found in the sperm whale (*Physeter catodon*) and in the sei whale (*Balaenoptera borealis*). Information regarding the geographical location of hosts was not provided by authors.

From Delyamure, 1955 - If *T. wilsoni* = *T. affinis*,

then this parasite was found in the sei whale (*Balaenoptera borealis*), the blue whale (*Balaenoptera musculus*), and the fin whale (*Balaenoptera physalus*). Geographical distribution includes Europe (coast of Norway), South Africa (Cape Town), New Zealand, and Antarctica (South Shetlands Islands).

From Leiper and Atkinson, 1914 - Found in the sei whale (*Balaenoptera borealis*) from New Zealand (Bay of Islands).

From Markowski, 1955 - Found in the sei whale (*Balaenoptera borealis*) and blue whale (*Balaenoptera musculus*) from Durban, South Africa, and South Georgia.

From Rees, 1953 - Found in the sperm whale (*Physeter catodon*) from the Ross Sea.

Remarks:

Delyamure (1955) discusses *T. wilsoni* in his brief historical review of *T. affinis*.

Tetraphyllidean sp.

Hosts and Locality:

From Markowski, 1955 – A larva of this parasite was found in a sperm whale (*Physeter catodon*) from South Georgia.

Trigonocotyle sp.

Hosts and Locality:

From Dailey and Brownell, 1972 - Found in the sperm whale (*Physeter catodon*) and the giant bottlenosed whale (*Berardius bairdi*). Information regarding the geographical location of hosts was not provided by authors. See Remarks.

From Delyamure, 1955 - Representatives from this genus were found by Gubanov, 1952, in the sperm whale (*Physeter catodon*) and in the bottlenosed whale (*Hyperoodon ampullatus*) from the Sea of Okhotsk and Pacific Ocean (Kurile Islands region).

Remarks:

Delyamure (1955) lists the bottlenosed whale (*Hyperoodon ampullatus*) and the sperm whale (*Physeter catodon*) as hosts of

Trigonocotyle sp.; there is no mention of the giant bottlenosed whale (*Berardius bairdi*) being a host.

Trigonocotyle globicephalae

Synonymy:

From Markowski, 1955 - *Prosthecocotyle monticelli* Linton, 1923; *Trigonocotyle monticelli* Baer, 1932; *Trigonocotyle lintoni* Yamaguti, 1942.

Hosts and Locality:

From Delyamure, 1955 - If *T. globicephala* = *T. lintoni*, then found in the North Atlantic pilot whale (*Globicephala melaena*) from the Massachusetts coast (Martha's Vineyard), and in the Mediterranean Sea (off coasts of Spain and France).

From Markowski, 1955 - Found in *Globicephala edwardi* from South Africa (off Cape Town).

Trigonocotyle lintoni

Synonymy:

From Delyamure, 1955 - *Prosthecocotyle monticelli* Linton, 1923 (nec Fuhrmann, 1899); *Triggonocotyle monticelli* Baer, 1932.

From Markowski, 1955 - *Triggonocotyle globicephalae* Yamaguti, 1942.

Hosts and Locality:

From Dailey and Brownell, 1972 - Found in the North Atlantic pilot whale (*Globicephala melaena*). Information regarding the geographical location of host was not provided by authors.

From Delyamure, 1955 - Found in the North Atlantic pilot whale (*Globicephala melaena*) from the Massachusetts coast (Martha's Vineyard), and in the Mediterranean Sea (off coasts of Spain and France).

From Markowski, 1955 - If *T. lintoni* = *T. globicephala*, then found in the North Atlantic pilot whale *Globicephala melaena* [= *edwardi*] from South Africa (off Cape Town).

Trigonocotyle monticellii

Synonymy:

From Baylis, 1932 - *Prosthecocotyle monticellii* Linton, 1923 (nec Fuhrmann, 1899).

Hosts and Locality:

From Baylis, 1932 - Found in pilot whale (*Globicephala melaena*). Information regarding the geographical location of host was not provided by author.

Trigonocotyle prudhoei

Hosts and Locality:

From Markowski, 1955 - Found in the rough-tooth dolphin (*Steno bredanensis*), the dusky or piebald dolphin (*Lagenorhynchus obscurus*), and in the dolphin (*Langenorhynchus australis*). All hosts were from the Antarctic (14° 45′ N, 18° 34′ E); East Falkland Islands (southernmost point of Bay of Harbours).

Trigonocotyle skrjabini

Hosts and Locality:

From Dailey and Brownell, 1972 - Found in the ringed seal (*Phoca hispida*). Information regarding the geographical location of host was not provided by authors.

From Delyamure, 1955 - Found in the Othotsk ringed seal (*Phoca hispida ochotensis*) from the Sea of Okhotsk (Aniva Gulf).

From King, 1964 - Found in the ringed seal (*Phoca hispida*). Information regarding the geographical location of host was not provided by author.

Trigonocotyle spasskyi

Hosts and Locality:

From Dailey and Brownell, 1972 - Found in the killer whale (*Orcinus orca*). Information regarding the geographical location of host was not provided by authors.

From Delyamure, 1955 - Found in the killer whale (*Orca orca*) from the Sea of Okhotsk (Kurile Islands region).

Nematoda

Nematodes or round worms are common parasites in the stomach and intestines of marine mammals and occasionally sea turtles. They can also be found in tissues like the lungs, mammary glands, or surrounding the peri-auditory sinuses of cetaceans. Small numbers are often well tolerated, but interactions that cause excessive inflamation, ulcerate or perforate the stomach, occlude air passages, or erode the bone of skull can cause significant pathology.

Species of the ubiquitous Anisakidae mature and reproduce only in marine mammals, but their larval forms are found in invertebrates, fish, and even humans. Since the larval worms have economic impact thru additional processing or condemnation of fish, and zoonotic potential they are among the best studied marine mammal parasites. The life cycle of many species in this group is well established. Morphological species identification requires examining adult male worms which can be difficult even in patent infections, fortunately molecular methods can now be employed, but this has not yet brought widespread clarity to these cases, as the molecular techniques are not standardized or commercially available. The genera of interest are *Anisakis*, *Contracaecum*, and *Pseudoterranova*. While ingesting larval anisakid worms in fish can be risky, the adults do not cause human infection. In marine mammals, lungworms mostly belong to Pseudaliidae, and can cause inflammation and obstruction of airpassages in cetaceans and pulmonary disease in seals. A family of nematodes restricted to marine mammals is Crassicaudidae which contains the largest nematode *Crassicauda boopis* from the excretory system of the fin whale (*Balaenoptera physalus*). Other members of this genus are found in subcutaneous tissues, the peribullar sinus, and mammary tissue. Filaroid nematodes are also represented in tissue worms and as heartworm of seals.

Anisakis sp.

Hosts and Locality:

From Baylis, 1929 - Found in the humpback whale (*Megaptera nodosa*) from Durban.

From Baylis, 1932 - Larvae found in the humpback whale (*Megaptera nodosa*). Information regarding geographical location of hosts was not provided by author.

From Beverley-Burton, 1978 - Found in the Atlantic white-sided dolphin (*Lagenorhynchus acutus*) from Lingley Cove, Edmunds, Maine.

From Dailey and Brownell, 1972 - Found in the Tasmanian fur seal (*Arctocephalus tasmanicus*), the rough-toothed dolphin (*Steno bredanensis*), the short finned pilot whale (*Globicephala macrorhyncha*), the killer whale (*Orcinus orca*), the Dall porpoise (*Phocoenoides dalli*), the sei whale (*Balaenoptera borealis*), the humpback whale (*Megaptera novaengliae*), and in the striped dolphin (*Stenella caeruleoalba*). Information regarding geographical location of hosts was not provided by authors.

From Johnston and Mawson, 1941 - Found in the Tasmanian fur seal (*Gypsophoca tasmanica*) from Franklin Island, Derwent Heads, Tasmania (Australia).

From King, 1964 - Found in the Tasmanian fur seal (*Arctocephalus tasmanicus*). Information regarding the geographical locality of host was not provided by author.

From Lyster, 1940 - Found in the white whale (*Delphinapterus leucas*) from Ellesmere Island, Lake Harbor and Baffin Island.

From Margolis and Dailey, 1972 - Found in the sei whale (*Balaenoptera borealis*), the fin whale (*Balaenoptera physalus*), the North Pacific giant bottle-toothed nose whale (*Berardius bairdi*), the humpback whale (*Megaptera novaengliae*), the killer whale (*Orcinus orca*), the sperm whale (*Physeter catodon*), and in the goose-beaked whale (*Ziphius cavirostris*). Geographical distribution included Alaska, British Columbia, Washington, and California.

From Margolis and Pike, 1955 - Found in the fin whale (*Balaenoptera physalus*) from the North Sea.

From Migaki et al, 1971 - Found in the California sea lion (*Zalophus californianus*) from California.

From Rice, 1963 - Found in the sei whale (*Balaenoptera borealis*), the humpback whale (*Megaptera novaengliae*), the fin whale (*Balaenoptera physalus*), and in the sperm whale (*Physeter catodon*). All hosts were from the California coastline.

Anisakis alata

Synonymy:

From Davey, 1971 - *Anisakis simplex* Rudolphi, 1809, det. Krabbe, 1878.

From Delyamure, 1955 - *Anisakis rosmari* Baylis, 1920; *Ascaris bicolor* Baird, 1868 nec Rudolphi, 1793; *Ascaris rosmari* Baylis, 1916.

Hosts and Locality:

From Dailey and Brownell, 1972 - Found in a captive (zoo) walrus (*Odobenus romarus*). Information regarding geographical location of host was not provided by authors.

From King, 1964 - Found in the walrus (*Odobenus romarus*). Information regarding geographical location of host was not provided by author.

From Yamaguti, 1961 - Found in the walrus (*Odobenus rosmarus*) from a zoo in Hamburg, Germany.

Anisakis alexandri

Synonymy:

From Yamaguti, 1961 - *Filocapsularia alexandri* Hsü and Hoeppli, 1933.

Hosts and Locality:

From Dailey and Brownell, 1972 - Found in the Chinese white-sided dolphin (*Sousa chinensis*). Information regarding geographical location of host was not provided by authors.

From Delyamure, 1955 - Found in the Chinese white-sided dolphin (*Sousa chinensis*) from the Pacific Ocean (China).

Anisakis bicolor

Synonymy:

From Delyamure, 1955 - *Anisakis rosmarus* (Baylis, 1916) Baylis, 1920; *Ascaris bicolor* Baird, 1868 nec Rudolphi, 1793; *Anisakis alata* Hsü, 1933.

See Remarks.

Hosts and Locality:

From Dailey and Brownell, 1972 - Found in the walrus (*Odobenus romarus*). Information regarding geographical location of host was not provided by authors.

From King, 1964 - Found in the walrus (*Odobenus romarus*). Information regarding geographical location of host was not provided by author.

From Stiles and Hassall, 1899 - Found in the walrus (*Odobenus romarus*) that died in a London Zoo in England.

Remarks:

There seems to be general agreement that this is not a valid species. In introducing the species, Stiles and Hassall (1899) expressed doubts about its validity. Delyamure (1955) mentions it as a synonym of *Anisakis remarus*, and Davey (1971), in his extensive revision of the genus *Anisakis*, does not mention this parasite and equates *Anisakis rosmarus* and *Anisakis alata* with *Anisakis simplex*.

Anisakis catodontis

Hosts and Locality:

From Baylis, 1932 - Found in the sperm whale (*Physeter catodon*). Information regarding geographical location of host was not provided by author.

Anisakis delphini

Synonymy:

From Baylis, 1932 - "(? Synonym of *Contracaecum lobulatum*)"

Hosts and Locality:

From Baylis, 1932 - Found in the Gangetic dolphin (*Platanista gangetica*). Information regarding geographical location of host was not provided by author.

Anisakis dussumierii

Synonymy:

From Baylis, 1932 - *Ascaris (Anisakis) simplex* of Dujardin, 1845, nec Rudolphi, 1809; *Ascaris dussumierii* van Beneden, 1870.

Hosts and Locality:

From Baylis, 1932 - Found in the dolphin (*Delphinus sp.*). Information regarding the geographical location of host was not provided by author.

Anisakis insignis

Synonymy:

From Baylis, 1932 - *Peritrachelius insignis* Diesing, 1851; *Ascaris insignis* Jägerskiöld, 1893.

From Yamaguti, 1961 - *Filocapsularia insignis* Diesing, 1851; *Peritrachelius insignis* Diesing, 1851.

Hosts and Locality:

From Baylis, 1932 - Found in the Bouto (*Inia geoffrensis*) [= *Delphinis amazonicus*]. Information regarding geographical location of hosts was not provided by author.

From Dailey and Brownell, 1972 - Found in the Amazon River dolphin (*Inia geoffrensis*). Information regarding geographical location of host was not provided by authors.

From Layne and Caldwell, 1964 - Found in an Amazon River dolphin (*Inia geoffrensis*) [= *Delphinis amazonicus*] that was captured in the Amazon River (near Leticia) but died in Florida.

Remarks:

Davey (1971) considers this parasite to be *species inquirendae* for lack of valid information.

Anisakis ivanizkii

Synonymy:

From Davey, 1971 - *Anisakis simplex* Rudolphi, 1809.

From Yamaguti, 1961 - *Filocapsularia ivanizkii* Mozgovi, 1949.

Hosts and Locality:

From Dailey and Brownell, 1972 - Found in the sperm whale (*Physeter catodon*). Information regarding geographical location of host was not provided by authors.

From Delyamure, 1955 - Found in the sperm whale (*Physeter catodon*) from the Pacific Ocean (Commander Island region of USSR).

Anisakis kükenthalii

Synonymy:

From Baylis, 1932 - "Possibly a synonym of *A. simplex*"; *Anisakis kükenthalii* Cobb 1888.

Hosts and Locality:

From Baylis, 1932 - Found in the white whale (*Delphinapterus leucas*). Information regarding geographical location of host was not provided by author.

~~~~~~

Anisakis patagonica

Synonymy:

From Davey, 1971 - *Anisakis simplex* (Rudolphi, 1809, det. Krabbe, 1878).

From Delyamure, 1955 - *Ascaris patagonica* Linstow, 1880.

Hosts and Locality:

From Dailey and Brownell, 1972 - Found in the South American sea lion (*Otaria byronia*), and in the southern elephant seal (*Mirounga leonina*). Information regarding geographical location of hosts was not provided by authors.

From Delyamure, 1955 - Found in the South American sea lion (*Otaria byronia*) from Patagonia.

From King, 1964 - Found in the southern elephant seal (*Mirounga leonina*), the Steller sea lion (*Eumetopias jubata*) and in the South American sea lion (*Otaria byronia*). Information regarding geographical location of hosts was not provided by author.

From Yamaguti, 1961 - Found in the Steller sea lion (*Eumetopias jubata*) from Patagonia.

Anisakis pegreffii

Synonymy:

From Davey, 1971 - *Anisakis simplex* Rudolphi, 1809.

From Delyamure, 1955 - *Skrjabinisakis schupakovi* Mozgovoi, 1953; *Anisakis sp.* Schupakov, 1936.

From Yamaguti, 1961 - *Filocapsularia pegreffi* Campana-Rouget and Biocca, 1955.

Hosts and Locality:

From Dailey and Brownell, 1972 - Found in the Mediterranean monk seal (*Monachus monachus*). Information regarding geographical location of host was not provided by authors.

From King, 1964 - Found in the Mediterranean monk seal (*Monachus monachus*). Information regarding geographical location of host was not provided by author.

From Yamaguti, 1961 - Found in the Mediterranean monk seal (*Monachus monachus*) from the Mediterranean Sea.

Anisakis physeteris

Synonymy:

From Davey, 1971 - *Anisakis skryabini* Mozgovoi, 1949; *Anisakis oceanica* Johnston and Mawson, 1951; *Anosakis brevispiculata* Dollfus, 1968.

From Yamaguti, 1961 - *Filocapsularia physeteris*. See Remarks.

Hosts and Locality:

From Baylis, 1932 - Found in the sperm whale (*Physeter catodon*). Information regarding geographical location of host was not provided by author.

From Dailey and Brownell, 1972 - Found in the sperm whale (*Physeter catodon*). Information regarding geographical location of host was not provided by authors.

From Davey, 1971 - Found in the sperm whale (*Physeter catodon*), the pigmy sperm whale (*Kogia breviceps*), the pilot whale (*Globicephalus ventricosus*), and in the bottlenosed whale (*Hyperoodon ampullatus*). Geographical distribution is worldwide.

From Delyamure, 1955 - Found in the sperm whale (*Physeter catodon*) from the Atlantic Ocean (Saldanha Bay, South West Africa), South Georgia, and the Indian Ocean (Durban, eastern South Africa).

Fron Kagei et al, 1967 - Found in the sperm whale (*Physeter catodon*) from the coast of Japan.

From Margolis and Dailey, 1972 - Found in the sperm whale (*Physeter catodon*) from Alaska and British Columbia.

From Margolis and Pike, 1955 - Found in the sperm whale (*Physeter catodon*) from Alaska and British Columbia.

Remarks:

Yamaguti (1961) considers the genus *Filocapsularia* to be synonymous with *Anisakis*.

Anisakis rosmari

Synonymy:

From Davey, 1971 - *Anisakis simplex* Baylis, 1920.

From Delyamure, 1955 - *Ascaris bicolor* Baird, nec Rudolphi, 1793; *Ascaris rosmari* Baylis, 1916; *Anisakis alata* Hsü, 1933.

Hosts and Locality:

From Dailey and Brownell, 1972 - Found in the walrus (*Odobenus romarus*) and in the ringed seal (*Pusa hispida*). Information regarding geographical location of hosts was not provided by authors.

From Delyamure, 1955 - Found in the walrus (*Odobenus rosmarus*). Geographical distribution "apparently" includes the North Atlantic - Arctic region.

From King, 1964 - Found in the ringed seal (*Pusa hispida*), and the walrus (*Odobenus rosmarus*). Information regarding geographical location of hosts was not provided by author.

Anisakis schupakovi

Synonymy:

From Delyamure, 1955 - *Skrjabinisakis schupakovi* Mozgovoi, 1953; *Anisakis sp.* Schupakov, 1936.

From Yamaguti, 1961 - *Filocapsularia schupakovi* Mozgovoi, 1953.

Hosts and Locality:

From Dailey and Brownell, 1972 - Found in the Caspian seal (*Pusa caspica*). Information regarding geographical location of host was not provided by authors.

From Delyamure, 1955 - Found in the Caspian seal (*Pusa caspica*) from the Caspian Sea (Chechen Island).

From King, 1964 - Found in the Caspian seal (*Pusa caspica*). Information regarding geographical location of host was not provided by author.

Anisakis similis

Synonymy:

From Davey, 1971 - *Anisakis simplex* Rudolphi, 1809; *Anisakis alata* Hsü, 1933; *Anisakis ivanizkii* Mozgovoi, 1949; *Anisakis kogiae* Johnston and Mawson, 1939; *Anisakis kukenthalii* Cobb, 1888; *Anisakis patagonica* von Linstow, 1880; *Anisakis pegreffii* Campana - Rouget and Biocca, 1955; *Anisakis rosmari* Baylis, 1916; *Anisakis tridentata* Kreis, 1939.

From Delyamure, 1955 - *Ascaris similis* Baird, 1853.

From Johnston and Mawson, 1945 - *Stomachus similis* (Baird); *Ascaris similis* Baylis 1920; *Ascaris patagonica* Linstow 1880; *Anisakis patagonia* Baylis 1923; *Capsularia similis* Johnston and Mawson 1943.

From Yamaguti, 1961 - *Ascaris patagonica* Linstow, 1880; *Filocapsularia similis* Baird, 1853.

Hosts and Locality:

From Baylis, 1929 - Found in the southern elephant seal (*Mirounga leonia*) from North Bay, Ice Fjord, and South Georgia (Antarctica).

From Caballero and Peregrina, 1938 - Found in the northern elephant seal (*Mirounga angustirostris*) from the San Diego Zoo, California.

From Dailey and Brownell, 1972 - Found in the South American sea lion (*Otaria byronia*), the harbor seal (*Phoca vitulina*), the northern elephant seal (*Mirounga angustirostris*), the southern elephant seal (*Mirounga leonina*), the leopard seal (*Hydrurga leptonyx*), and in the California sea lion (*Zalophus californianus*). Information regarding geographical location of hosts was not provided by authors. See Remarks.

From Delyamure, 1955 - Found in the gray seal (*Halichoerus grypus*) and the southern elephant seal (*Mirounga leonina*). Geographical distribution includes the Atlantic Ocean (England, Falkland, South Georgia), the North Sea, Switzerland (Basle Zoo) and Australia (Pacific Ocean).

From Johnston, 1937c - Found in the elephant seal (*Mirounga leonina*) from Commonwealth Bay and Macquarie Island (Antarctica), and in the sea leopard (*Hydrurga leptonyx*) from Macquarie Island (Antarctica).

From Johnston and Mawson, 1941 - Found in the leopard seal (*Hydrurga leptonyx*) from Port River, Port Adelaide (Australia).

From Johnston and Mawson, 1945 - If *Anisakis similis* = *Stomachus similis*, then found in the southern elephant seal (*Mirounga leonia*) from the Antarctic (Macquarie Island and Commonwealth Bay), and in the leopard seal (*Hydrurga leptonyx*) from Macquarie Island (Antarctica).

From King, 1964 - Found in the gray seal (*Halichoerus grypus*), the leopard seal (*Hydrurga leptonyx*), the northern elephant seal (*Mirounga angustirostris*), the southern elephant seal (*Mirounga leonina*), the South American fur seal (*Arctocephalus australis*), the Steller sea lion (*Eumetopias jubata*), the California sea lion (*Zalophus californianus*), the South American sea lion (*Otaria byronia*), and in the harbor seal (*Phoca vitulina*). Information regarding geographical location of hosts was not provided by author.

From Margolis and Dailey, 1972 - Found in the Steller sea lion (*Eumetopias jubata*), the northern elephant seal (*Mirounga angustirostris*), and in the California sea lion (*Zalophus californianus*). Geographical distribution includes California (San Diego Zoo), Baja California, and Switzerland (Basel Zoo).

From Yamaguti, 1961 - Found in the gray seal (*Halichoerus grypus*) from the Falklands and Cornwall Islands. Also found in the California sea lion (*Zalophus californianus*), the leopard seal (*Hydrurga leptonyx*), the Steller sea lion (*Eumetopias jubata*), and in a seal (*Phoca sp*). Geographical distribution includes California, Antarctic, South Australia, New Zealand, Patagonia, and the Gulf of St. Lawrence.

Remarks:

Dailey and Brownell (1972) list the Steller sea lion (*Eumetopias jubata*), the South American fur seal (*Arctocephalus australis*) and the gray seal (*Halichoerus grypus*) as hosts to this parasite and give Baylis, 1920a as a reference source. However, the only host listed in the referenced Baylis (1920a) paper for *Anisakis similis* is an unidentified seal from Antarctica.

The geographical distribution of *Anisakis similis* is much more extensive if Davey's (1971) opinion that *A. similis* is synonymous with *A. simplex* is correct.

Anisakis simplex

Synonymy:

From Baylis, 1932 - *Ascaris simplex* Rudolphi, 1804 ("not *Ascaris* [*Anisakis*] *simplex*, Dujardin, 1845"); *Ascaris angulivalvis* Creplin, 1851.

From Dailey and Brownell, 1972 - *Anisakis tursonis* Crusz, 1946; *Ascaris angulivalis*.

From Davey, 1971 - *Anisakis alata* Hsü,, 1933; *Anisakis catodontis* Baylis, 1929; *Anisakis ivanizkii* Mozgovoi, 1949; *Anisakis kogiae* Johnston and Mawson, 1939; *Anisakis kükenthalii* Cobb, 1888; *Anisakis pegreffii* Campana - Rouget and Biocca, 1955; *Anisakis patagonica* von Linstow, 1880; *Anisakis rosmari* Baylis, 1916; *Anisaki similis* Baird, 1853; *Anisakis tridentata* Kreis, 1939. See Remarks.

From Delyamure, 1955 - *Ascaris simplex* Rudolphi, 1809 nec *Ascaris simplex*, Dujardin 1845; *Ascaris angulivalvis* Creplin, 1851; *Anisakis salaries* (Gmelin, 1790) Yamaguti, 1935.

From Yamaguti, 1961 - *Filocapsularia dussumierii*.

Hosts and Locality:

From Baylis, 1932 - Found in the piked whale (*Balaenoptera acutorostrata*), the sei whale (*Balaenoptera borealis*), the blue whale (*Balaenoptera musculus*), the white whale (*Delphinapterus leucas*), the dolphin (*Delphinus sp.*), the bottled-nose dolphin (*Hyperoodon rostratus*), the white-beaked dolphin (*Lagenorhynchus albirostris*), the Sowerby dolphin (*Mesoplodon bidens*), the narwhal (*Monodon monoceros*), the finned porpoise (*Phocoena phocoena*), and in the Gangetic dolphin (?) sic *Platanista gangetica*. Information regarding the geographical locality of hosts was not provided by author.

From Dailey and Brownell, 1972 - Found in the Steller sea lion (*Eumetopias jubata*), the bottlenosed dolphin (*Tursiops truncatus*), the dusky dolphin (*Lagenorhynchus obscurus*), the long-beaked dolphin (*Stenella longirostris*), the eastern pacific spotted dolphin (*Stenella graffmani*), the common dolphin (*Delphinus delphis*), a dolphin (unspecified species), the false killer whale (*Pseudorca crassidens*), the North Atlantic pilot whale (*Globicephala melaena*), the harbor porpoise (*Phocoena phocoena*), the narwhal (*Monodon monoceros*), the white whale (*Delphinapterus leucas*), the sperm whale (*Physeter catodon*), the pigmy sperm whale (*Kogia breviceps*), the Sowerby beaked whale (*Mesoplodon bidens*), the giant bottlenosed whale (*Berardius bairdi*), the northern bottlenosed whale (*Hyperoodon ampullatus*), the little piked whale (*Balaenoptera acutorostrata*), the fin whale (*Balaenoptera physalus*), the blue whale (*Balaenoptera musculus*), and the white-beaked dolphin (*Lagenorhynchus albirostris*). Information regarding the geographical locality of hosts was not provided by authors. See Remarks.

From Dailey and Perrin, 1973 - Found in the long-beaked dolphin (*Stenella longirostris*), and the eastern pacific spotted dolphin (*Stenella graffmani*). Both hosts were captured at Lat. 12° 51′N, Long. 90° 18′ W; Lat 7° 11′ N, Long. 90° 32′ W; Lat approx. 8° N., 107° W. An addition, *Anisakis simplex* was found in a *Stenella longirostris* from Lat approx. 8° N, Long 109° 45′ W and in a *Stenella graffmani* from Lat approx. 14° N, Long 100° W.

From Delyamure, 1955 - Found in the Steller sea lion (*Eumetopias jubata*), the bottlenosed whale (*Hyperoodon ampullatus*), the Sowerby dolphin (*Mesoplodon bidens*), the white whale (*Delphinapterus leucas*), the narwhal (*Monodon monoceros*), the common dolphin (*Delphinus delphis*), the white-beaked dolphin (*Lagenorhynchus albirostris*), the piebald dolphin (*Lagenorhynchus obscurus*); the killer whale (*Orcinus orca*), the false killer whale (*Pseudorca crassidens*), the finned porpoise (*Phocoena phocoena*), the blue whale (*Balaenoptera musculus*), the piked whale (*Balaenoptera acutorostrata*), and in the sperm whale (*Physeter catodon*). Geographical distribution includes the North Sea (Denmark, England, Germany), the Pacific Ocean (Japan, New Zealand), and USSR (Morzhovoi Bay, Kronotskii Bay, Olyutorskii Bay).

From Johnston and Best, 1942 - Found in the dusky dolphin (*Lagenorhynchus obscurus*) from Cook Strait (New Zealand).

From Johnston and Mawson, 1941 - Found in the dolphin (*Delphinus forsteri*) from Sydney Harbor (Australia). See Remarks.

From Kagei et al, 1967 - Found in the rough porpoise (*Steno bredanensis*), the blue white dolphin (*Stenella caeruleoalba*), the short finned pilot whale (*Globicephala macrorhyncha*), and the Dall porpoise (*Phocoenoides dalli*) the sperm whale (*Physeter catodon*), and in the fur seal (*Callorphinus ursinus*). All hosts were from the coast of Japan.

From King, 1964 - Found in the Steller sea lion (*Eumetopias jubata*). Information regarding the geographical locality of host was not provided by author.

From Lyster, 1940 - Found in the white whale (*Delphinapterus leucas*) from the Gulf of St. Lawrence, Canada.

From Margolis and Dailey, 1972 - Found in the sei whale (*Balaenoptera borealis*), the North Pacific giant bottle-toothed nose whale (*Berardius bairdi*), the killer whale (*Orcinus orca*), the Dall porpoise (*Phocoenoides dalli*), and in the sperm whale (*Physeter catodon*). All hosts were from British Columbia.

From Wulker, 1930 - Found in the fin whale (*Balaenoptera physalus*) from northern Norway.

From Yamaguti, 1961 - If *Filocapsularia dussumierii* = *Anisakis simplex*, then found in the dolphin *Delphinus sp.* and the sperm whale (*Physeter catodon*) from Maldive Isl., Indian Ocean and the Pacific Ocean.

Remarks:

Dailey and Brownell (1972) list the bottle-nosed dolphin (*Tursiops truncatus*) as a host of *Anisakis simplex* based on the opinion that *A. simplex* is synonymous with *Anisakis tursionis* (Crusz, 1946). They cite Delyamure (1955) as a source reference to support this. However, Delyamure does not list *Tursiops truncatus* as a host of *A. simplex* and claims *A. tursionis* cannot be accurately described due to lack of information. Dailey and Brownell (1972) also list the Steller sea lion (*Eumetopias jubata*) as a host of *A. simplex* and cite Baylis 1920a as a source reference. However, no mention this host could be founded in the Baylis (1920a) paper.

Davey (1971) lists a number of hosts based on his opinion that *Anisakis simplex* is synonymous with other species of *Anisakis*. These host species include the humpback whale (*Megaptera novaengliae*), the Bryde whale (*Balaenoptera brydei*), the ringed seal (*Pusa hispida*), the gray seal (*Halichoerus grypus*), the Mediterranean sea monk (*Monachus monachus*), and the northern elephant seal (*Mirounga angustirostris*). Many of these hosts were identified by other investigators as hosts of other species of *Anisakis* that Davey considers to be synonymous with *Anisakis simplex*. Davey also considers the distribution of *A. simplex* to be worldwide, particularly in the colder temperate and polar waters.

Johnston and Mawson (1941) re-examined a previously collected nematode taken from a *Delphinus forsteri* at Sydney Harbour, Australia (originally identified as *Anisakis sp.*) and determined it was an *Anisakis simplex*.

Anisakis skrjabini

Synonymy:

From Davey, 1971 - *Anisakis physeteris* Baylis, 1923; *Anisakis oceanica* Johnston and Mawson, 1951; *Anisakis brevispiculata* Dollfus, 1968.

Hosts and Locality:

From Dailey and Brownell, 1972 - Found in the sperm whale (*Physeter catodon*), and the giant bottlenosed whale (*Berardius bairdi*). Information regarding geographical location of hosts was not provided by authors.

From Delyamure, 1955 - Found in the sperm whale (*Physeter catodon*) and the bottlenosed whale (*Hyperoodon ampullatus*). Geograph-

ical distribution includes the Pacific Ocean (Commander Islands region), the Sea of Okhotsk, and Antarctica.

From Yamaguti, 1961 - Found in the sperm whale (*Physeter catodon*) from the Kommandorski Islands.

Anisakis tridentata

Synonymy:

From Davey, 1971 - *Anisakix simplex* Krabbe, 1878.

Hosts and Locality:

From Dailey and Brownell, 1972 - Found in the Steller sea lion (*Eumetopias jubata*). Information regarding geographical location of host was not provided by authors.

From King, 1964 - Found in the Steller sea lion (*Eumetopias jubata*). Information regarding geographical location of host was not provided by author.

From Kreis, 1938 - Found in a captive Steller sea lion (*Eumetopias jubata*) from the Zoological Gardens, Basel (Switzerland).

Anisakis typica

Synonymy:

From Baylis, 1932 - *Conocephalus typicus* Diesing, 1861; *Ascaris typica* Jägerskiöld, 1894; *Ascaris (Peritracheilus) typicus* Jägerskiöld, 1894. *Peritracheilus typicus* Jägerskiöld, 1894.

From Davey, 1971 - *Anisakis tursiopis* Crusz, 1946.

From Delyamure, 1955 - *Conocephalus typicus* Diesing, 1860; *Ascaris typica* (Diesing, 1860) Jägerskiöld, 1894; *Peritracheilus typicus* (Diesing, 1860) Jägerskiöld, 1894.

Hosts and Locality:

From Baylis, 1929 - Found in the dusky dolphin (*Lagenorhynchus obscurus*) from southwest Africa (north of Salanha Bay).

From Baylis, 1932 - Found in the common dolphin (*Delphinus delphis*), the pilot whale

(*Globicephalus melas*), the dusky dolphin (*Lagenorhynchus obscurus*), the common porpoise (*Phocoena phocoena*), and in the dolphin (*Prodelphinus sp.*). Information regarding the geographical location of hosts was not provided by author.

From Davey, 1971 - Found in the blue white dolphin (*Stenella caeruleoalba*), the common dolphin (*Delphinus delphis*), the dolphin (*Prodelphinus sp.* Krabbe 1878), the bottlenose dolphin (*Tursiops truncatus*), the Gray's dolphin (*Lagenorhynchus obscurus*), the pilot whale (*Globicephalus melas*), the common porpoise (*Phocoena phocoena*), and the Dall porpoise (*Phocoenoides dalli*). Geographical distribution includes warmer temperature and tropical waters between 40° N and 36° S.

From Delyamure, 1955 - Found in the common dolphin (*Delphinus delphis*), the pilot whale (*Globicephalus melas*), the finned porpoise (*Phocoena phocoena*), and in the piebald dolphin (*Lagenorhynchus obscurus*). Geographical distribution includes the North Sea (Germany), and the Atlantic Ocean (north of Saldanah Bay, South East Africa).

Ascaris dehiscens

Hosts and Locality:

From Dailey and Brownell, 1972 - Found in the ringed seal (*Pusa hispida*). Information regarding the geographical location of host was not provided by authors.

From King, 1964 - Found in the ringed seal (*Pusa hispida*). Information regarding the geographical location of host was not provided by author.

Ascaris delphini

Synonymy:

See Remarks.

Hosts and Locality:

From Baylis, 1932 - Found in the Susu or blind river dolphin (*Platanista gangetica*).

Remarks:

Baylis (1932) questions whether this parasite is synonymous with *Contracaecum lobulatum*.

Ascaris lobulata

Hosts and Locality:

From Linstow, 1907 - Found in the Susu or blind river dolphin (*Platanista gangetica*).

Ascaris osculata

Hosts and Locality:

From Linstow, 1906 - Found in the Weddell seal (*Leptonychotes weddelli*) from Antarctica.

Ascaris radiata

Hosts and Locality:

From Linstow, 1906 - Found in the Weddell seal (*Leptonychotes weddelli*) from Antarctica.

Ascaris rectangula

Hosts and Locality:

From Linstow, 1906 - Found in the Weddell seal (*Leptonychotes weddelli*) from South Orkneys (Antarctica).

Contracaecum sp.

Hosts and Locality:

From Baylis, 1929 - Found in the fin whale (*Balaenoptera physalus*) from South Georgia (Antarctica).

From Baylis, 1932 - Larvae found in the fin whale (*Balaenoptera physalus*). Information regarding the geographical location of host was not provided by author.

From Dailey and Brownell, 1972 - Found in the La Plata dolphin or Franciscana (*Pontoporia blainvillei*) and in the fin whale (*Balaenoptera physalus*). Information regarding the geographical location of host was not provided by authors.

From Margolis and Dailey, 1972 - Found in the Pacific white-sided dolphin (*Lagenorhynchus obliquidens*) from California. *Contracaecum sp.* larvae were also found in the ringed seal (*Pusa hispida*) from Alaska.

From Martin et al, 1970 - Found in the striped dolphin (*Lagenorhynchus obliquidens*) from the Palos Verdes Peninsula, California.

From Wilson and Stockdale, 1970 - Found in a captive harp seal (*Pagophilus groenlandicus*). Information regarding the geographical location of host was not provided by authors.

Contracaecum callotariae

Hosts and Locality:

From Dailey and Brownell, 1972 - Found in the northern fur seal (*Callorhinus ursinus*). Information regarding geographical location of host was not provided by authors.

From King, 1964 - Found in the northern fur seal (*Callorhinus ursinus*). Information regarding geographical location of host was not provided by author.

Contracaecum corderoi

Hosts and Locality:

From Dailey and Brownell, 1972 - Found in the South American fur seal (*Arctocephalus australis*). Information regarding geographical location of host was not provided by authors.

From Delyamure, 1955 - Found in the South American fur seal (*Arctocephalus australis*) from the Atlantic Ocean off Uruguay.

From King, 1964 - Found in the South American fur seal (*Arctocephalus australis*). Information regarding geographical location of host was not provided by author.

Contracaecum gypsophocae

Hosts and Locality:

From Johnston and Mawson, 1941 - Found in the Tasmanian fur seal (*Gypsophoca tasmanica*) from Derwent Heads (Tasmania, Australia).

Contracaecum lobulatum

Synonymy:

From Baylis, 1932 - *Ascaris lobulata* Schneider, 1866; *Ascaris delphini* Rudolphi, 1819 (*vide infra*); "?" *Ascaris simplex* of Diesing, 1851 (part).

From Delyamure, 1955 - *Ascaris delphini* Rudolphi, 1819; *Ascaris lobulata* Schneider, 1866.

Hosts and Locality:

From Baylis, 1932 - Found in the Gangetic dolphin (*Platanista gangetica*). Information regarding geographical location of host was not provided by author.

From Dailey and Brownell, 1972 - Found in the Susu or blind river dolphin (*Platanista gangetica*). Information regarding geographical location of host was not provided by authors.

From Delyamure, 1955 - Found in the Susu or blind river dolphin (*Platanista gangetica*) from the Indian Ocean (Ceylon, Burma).

From Linstow, 1907 - Found in the Gangetic dolphin (*Platanista gangetica*).

From Yamaguti, 1961 - Found in the dolphin *Delphinus* (= *Platanista*) *gangeticus* from India.

Contracaecum ogmorhini

Hosts and Locality:

From Dailey and Brownell, 1972 - Found in the leopard seal (*Hydrurga leptonyx*). Information regarding geographical location of host was not provided by authors.

From Johnston and Mawson, 1941 - Found in the leopard seal (*Hydrurga leptonyx*) from Port Adelaide (Australia).

From King, 1964 - Found in the leopard seal (*Hydrurga leptonyx*). Information regarding geographical location of host was not provided by author.

Contracaecum osculatum

Hosts and Locality:

From Caballero and Peregrina, 1938 - Found in a captive northern elephant seal (*Mirounga angustirostris*) from the San Diego Zoo, California.

From Dailey and Brownell, 1972 - Found in the South American sea lion (*Otaria byronia*), the California sea lion (*Zalophus californianus*), the Australian sea lion (*Neophoca cinerea*), the northern fur seal (*Callorhinus ursinus*), the walrus (*Odobenus rosmarus*), the harbor seal (*Phoca vitulina*), the bearded seal (*Erignathus barbatus*), the hooded seal (*Cystophora cristata*), the gray seal (*Halichoerus grypus*), the harp seal (*Phoca groenlandica*), the northern elephant seal (*Mirounga angustirostris*), the southern elephant seal (*Mirounga leonina*), the crab-eating seal (*Lobodon carcinophagus*), the leopard seal (*Hydrurga leptonyx*), the Weddell seal (*Leptonychotes weddelli*), the Mediterranean monk seal (*Monachus monachus*), and in the Steller sea lion (*Eumetopias jubata*). Information regarding geographical location of hosts was not provided by authors. See Remarks.

From Dailey and Hill, 1970 - Found in the Steller sea lion (*Eumetopias jubata*) and the California sea lion (*Zalophus californianus*). Both hosts were from the southern to central California region (Alamitos Bay to Año Nuevo Island).

From Delyamure, 1955 - See Remarks.

From Johnston, 1937c - Found in the Weddell seal (*Leptonychotes weddelli*) from Commonwealth Bay (Antarctica), the Ross seal (*Ommatophoca rossi*) from Antarctica, the sea elephant (*Mirounga leonina*) from Macquarie Island (Antarctica), and in the sea leopard (*Hydrurga leptonyx*) from Macquarie Island and the Antarctic.

From Johnston, 1937e - Erroneously reported to be found in the Australian hair seal (*Arctocephalus forsteri*) from Pearson Island, South Australia. See Remarks.

From Johnston and Mawson, 1941 - Found in the Australian sea lion (*Neophoca cinerea*) and in the leopard seal (*Hydrurga leptonyx*) from Pearson Island and Port Adelaide (Australia).

From Johnston and Mawson, 1945 - Found in the southern elephant seal (*Mirounga leonia*)

from Heard Island, Possession Islands and the Crozets (Antarctica); the crab-eating seal (*Lobodon carcinophagus*) from Antarctica (64° 49'); the leopard seal (*Hydrurga leptonyx*) from Heard Island (Antarctica); the Weddell seal (*Leptonychotes weddelli*) from Enderby Land (Antarctica); and in the Ross seal (*Ommatophoca rossi*) from Antarctica.

From Keyes, 1965 - Found in the northern fur seal (*Callorhinus ursinus*) from the Pribilof Islands, Alaska.

From King, 1964 - Found in the bearded seal (*Erignathus barbatus*), the gray seal (*Halichoerus grypus*), the harbor seal (*Phoca vitulina*), the ringed seal (*Pusa hispida*), the Baikal seal (*Phoca sibirica*), the harp seal (*Phoca groenlandica*), the leopard seal (*Hydrurga leptonyx*), the Weddell seal (*Leptonychotes weddelli*), the crab-eating seal (*Lobodon carcinophagus*), the Ross seal (*Ommatophoca rossi*), the Mediterranean monk seal (*Monachus monachus*), the hooded seal (*Cystophora cristata*), the southern elephant seal (*Mirounga leonia*), the northern elephant seal (*Mirounga angustirostris*), the northern fur seal (*Callorhinus ursinus*), the South American fur seal (*Arctocephalus australis*), the Kerguelen fur seal (*Arctocephalus tropicalis*), the South African fur seal (*Arctocephalus pusillus*), the walrus (*Odobenus rosmarus*), the California sea lion (*Zalophus californianus*), the Steller sea lion (*Eumetopias jubata*), the South American sea lion (*Otaria byronia*), and in the Australian sea lion (*Neophoca cinerea*). Information regarding geographical location of hosts was not provided by author.

From Linstow, 1892 - Found in the leopard seal (*Hydrurga leptonyx*) from South Georgia (Antarctica).

From Lyster, 1940 - Found in the ringed seal (*Phoca hispida*) and in the harbor seal (*Phoca vitulina*). Geographical distribution includes Dundas Harbor, Devon Island, and intermediate points from Craig Harbor in the north to Havre St. Pierre (Quebec) in the south (Lake Harbor, Clyde River in Baffin Island, Stupart Bay, Wolstenholme).

From Margolis and Dailey, 1972 - Found in the northern fur seal (*Callorhinus ursinus*), the Steller sea lion (*Eumetopias jubata*), the northern elephant seal (*Mirounga angustiros-*

tris), the harbor seal (*Phoca vitulina richardi*), and in the California sea lion (*Zalophus californianus*). Geographical distribution includes Alaska, British Columbia, California, Baja California, and the Baltimore Zoo.

From Myers, 1957 - Found in the harbor seal (*Phoca vitulina*) from southwest Baffin Island; the ringed seal (*Pusa hispida*) from Port Burwell, Ungava Bay, Herschel Islands, and southwest Baffin Bay; the bearded seal (*Erignathus barbatus*) from Tunnusaksuk in Ungava Bay, Diana Bay, Coral Harbor, and Southampton Island; and in the harp seal (*Phoca groenlandica*) from Buttons Islands and the Magdalen Islands (Province of Quebec).

From Railliet and Henry, 1907 - Found in the crab-eating seal (*Lobodon carcinophagus*) from Booth-Wandle Island and Graham Island (Antarctica).

From Stiles and Hassall, 1899 - Found in the Steller sea lion (*Eumetopias jubata*) from the Bering Sea; the South American sea lion (*Otaria byronia*) from Patagonia; the walrus (*Odobenus rosmarus*) from Greenland; the harbor seal (*Phoca vitulina*) from Greifswald, Oresund; the bearded seal (*Erignathus barbatus*) from Greenland, Iceland and Baffin Bay; the gray seal (*Halichoerus grypus*) from Rugen; the harp seal (*Phoca groenlandica*) from Greenland; the hooded seal (*Cystophora cristata*) from Greenland; and in the Weddell seal (*Leptonychotes weddelli*) from Orkneys and Commonwealth Bay (Antarctica).

Remarks:

Dailey and Brownell (1972) also list the South American fur seal (*Arctocephalus australis*), the South African fur seal (*Arctocephalus pusillus*), the Australian fur seal (*Arctocephalus doriferus*), the Australian sea lion (*Neophoca cinerea*), and the Kerguelen fur seal (*Arctocephalus tropicalis*) as hosts of *Contracaecum osculatum* and cite Baylis (1920a) as a source reference. However, no mention of these hosts could be found in the Baylis (1920a) paper. Baylis does equate *Kathleena osculata* with *Contracaecum* and notes this parasite was found in the leopard seal (*Hydrurga leptonyx*). However the only mention of *Contracaecum osculatum* infection was in unspecified "seals".

Delyamure (1955) breaks down this species into two sub-species: *Contracaecum osculatum baicalensis* and *Contracaecum osculatum osculatum*. See below.

Johnston (1937e) erroneously lists the New Zealand fur seal (*Arctocephalus forsteri*) as a host of *Contracaecum osculatum*. In a subsequent paper by Johnston and Mawson (1941) the authors correct the error by noting the examined host was actually an Australian sea lion (*Neophoca cinerea*).

Contracaecum osculatum baicalensis

Hosts and Locality:

From Dailey and Brownell, 1972 - Found in the Baikal seal (*Pusa sibirica*). Information regarding geographical location of host was not provided by authors.

From Delyamure, 1955 - Found in the Baikal seal (*Phoca sibirica*) from Lake Baikal (USSR).

Contracaecum osculatum osculatum

Synonymy:

From Delyamure, 1955 - *Ascaris osculatum* Rudolphi, 1802; *Kathleena osculatum* (Rudolphi 1802) Leiper and Atkinson 1915; *Contracaecum antarcticum* Johnston 1938; *Contracaecum ogmorhini* Johnston and Mawson 1941; *Contracaecum gypsophocae* Johnston and Mawson 1941; and *Phocascaris hydrurgae* Johnston and Mawson 1941.

Hosts and Locality:

From Delyamure, 1955 - Found in the Australian fur seal (*Arctocephalus doriferus*), the South American sea lion (*Otaria byronia*), the walrus (*Odobenus rosmarus romarus*), the Greenland seal (*Pagophoca groenlandica*), the ringed seal (*Pusa hispida*), the Okhotsk ringed seal (*Phoca hispida ochotensis*), the common seal (*Phoca vitulina*), the gray seal (*Halichoerus grypus*), the bearded seal (*Erignathus barbatus*), the crab-eating seal (*Lobodon carcinophagus*), the leopard seal (*Hydrurga leptonyx*), the Weddell seal (*Leptonychotes weddelli*), the monk seal (*Monachus monachus*), the crested seal (*Cystophora cristata*), and in the elephant seal (*Mir-*

ounga leonina). Geographical distribution includes Greenland, Spitzbergen, England, North America, Canada, Bering Sea, Ceylon, Egypy, Antarctica, and Russia (White Sea, Novaya Zemlya, Hooker Island, Bukhta Tikhaya, Franz-Josef Land, Kara Strait, Loginov Island, and Novosibirsk Island).

Contracaecum radiatum

Synonymy:

From Delyamure, 1955 - *Ascaris radiata* Linstow, 1907; *Ascaris radiata* Linstow, 1907; *Ascaris falcigera* Railliet and Henry, 1907; *Kathleena radiata* (Linstow, 1907) Leiper and Atkinson, 1914.

From Johnston, 1937c - *Ascaris radiata* Linstow, 1907; *Ascaris falcigera* Railliet and Henry, 1907; *Ascaris falcigera* Garin 1913; *Kathleena radiata* Leiper and Atkinson, 1914; *Ascaris osculate* of Linstow, 1892; *Contracaecum radiatum* Baylis, 1920; and *Contracaecum falcigerum* Baylis, 1920.

From Linstow, 1892 - *Ascaris osculate.*

Hosts and Locality:

From Baylis, 1929 - Found in the leopard seal (*Hydrurga leptonyx*) from the South Sandwich region, and in the crab-eating seal (*Lobodon carcinophagus*) from the Palmer Archipelago (Antarctica).

From Dailey and Brownell, 1972 - Found in the southern elephant seal (*Mirounga leonina*), the leopard seal (*Hydrurga leptonyx*), the Weddell seal (*Leptonychotes weddelli*), the Ross seal (*Ommatophoca rossi*), and in the crab-eating seal (*Lobodon carcinophagus*). Information regarding geographical location of hosts was not provided by authors.

From Delyamure, 1955 - Found in the Weddell seal (*Leptonychotes weddelli*), the leopard seal (*Hydrurga leptonyx*), and in the Ross seal (*Ommatophoca rossi*). Geographical distribution includes the Antarctic.

From Johnston, 1937c - Found in the Weddell seal (*Leptonychotes weddelli*) and the crab-eating seal (*Lobodon carcinophagus*) from Commonwealth Bay (Antarctica).

From Johnston and Mawson, 1945 - Found in the leopard seal (*Hydrurga leptonyx*) from Heard Island, and the crab-eating seal (*Lobodon carcinophagus*) from Commonwealth Bay (64° 49').

From King, 1964 - Found in the leopard seal (*Hydrurga leptonyx*), the Weddell seal (*Leptonychotes weddelli*), the crab-eating seal (*Lobodon carcinophagus*), the Mediterranean monk seal (*Monachus monachus*), the Ross seal (*Ommatophoca rossi*), and in the southern elephant seal (*Mirounga leonina*). Information regarding geographical location of hosts was not provided by author.

From Linstow, 1892 - If *Contracaecum radiatum* = *Ascaris osculata*, then found in the leopard seal (*Hydrurga leptonyx*) from South Georgia (Antarctica).

From Linstow, 1906 - If *Contracaecum radiatum* = *Ascaris radiate,* then found in the Weddell seal (*Leptonychotes weddelli*) from the Antarctic.

From Railliet and Henry, 1907 - Found in the Weddell seal (*Leptonychotes weddelli*) from Graham's Garin (Antarctica).

From Yamaguti, 1961 - Found in the southern elephant seal (*Mirounga leonia*) from the Antarctic.

Contracaecum rectangulum

Synonymy:

From Delyamure, 1955 - *Ascaris rectangula* Linstow, 1907; *Kathleena rectangula* (Linstow, 1907) Leiper and Atkinson, 1914.

From Johnston, 1937c - *Porrocaecum decipiens.*

Hosts and Locality:

From Baylis, 1929 - Found in the crab-eating seal (*Lobodon carcinophagus*) and the leopard seal (*Hydrurga leptonyx*). Both host species were from the Palmer Archipedago.

From Dailey and Brownell, 1972 - Found in the South American sea lion (*Otaria byronia*), the southern elephant seal (*Mirounga leonina*), the crab-eating seal (*Lobodon carcinophagus*), and in the leopard seal (*Hydrurga leptonyx*). Information regarding geographical location of hosts was not provided by authors.

From Delyamure, 1955 - Found in the leopard seal (*Hydrurga leptonyx*), the Weddell seal (*Leptonychotes weddelli*), and in the crab-eating seal (*Lobodon carcinophagus*). Geographical distribution includes the Sandwich Islands, Antarctica.

From Hamilton, 1934 - Found in the South American sea lion (*Otaria byronia*) from the Falkland Islands.

From King, 1964 - Found in the leopard seal (*Hydrurga leptonyx*), the Weddell seal (*Leptonychotes weddelli*), the crab-eating seal (*Lobodon carcinophagus*), the South American fur seal (*Arctocephalus australis*), the South American sea lion (*Otaria byronia*), and in the southern elephant seal (*Mirounga leonina*). Information regarding geographical location of hosts was not provided by author.

From Yamaguti, 1961 - Found in the leopard seal (*Hydrurga leptonyx*), the Weddell seal (*Leptonychotes weddelli*), and in the South American sea lion (*Otaria byronia*).

Remarks:

Dailey and Brownell (1972) list the South American fur seal (*Arctocephalus australis*), and the Weddell seal (*Leptonychotes weddelli*) as hosts of *Contracaecum rectangulum* and give Baylis (1920a) as a source reference. However, no mention of these hosts in connection with this parasite could be found in the Baylis (1920a) paper. Only a note states *Contracaecum rectangulum* were collected "from seals".

Contracaecum stenocephalum

Synonymy:

From Delyamure, 1955 - *Ascaris stenocephala* Railliet and Henry, 1907.

Hosts and Locality:

From Dailey and Brownell, 1972 - Found in the leopard seal (*Hydrurga leptonyx*) and the Weddell seal (*Leptonychotes weddelli*). Information regarding the geographical location of hosts was not provided by authors.

From Johnston, 1937c - Found in the Weddell seal (*Leptonychotes weddelli*) from Commonwealth Bay (Antarctica) and in the leopard seal (*Hydrurga leptonyx*) from the Antarctic.

From Johnston and Mawson, 1945 - Found in the leopard seal (*Hydrurga leptonyx*) and the Weddell seal (*Leptonychotes weddelli*). Both host species were from Commonwealth Bay (Antarctica).

From King, 1964 - Found in the leopard seal (*Hydrurga leptonyx*) and the Weddell seal (*Leptonychotes weddelli*). Information regarding geographical location of hosts was not provided by author.

Contracaecum turgidum

Hosts and Locality:

From Dailey and Brownell, 1972 - Found in the Hawaiian monk seal (*Monachus schauinslandi*). Information regarding the geographical location of host was not provided by authors.

From Delyamure, 1955 - Found in the Hawaiian monk seal (*Monachus schauinslandi*) from Hawaii and the Laysan Islands.

From King, 1964 - Found in the Hawaiian monk seal (*Monachus schauinslandi*). Information regarding the geographical location of host was not provided by author.

Crassicauda sp.

Hosts and Locality:

From Dailey and Brownell, 1972 - Found in the Hawaiian monk seal (*Monachus schauinslandi*) and the eastern Pacific spotted dolphin (*Stenella graffmani*). Information regarding the geographical location of hosts was not provided by authors.

From Margolis and Dailey (1972) - Found in the humpback whale (*Megaptera novaengliae*) from California.

From Rice, 1963 - Found in the sei whale (*Balaenoptera borealis*) and the fin whale (*Balaenoptera physalus*). Both hosts were from California.

Crassicauda anthonyi

Hosts and Locality:

From Chabaud, 1963 - Found in the True's beaked whale (*Mesoplodon mirus*). Information regarding the geographical location of host was not provided by author.

From Dailey and Brownell, 1972 - Found in the True's beaked whale (*Mesoplodon mirus*). Information regarding the geographical location of host was not provided by authors.

Crassicauda bennetti

Synonymy:

From Baylis, 1932 - *Crassicauda sp.* of Baylis, 1920. See Remarks.

Hosts and Locality:

From Baylis, 1920b - Found in the southern bottlenosed whale (*Hyperoodon planifrons*) from the South Orkneys Islands (Antarctica). See Remarks.

From Baylis, 1932 - Found in the bottlenosed whale (*Hyperoodon sp.* ["probably *planifrons*"]). Information regarding the geographical location of host was not provided by author.

From Dailey and Brownell, 1972 - Found in the southern bottlenosed whale (*Hyperoodon planifrons*). Information regarding the geographical location of host was not provided by authors.

From Delyamure, 1955 - Found in "*Hyperoodon sp.* (probably *H. planifrons*-bottlenosed whale". Information regarding the geographical location of host was not provided by author.

From Spaul, 1926 - Found in the bottle-nosed whale (*Hyperoodon sp.*). Information regarding the geographical location of host was not provided by author.

Remarks:

Baylis (1920b) does not actually mention *Crassicauda bennetti* in his paper. Instead, he notes the examination of a nematode that was unlike others in the sample to the point where it may be a new species. By the time Baylis published his paper in 1932 (Baylis, 1932), he had determined that the species in question was indeed a new species. Spaul (1926) actually proposed the name *Crassicauda bennetti*.

Crassicauda boopis

Synonymy:

From Baylis, 1932 - *Crassicauda crassicauda* Leiper and Atkinson, 1914.

Hosts and Locality:

From Baylis, 1916b - Found in the goose beaked whale or Cuvier beaked whale (*Ziphius cavirostris*) from the coast of Ireland (near Bannow Bay).

From Baylis, 1920b - Found in the humpback whale (*Megaptera nodosa*) from the Antarctic. See Remarks.

From Baylis, 1932 - Found in the humpback whale (*Megaptera nodosa*) and "doubtfully" in the Cuvier's whale (*Ziphius cavirostris*). Information regarding the geographical locality of hosts was not provided by author.

From Dailey and Brownell, 1972 - Found in the fin whale (*Balaenoptera physalus*), the humpback whale (*Megaptera novaengliae*), and in the goose beaked whale or Cuvier beaked whale (*Ziphius cavirostris*). Information regarding the geographical locality of hosts was not provided by authors.

From Delyamure, 1955 - Found in the humpback whale (*Megaptera novaengliae*), and the fin whale (*Balaenoptera physalus*). Geographical distribution includes the Atlantic Ocean and the Sea of Okhotsk (Kurile Islands region).

Remarks:

Baylis (1920b) proposed this as a new species upon further examination of samples collected by Leiper and Atkinson (1914) from the humpback whale inhabiting the Shetland Islands of Antarctica.

Crassicauda crassicauda

Synonymy:

From Baylis, 1932 - *Filaria crassicauda* Creplin, 1829.

Hosts and Locality:

From Baylis, 1916b - Found in the sei whale (*Balaenoptera borealis*) and the blue whale (*Balaenoptera musculus*). Both hosts were from New Zealand.

From Baylis, 1920b - Found in the fin whale (*Balaenoptera physalus*) and the blue whale (*Balaenoptera musculus*) from Antarctica (Deception Island, South Shetlands Islands).

From Baylis, 1929 - Found in the fin whale (*Balaenoptera physalus*) from South Africa (Saldanha Bay).

From Baylis, 1932 - Found in the fin whale (*Balaenoptera physalus*), the blue whale (*Balaenoptera musculus*), the bottlenosed dolphin (*Tursiops truncatus*), and (? sic) in the sei whale (*Balaenoptera borealis*). Information regarding the geographical locality of hosts was not provided by author.

From Dailey and Brownell, 1972 - Found in the bottlenosed dolphin (*Tursiops truncatus*), the goose beaked whale or Cuvier beaked whale (*Ziphius cavirostris*), the Greenland right whale (*Balaena mysticetus*), the little piked whale (*Balaenoptera acutorostrata*), the sei whale (*Balaenoptera borealis*), the fin whale (*Balaenoptera physalus*), the blue whale (*Balaenoptera musculus*), and in the humpback whale (*Megaptera novaengliae*). Information regarding the geographical locality of hosts was not provided by authors.

From Delyamure, 1955 - Found in the Greenland whale (*Balaena mysticetus*), the blue whale (*Balaenoptera musculus*), the sei whale (*Balaenoptera borealis*), the piked whale (*Balaenoptera acutorostrata*), the fin whale (*Balaenoptera physalus*), the humpback whale (*Megaptera novaengliae*), the Cuvier's beaked whale (*Ziphius cavirostris*), and in the bottlenosed dolphin (*Tursiops truncatus*). Geographical distribution includes the Atlantic Ocean (northern and southern hemispheres).

Crassicauda delamureana

Hosts and Locality:

From Dailey and Brownell, 1972 - Found in the sei whale (*Balaenoptera borealis*). Information regarding the geographical locality of host was not provided by authors.

Crassicauda duguyi

Hosts and Locality:

From Dailey and Brownell, 1972 - Found in the pigmy sperm whale (*Kogia breviceps*). Information regarding the geographical locality of host was not provided by authors.

Crassicauda fuelleborni

Synonymy:

From Baylis, 1932 - *Onchocerca fulleborni* Hoeppli and Hsü, 1929.

From Delyamure, 1955 - *Onchocerca fulleborni* Hoeppli and Hsü, 1929.

Hosts and Locality:

From Baylis, 1932 - Found in the common Chinese porpoise (*Neomeris phocaenoides*). Information regarding geographical location of host was not provided by author.

From Dailey and Brownell, 1972 - Found in the black finless porpoise or the common Chinese porpoise (*Neophocoena phocaenoides*). Information regarding geographical location of host was not provided by authors.

From Delyamure, 1955 - Found in the finless porpoise (*Neomeris phocaenoides*) from the Pacific Ocean (near Ama Island).

Remarks:

A brief historical account of this parasite is provided by Delyamure (1955).

Crassicauda giliakiana

Hosts and Locality:

From Dailey and Brownell, 1972 - Found in the white whale (*Delphinapterus leucas*) and the giant bottlenosed whale (*Berardius bairdi*).

Information regarding geographical location of hosts was not provided by authors.

From Delyamure, 1955 - Found in the white whale (*Delphinapterus leucas*) and the bottlenosed dolphin (*Hyperoodon ampullatus*). Geographical distribution includes the Sea of Okhotsk (Amur estuary and Kurile Islands region).

Remarks:

Dailey and Brownell (1972) list the giant bottlenosed whale (*Berardius bairdi*) as a host of *Crassicauda giliakiana* and give Delyamure (1955) as a source reference. However, no mention of this host being associated with *Crassicauda giliakiana* could be found in the Delyamure (1955) paper. However, although Delyamure does not mention of *Berardius bairdi*, he does refer to *Hyperoodon ampullatus* as a "bottlenosed whale". This reference to the "bottlenosed whale" as being *Hyperoodon ampullatus* also is found in Delyamure's reference to the nematode *Delamurella hyperoodoni*.

Crassicauda grampicola

Hosts and Locality:

From Dailey and Brownell, 1972 - Found in the Risso dolphin (*Grampus griseus*). Information regarding the geographical locality of host was not provided by authors.

From Johnston and Mawson, 1941 - Found in the Risso dolphin (*Grampus griseus*) from Manly, Australia (New South Wales).

Remarks:

A brief historical account of this parasite is provided by Delyamure (1955).

Crassicauda magna

Hosts and Locality:

From Dailey and Brownell, 1972 - Found in the pigmy sperm whale (*Kogia breviceps*). Information regarding the geographical locality of host was not provided by authors.

From Delyamure, 1955 - Found in the pigmy sperm whale (*Kogia breviceps*) from South Australia.

Crassicauda pacifica

Hosts and Locality:

From Dailey and Brownell, 1972 - Found in the fin whale (*Balaenoptera physalus*). Information regarding the geographical locality of host was not provided by authors.

From Margolis and Dailey, 1972 - Found in the fin whale (*Balaenoptera physalus*) from British Columbia.

From Margolis and Pike, 1955 - Found in the fin whale (*Balaenoptera physalus*) from British Columbia, Northern European seas, Atlantic coast of South Africa, Antarctica (South Georgia) and the Ross Sea area.

Delamurella hyperoodoni

Hosts and Locality:

From Dailey and Brownell, 1972 - Found in the giant bottlenosed whale (*Berardius bairdi*). Information regarding the geographical locality of host was not provided by authors.

From Delyamure, 1955 - Found in the northern bottlenosed whale (*Hyperoodon ampullatus*). Geographical distribution includes the Sea of Okhotsk (Kurile Islands region).

Remarks:

Dailey and Brownell (1972) list the giant bottlenosed whale (*Berardius bairdi*) as a host of this parasite and give Delyamure (1955) as a source reference. However, Delyamure's 1955 paper only list *Hyperoodon ampullatus* as a host of this parasite. However, although Delyamure does not mention of *Berardius bairdi* in his paper, he does refer to *Hyperoodon ampullatus* as a "bottlenosed whale". This reference to the "bottlenosed whale" as being *Hyperoodon ampullatus* also is found in Delyamure's reference to the nematode *Crassicauda giliakiana*.

Dioctophyme renale

Hosts and Locality:

From Dailey and Brownell, 1972 - Found in the gray seal (*Halichoerus grypus*). Information regarding geographical location of host was not provided by authors.

From King, 1964 - Found in the gray seal (*Halichoerus grypus*). Information regarding the geographical location of host was not provided by author.

Dipetalonema odendhali

Hosts and Locality:

From Dailey and Brownell, 1972 - Found in the California sea lion (*Zalophus californianus*). Information regarding geographical location of host was not provided by authors.

From Dailey and Hill, 1970 - Found in the California sea lion (*Zalophus californianus*) from Santa Cruz Island, Año Nuevo Island, and the San Diego Zoo, California.

From Margolis and Dailey, 1972 - Found in the California sea lion (*Zalophus californianus*) from California.

From Perry, 1967 - Found in a captive California sea lion (*Zalophus californianus*) from Sacramento, California. The host was captured six years earlier at Santa Cruz Island, California. See Remarks.

Remarks:

Perry (1967) notes that the parasite taken from a northern sea lion (*Callorhinus ursinus*), and identified as *Dipetalonema spirocauda* by Anderson (1959), may have been a *Dipetalonema odendhali*.

Dipetalonema spirocauda

Synonymy:

From Anderson, 1959 - *Filiria spirocaucada* Leidy 1858; *Skrjabinaria spirocaucada* (Leidi) Lubimov 1927; *Skrjabinarir heteromorpha* Kreis, 1953.

Hosts and Locality:

From Anderson, 1959 - Found in the harbor seal (*Phoca vitulina concolor*) from Maine, and "possibly" in the northern fur seal (*Callorhinus ursinus*) from Alaska. See Remarks.

From Dailey and Brownell, 1972 - Found in the

northern fur seal (*Callorhinus ursinus*) and the ringed seal (*Pusa hispida*). Information regarding geographical location of hosts was not provided by authors.

From Margolis and Dailey, 1972 - Found in the northern fur seal (*Callorhinus ursinus*) and the harbor seal (*Phoca vitulina richardi*) from Alaska "?" [sic] and California (captive harbour seals).

From Taylor et al, 1961 - Found in captive harbor seals (*Phoca vitulina geronimensis*) from Marineland of the Pacific, California. Host species were captured off the coast of Southern California (Paradise Cove, Malibu, Los Angeles Co., China Point, Santa Catalina Island, and Manhattan Beach, Los Angeles Co).

Remarks:

Dailey and Brownell (1972) list the ringed seal (*Pusa hispida*) as a host of *Dipetlonema spirocauda* and cite Taylor et al, 1961 as a source reference. However, no mention of *Pusa hispida* could be found in the Taylor et al (1961) paper.

Both Perry (1967) and Margolis and Dailey (1972) note the parasite identified by Anderson (1959) as *Dipetlonema spirocauda* may have been *Dipetalinema odendhali*. Anderson (1959) questions the occurrence of this parasite in the northern fur seal (*Callorhinus ursinus*).

Dirofilaria immitis

Synonymy:

From Delyamure, 1955 - *Dirofilaria spirocauda* Faust, 1937 nec Leidy, 1858; *Dirofilaria fausti* Skrjabin and Schikhobalova, 1948.

Hosts and Locality:

From Dailey and Brownell, 1972 - Found in the California sea lion (*Zalophus californianus*), and in the hooded seal (*Cystophora cristata*). Information regarding geographical location of hosts was not provided by authors.

From King, 1964 - Found in the harbor seal (*Phoca vitulina*), the California sea lion (*Zalophus californianus*), and in the hooded seal

(*Cystophora cristata*). Information regarding geographical location of hosts was not provided by author.

From Margolis and Dailey, 1972 - Found in the California sea lion (*Zalophus californianus*) from the Zoological Garden, New Orleans, Louisiana. Animal was captured at Sea Cliffs, California.

From Taylor et al, 1961 - Found in captive California sea lions (*Zalophus californianus*) from the Marineland of the Pacific, California. See Remarks.

Remarks:

Perry (1967) feels that since *Dirofilaria immitis* is enzootic in New Orleans and probably not in California, the California sea lion infected with this parasite probably acquired it while in New Orleans. Delyamure (1955) points out that this parasite is commonly found in dogs, cats, and other carnivores in almost all tropical and subtropical countries, as well as in USSR.

Taylor et al (1961) tentatively identified the microfilariae recovered from captive *Zalophus californianus* as *Dirofilaria immitis*.

Dirofilaria spirocauda

Synonymy:

From Delyamure, 1955 - *Dirofilaria immitis* Leidy, 1856; *Dirofilaria fausti* Skrjabin and Schikhobalova, 1948.

Hosts and Locality:

From Dailey and Brownell, 1972 - Found in a captive (zoo) common seal (*Phoca vitulina*). Information regarding geographical location of host was not provided by authors.

From Delyamure, 1955 - Found in a captive harbor seal (*Phoca vitulina*). See Remarks.

From King, 1964 - Found in the harbor seal (*Phoca vitulina*). Information regarding geographical location of host was not provided by author.

Remarks:

This species is accepted as a synonym of *Dirofilaria immitis* by Delyamure (1955) and

Margolis and Dailey (1972). Dailey and Brownell (1972) list a captive harbor seal (*Phoca vitulina*) as a host of this parasite and cite Taylor et al (1961) as a source reference. However, Taylor et al (1961) discusses the infection of a captive sea lion (*Phoca vitulina*) with *Dipetalonema spirocauda*, and not *Dirofilaria spirocauda*. Taylor et al (1961) does discuss the heart worm *Dirofilaria immitis*, but not *Dirofilaria spirocauda*.

Dujardinia sp.

Hosts and Locality:

From Dailey and Brownell, 1972 - Found in the California sea lion (*Zalophus californianus*). Information regarding geographical location of host was not provided by authors.

From King, 1964 - Found in the California sea lion (*Zalophus californianus*). Information regarding geographical location of host was not provided by author.

From Margolis and Dailey, 1972 - Found in the California sea lion (*Zalophus californianus*) from the San Diego Zoo, California.

Echinocephalus uncinatus

Hosts and Locality:

From Johnston and Mawson, 1941 - Found in the common dolphin (*Delphinus delphis*) from St. Vincent Gulf, Australia.

Eustrongylides excisus

Hosts and Locality:

From Dailey and Brownell, 1972 - Found in the Caspian seal (*Pusa caspica*). Information regarding geographical location of host was not provided by authors.

From King, 1964 - Found in the Caspian seal (*Pusa caspica*). Information regarding the geographical location of host was not provided by author.

Filaria sp.

Hosts and Locality:

From Dailey and Brownell, 1972 - Found in the southern elephant seal (*Mirounga leonina*). Information regarding geographical location of host was not provided by authors.

From King, 1964 - Found in the elephant seal (*Mirounga leonina*). Information regarding the geographical location of host was not provided by author.

Filaria hebetata

Hosts and Locality:

From King, 1964 - Found in the hooded seal (*Cystophora cristata*). Information regarding geographical location of host was not provided by author.

Halocercus sp.

Hosts and Locality:

From Benson and Groody, 1942 - Found in the Dall porpoise (*Phocoenoides dalli*) from San Quentin Point, San Francisco, California.

From Dailey and Brownell, 1972 - Found in the broad-beaked dolphin (*Peoponcephala electra*) and the Amazon River dolphin or Bouta (*Inia geoffrensis*). Information regarding the geographical location of hosts was not provided by authors.

From Migaki et al, 1971 - Found in the California sea lion (*Zalophus californianus*) from California.

Halocercus brasiliensis

Hosts and Locality:

From Dailey and Brownell, 1972 - Found in the Guiana dolphin (*Sotalia guianensis*). Information regarding geographical location of host was not provided by authors. See Remarks.

From Delyamure, 1955 - Found in the Guiana dolphin (*Sotalia guianensis*) from the Atlantic Ocean (Brazil, near Rio de Janeiro).

Remarks:

Dailey and Brownell (1972) list this parasite as a trematode infecting the Guiana dolphin (*Sotalia guianensis*).

Halocercus delphini

Hosts and Locality:

From Baylis, 1932 - Found in the common dolphin (*Delphinus delphis*). Information regarding geographical location of host was not provided by author.

From Dailey and Brownell, 1972 - Found in the common dolphin (*Delphinus delphis*). Information regarding geographical location of host was not provided by authors.

From Delyamure, 1955 - Found in the common dolphin (*Delphinus delphis*) from the Atlantic Ocean (British Isles).

Halocercus gymnurus

Synonymy:

From Delyamure, 1955 - *Parafilaroides gymnurus* (Railliet, 1899) Dougherty, 1946; *Pseudalius gymnurus* Railliet, 1899; *Filaroides gymnurus* Railliet, 1899, Dougherty, 1943.

Hosts and Locality:

From Dailey and Brownell, 1972 - Found in the ringed seal (*Pusa hispida*). Information regarding geographical location of host was not provided by authors.

From King, 1964 - Found in the harbor seal (*Phoca vitulina*), and in the ringed seal (*Pusa hispida*). Information regarding the geographical location of hosts was not provided by author.

Halocercus inflexocaudatus

Synonymy:

From Arnold and Gaskin, 1975 - *Halocercus taurica* Delyamure 1942.

From Baylis, 1932 - *Filaria inflexocaudatus* Siebold, 1842; *Pseudalius tumidus* Schneider, 1866; (?) sic *Strongylus vegans* Eschricht,

1841; (?) sic *Strongylus invaginatus* Quekett, 1842.

Hosts and Locality:

From Baylis, 1932 - Found in the common porpoise (*Phocoena phocoena*). Information regarding geographical location of host was not provided by author.

Halocercus invaginatus

Synonymy:

From Arnold and Gaskin, 1975 - *Strongylus invaginatus* Quekett, 1841; *Filaria inflexocaudata* Siebold, 1842; *Pseudalis tumidus* Schneider, 1866; *Halocercus inflexocaudatus* (von Siebold) Baylis and Daubney, 1925; *Halocercus invaginatus* (Quekett) Dougherty 1943; *Halocercus ponticus* Delyamure 1946.

From Delyamure, 1955 - *Strongylus invaginatus* Quekett, 1841; *Filaria inflexocaudata* Siebold, 1842; *Pseudalis tumidus* Schneider, 1866; *Halocercus inflexocaudatus* (Siebold, 1842) Baylis and Daubney, 1925.

Hosts and Locality:

From Arnold and Gaskin, 1975 - Found in the harbor porpoise (*Phocoena phocoena*) from the Bay of Fundy, Canada; Vancouver Island, British Columbia, Canada.

From Dailey and Brownell, 1972 - Found in the harbor porpoise (*Phocoena phocoena*). Information regarding the geographical location of host was not provided by authors.

From Delyamure, 1955 - Found in the finned porpoise (*Phocoena phocoena*). Geographical distribution includes the Pacific coast of the United States (San Francisco Bay and Washington Bay), the Baltic Sea, and the Atlantic Ocean (British Isles).

From Margolis and Dailey, 1972 - Found in the harbor porpoise (*Phocoena phocoena*) from California and Washington.

Halocercus kirbyi

Synonymy:

From Margolis and Dailey, 1972 - *Halocercus sp.*

of Benson and Groody, 1942 and of Dougherty, 1943.

Hosts and Locality:

From Dailey and Brownell, 1972 - Found in the Dall porpoise (*Phocoenoides dalli*). Information regarding the geographical location of host was not provided by authors.

From Delyamure, 1955 - Found in the Dall porpoise (*Phocoenoides dalli*) from California (San Francisco Bay).

From Margolis and Dailey, 1972 - Found in the Dall porpoise (*Phocoenoides dalli*) from California.

Halocercus kleinenbergi

Synonymy:

From Delyamure, 1955 - *Halocercus (Posthalocercus) kleinenbergi* Delyamure, 1951.

Hosts and Locality:

From Dailey and Brownell, 1972 - Found in the common dolphin (*Delphinus delphis*), and the bottlenosed dolphin (*Tursiops truncatus*). Information regarding the geographical locality of hosts was not provided by authors.

From Delyamure, 1955 - Found in the common dolphin (*Delphinus delphis*) from the Black Sea (USSR).

Halocercus lagenorhynchus

Hosts and Locality:

From Baylis, 1932 - Found in the white-beaked dolphin (*Lagenorhynchus albirostris*). Information regarding the geographical locality of host was not provided by author.

From Dailey and Brownell, 1972 - Found in the bottlenosed dolphin (*Tursiops truncatus*) and the white-beaked dolphin (*Lagenorhynchus albirostris*). Information regarding the geographical locality of hosts was not provided by authors.

From Delyamure, 1955 - Found in the white beaked dolphin (*Lagenorhynchus albirostris*) and in the bottlenosed dolphin (*Tursiops truncatus*). Geographical distribution includes the Atlantic Ocean (Europe), and the coast of Australia.

From Johnston and Mawson, 1941 - Found in the bottlenosed dolphin (*Tursiops truncatus*) from Encounter Bay (Australia). See Remark.

Remarks:

Johnston and Mawson (1941) questioned whether the host species was a *Tursiops truncates* or a separate European species (*Tursiops maugeanus*).

Halocercus pingi

Hosts and Locality:

From Baylis, 1932 - Found in the common Chinese porpoise (*Neophocoena phocaenoides*). Information regarding the geographical location of host was not provided by author.

From Dailey and Brownell, 1972 - Found in the black finless porpoise or the common Chinese porpoise (*Neophocoena phocaenoides*). Information regarding the geographical location of host was not provided by authors.

From Delyamure, 1955 - Found in the black finless porpoise or common Chinese porpoise (*Neophocoena phocaenoides*) from the Pacific Ocean (China).

Halocercus ponticus

Hosts and Locality:

From Dailey and Brownell, 1972 - Found in the harbor porpoise (*Phocoena phocoena*). Information regarding the geographical location of host was not provided by authors.

From Delyamure, 1955 - Found in the harbor porpoise (*Phocoena phocoena*) from USSR (Black Sea, Azov Sea, Kerch Strait).

Halocercus taurica

Synonymy:

From Arnold and Gaskin, 1975 - *Halocercus inflexocaudatus* (of Schmidt-Ries 1939).

Hosts and Locality:

From Arnold and Gaskin, 1975 - Found in the harbor porpoise (*Phocoena phocoena*) from the Bay of Fundy, Canada; and Vancouver Island, British Columbia, Canada.

From Dailey and Brownell, 1972 - Found in the harbor porpoise (*Phocoena phocoena*). Information regarding the geographical location of host was not provided by authors.

From Delyamure, 1955 - Found in the harbor porpoise (*Phocoena phocoena*) from USSR (Azov Sea, Black Sea).

Mastigonema stenella

Hosts and Locality:

From Dailey and Perrin, 1973 - Found in the eastern Pacific spotted dolphin (*Stenella graffmani*) from the eastern tropical Pacific Ocean, and in the long beaked dolphin (*Stenella longirostris*) from Lat. 8° N, Long. 7° W.

Odontobius ceti

Hosts and Locality:

From Baylis, 1932 - Found in the southern right whale (*Balaena australis*), the blue whale (*Balaenoptera musculus*), the fin whale (*Balaenoptera physalus*), and in the humpback whale (*Megaptera nodosa*). Information regarding the geographical location of hosts was not provided by author.

Otophocaenurus oserskoi

Synonymy:

From Delyamure, 1955 - *Pharurus oserskoiaae* (Skrjabin, 1942) Dougherty, 1949.

From Dougherty, 1949b - *Pharurus oserskiaae* Skriabin, 1942.

From Margolis and Dailey, 1972 - *Pharurus oserkaiae* (Skrjabin, 1942) Dougherty, 1949.

Hosts and Locality:

From Babero and Thomas, 1960 - If *Otophocaenurus oserskoi* = *Phaeurus oserkaiae*, then found in the beluga or white whale (*Delphinapterus leucas*) from Kotzebue, Alaska.

From Dailey and Brownell, 1972 - Found in the white whale (*Delphinapterus leucas*). Information regarding the geographical location of host was not provided by authors.

From Delyamure, 1955 - Found in the white whale (*Delphinapterus leucas*) from the Pacific Ocean (Sakhalin).

Remarks:

Brief taxonomic accounts of this parasite are provided by Margolis and Dailey (1972), Dougherty (1949b), and Babero and Thomas (1960).

Otostrongylus andreewaae

Synonymy:

From Dailey and Brownell, 1972 - *Otostrongylus andreewoi* Skrjabin, 1933.

Hosts and Locality:

From Dailey and Brownell, 1972 - Found in the ringed seal (*Pusa hispida*) and the harp seal (*Phoca groenlandica*). Information regarding the geographical location of hosts was not provided by authors.

From Dougherty, 1949a - Found in the Okhotsk ringed seal (*Phoca hispida ochotensis*) and the White Sea ringed seal (*Phoca hispida pomororum*). Information regarding the geographical location of hosts was not provided by author.

From King, 1964 - Found in the ringed seal (*Pusa hispida*) and the harp seal (*Phoca groenlandica*). Information regarding the geographical location of hosts was not provided by author.

From Yamaguti, 1961 - Found in the ringed seal (*Pusa hispida*) from the Sea of Okhotsk.

Otostrongylus circumlitus

Synonymy:

From Delyamure, 1955 - *Strongylus circumlitus* Railliet, 1899; *Kutassicaulus andreewoi* Skrjabin, 1933.

Hosts and Locality:

From Dailey and Brownell, 1972 - Found in the common seal (*Phoca vitulina*) and the ringed seal (*Pusa hispida*). Information regarding the geographical location of hosts was not provided by authors.

From Delyamure, 1955 - Found in the common seal (*Phoca vitulina*), the Pomor ringed seal (*Pusa hispida pomororum*), and in the Okhotsk ringed seal (*Pusa hispida ochotensis*). Geographical distribution includes the North Sea (coast of France and Holland), the White Sea, and the Sea of Okhotsk.

From Dougherty, 1949a - Found in the common harbor seal (*Phoca vitulina vitulina*). Information regarding the geographical location of host was not provided by author.

From King, 1964 - Found in the common seal (*Phoca vitulina*) and the ringed seal (*Pusa hispida*). Information regarding geographical location of hosts was not provided by author.

Parafilaroides sp.

Hosts and Locality:

From Dailey and Brownell, 1972 - Found in the Steller sea lion (*Eumetopias jubata*). Information regarding geographical location of host was not provided by authors.

From Margolis and Dailey, 1972 - Found in the Steller sea lion (*Eumetopias jubata*) from British Columbia, and in both wild and captive Steller sea lions (*Eumetopias jubata*) from California.

Parafilaroides arcticus

Hosts and Locality:

From Dailey and Brownell, 1972 - Found in the ringed seal (*Pusa hispida*). Information regarding geographical location of host was not provided by authors.

Parafilaroides decorus

Synonymy:

From Margolis and Dailey, 1972 - *Filaroides sp.* of Dougherty, 1943; *Parafilaroides sp.* of Dougherty, 1946.

Hosts and Locality:

From Dailey, 1970 - Found in the California sea lion (*Zalophus californianus*) from California.

From Dailey and Brownell, 1972 - Found in the California sea lion (*Zalophus californianus*). Information regarding geographical location of host was not provided by authors.

From King, 1964 - Found in the California sea lion (*Zalophus californianus*). Information regarding geographical location of host was not provided by author.

From Margolis and Dailey, 1972 - Found in wild and captive California sea lions (*Zalophus californianus*) from California, the San Diego Zoo, and the Baltimore Zoo.

From Migaki et al, 1971 - Found in the California sea lion (*Zalophus californianus*) from California.

Parafilaroides gymnurus

Synonymy:

From Delyamure, 1955 - *Pseudalius gymnurus* Railliet, 1899; *Halocercus gymnurus* (Railliet, 1899) Baylis and Daubney, 1925; *Halocercus (Prohalocercus) gymnurus* (Railliet, 1899) Baylis and Daubney, 1925 in Skrjabin, 1942; *Filaroides gymnurus sp.* (Railliet, 1899) Baylis and Daubney, 1943.

Hosts and Locality:

From Dailey and Brownell, 1972 - Found in the common seal (*Phoca vitulina*). Information regarding geographical location of host was not provided by authors.

From Delyamure, 1955 - Found in the common seal (*Phoca vitulina*) from Europe.

From King, 1964 - Found in the common seal (*Phoca vitulina*). Information regarding geographical location of host was not provided by author.

Parafilaroides hydrurgae

Hosts and Locality:

From Dailey and Brownell, 1972 - Found in the leopard seal (*Hydrurga leptonyx*). Informa-

tion regarding geographical location of host was not provided by authors.

From King, 1964 - Found in the leopard seal (*Hydrurga leptonyx*). Information regarding geographical location of host was not provided by author.

From Mawson, 1953 - Found in the leopard seal (*Hydrurga leptonyx*) from Heard Island (Antarctica).

Parafilaroides nanus

Synonymy:

From Margolis and Dailey, 1972 - *Filaroides sp.* of Dougherty 1943; *Parafilaroides sp.* of Dougherty 1946.

Hosts and Locality:

From Dailey and Brownell, 1972 - Found in the Steller sea lion (*Eumetopias jubata*). Information regarding geographical location of host was not provided by authors.

From King, 1964 - Found in the Steller sea lion (*Eumetopias jubata*). Information regarding geographical location of host was not provided by author.

From Margolis and Dailey, 1972 - Found in the Steller sea lion (*Eumetopias jubata*) from the San Diego Zoo, California.

Parafilaroides prolificus

Synonymy:

From Margolis and Dailey, 1972 - *Filaroides sp.* of Dougherty, 1943; *Parafilaroides sp.* of Dougherty 1946.

Hosts and Locality:

From Dailey and Brownell, 1972 - Found in the Steller sea lion (*Eumetopias jubata*). Information regarding geographical location of host was not provided by authors.

From Dougherty and Hermann, 1947 - Found in the Steller sea lion (*Eumetopias jubata*) from the San Diego Zoo, California.

From King, 1964 - Found in the Steller sea lion (*Eumetopias jubata*). Information regarding geographical location of host was not provided by author.

From Margolis and Dailey, 1972 - Found in the Steller sea lion (*Eumetopias jubata*) from the San Diego Zoo, California.

Pharurus alatus

Synonymy:

From Arnold and Gaskin, 1975 - *Strongylus alatus* Leuckart, 1848; *Pharurus alatus* Leuckart 1848; *Prothecosacter alatus* (Leuckart) Diesing, 1851; *Strongylus (Pharurus) alatus* Diesing, 1851; *Pseudalius alatus* (Leuckart) von Linstow 1888; *Stenurus alatus* (Leuckart) Yorke and Maplestone 1926; *Torynurus alatus* (Leuchart) Deltamure 1952.

Hosts and Locality:

From Arnold and Gaskin, 1975 - Found in the narwhal (*Monodon monoceros*) from Baffin Island, Canada.

Pharurus convolutus

Synonymy:

From Delyamure, 1955 - *Torynurus convolutus* (Kuhn, 1829) Baylis and Daubney, 1825; *Strongylus convolutus* Kuhn, 1829; *Prosthecostrongylus convolutus* (Kuhn, 1829) Diesing, 1851; *Pseudalius convolutus* (Kuhn, 1829) Schneider, 1866; *Pseudalius bicostatus* Linstow, 1906.

Hosts and Locality:

From Dailey and Brownell, 1972 - Found in the North Atlantic pilot whale (*Globicephalus melaena*), the harbor porpoise (*Phocoena phocoena*), and in the short-finned pilot whale (*Globicephala macrorhyncha*). Information regarding geographical location of hosts was not provided by authors. See Remarks.

From Delyamure, 1955 - Found in the finned porpoise (*Phocoena phocoena*) and in a porpoise (*Phocoena sp.*). Geographical distribution includes the North Atlantic (Europe) and USSR (Sakhalin).

From Margolis and Dailey, 1972 - Found in the harbour porpoise (*Phocoena phocoena*) from Washington and California.

Remarks:

Dailey and Brownell (1972) note the host species *Globicephalus melas* also includes species identified as *Globicephalus scammoni*.

Pharurus inflexus

Synonymy:

From Delyamure, 1955 - *Strongylus inflexus* Rudolphi, 1809; *Strongylus inflexus* major Rospail, 1829; *Pseudalius filum* Dujardin, 1845; *Prosthecosacter inflexus* Diesing, 1851; *Prosthecosacter convolutus* Cobbold, 1846; *Pseudalius inflexus* Schneider, 1866; *Prosthecosacter convolutus* Cobbold, 1879; (nec *Stenurus inflexus* Dujardin, 1845).

Hosts and Locality:

From Delyamure, 1955 - Found in the finned porpoise (*Phocoena phocoena*). Geographical distribution includes the North Atlantic, coast of Europe, and the Asiatic coast of the Pacific Ocean.

Pharurus oserkaiae

Hosts and Locality:

From Babero and Thomas, 1960 - Found in the white whale (*Delphinapterus leucas*) from Alaska.

From Margolis and Dailey, 1972 - Found in the white whale *Delphinapterus leucas*) from Alaska. See Remarks.

Remarks:

From Margolis and Dailey (1972) provide a brief taxonomic history of this parasite.

Pharurus pallasii

Synonymy:

From Arnold and Gaskin, 1975 - *Strongylus pallasii* van Beneden 1870; *Strongylus arcticus* Cobb 1888; *Pseudalius arcticus* (Cobb) von

Linstow 1900; *Otophocoenurus* Dougherty 1943; *Otophocoenurus oserskoi* Skrjabin 1942; *Stenurus pallasii* (van Beneden) Dougherty 1943; *Pharurus oserskaiaae* (Skrjabin) Dougherty 1949; *Pharurus oserskaiaae* (Skrjabin) Dougherty 1951.

Hosts and Locality:

From Arnold and Gaskin, 1975 - Found in the white whale (*Delphinapterus leucas*) from the MacKenzie River Delta in Canada; New Brunswick, Canada; and from Churchill, Manitoba, Canada.

Phocanema sp.

Hosts and Locality:

From Dailey and Brownell, 1972 - Found in the white-beaked dolphin (*Lagenorhynchus albirostris*) and the pygmy sperm whale (*Kogia breviceps*). Information regarding geographical location of hosts was not provided by authors.

From Myers, 1957 - Found in the ringed seal (*Pusa hispida*) from Baffin Island.

From Van Thiel, 1966 - Found in the white beaked dolphin (*Lagenorhynchus albirostris*) from Katwijk Beach and the pygmy sperm whale (*Kogia breviceps*) from the west coast of France.

Phocanema decipiens

Synonymy:

From Myers, 1959 - *Ascaris bulbosa* Cobb, 1888; *Ascaris decipiens* Krabb, 1878; *Ascaris rectangular* von Linstow, 1907 nec Leiper and Atkinson, 1915; *Ascaris simplex* von Linstow, 1888; *Physaloptera guiarta* Garin, 1913; "?" *Porrocaecum azarsi* Yamaguti and Arima, 1942; "?" *Porrocaecum callotariae* Yamaguti, 1951; *Porrocaecum decipiens* (Krabbe, 1978 Baylis, 1920; *Terranova decipiens* (Krabbe, 1878) Mozzovoi, 1953; *Terranova piscium* (Rudolphi, 1809) Johnson and Mawson, 1943.

Hosts and Locality:

From Dailey and Brownell, 1972 - Found in the ringed seal (*Pusa hispida*) and the bearded

seal (*Erignathus barbatus*). Information regarding geographical location of hosts was not provided by authors.

From Johnson et al, 1966 - Found in the ringed seal (*Pusa hispida*) and the bearded seal (*Erignathus barbatus*) from the Cape Thompson region of Alaska.

From Myers, 1959 - Found in the hooded seal (*Cystophora cristata*), the bearded seal (*Erignathus barbatus*), the gray seal (*Halichoerus grypus*), the harp seal (*Phoca groenlandica*), the harbor seal (*Phoca vitulina*), and the ringed seal (*Phoca hispida soperi*). All host listed above were from the North Atlantic. From the north Pacific, *Phocanema decipiens* was found in the northern fur seal (*Callorhinus ursinus cynocephalus*), the sea otter (*Enhydra lutris neris*), the bearded seal (*Erignathus barbatus*), the harbor seal (*Phoca vitulina*), and in the California sea lion (*Zalophus californianus*). From the south Pacific, this parasite was found in the Kerguelen fur seal (*Arctocephalus gazella*), the Hooker's sea lion (*Arctocephalus hookeri*), the leopard seal (*Hydrurga leptonyx*), the Weddell seal (*Leptonychotes weddelli*), the southern sea lion (*Mirounga leonina*), and in the sea otter (*Enhydra lutris*).

Remarks:

A review of the taxonomy of this species is provided by Myers (1959).

Phocascaris ceptophora

Hosts and Locality:

From Dailey and Brownell, 1972 - Found in the hooded seal (*Cystophora cristata*). Information regarding geographical location of host was not provided by authors.

Phocascaris hydrurgae

Hosts and Locality:

From Dailey and Brownell, 1972 - Found in the leopard seal (*Hydrurga leptonyx*). Information regarding geographical location of host was not provided by authors.

From Johnston and Mawson, 1941 - Found in the leopard seal (*Hydrurga leptonyx*) from Port River and Port Adelaide (Australia).

From King, 1964 - Found in the leopard seal (*Hydrurga leptonyx*). Information regarding geographical location of host was not provided by author.

Phocascaris netsiki

Hosts and Locality:

From Dailey and Brownell, 1972 - Found in the common seal (*Phoca vitulina*) and the ringed seal (*Pusa hispida*). Information regarding geographical location of hosts was not provided by authors.

From Delyamure, 1955 - Found in the ringed seal (*Pusa hispida*) from the Arctic.

From King, 1964 - Found in the common seal (*Phoca vitulina*) and the ringed seal (*Pusa hispida*). Information regarding geographical location of hosts was not provided by author.

From Lyster, 1940 - Found in the ringed seal (*Phoca hispida*) from Craig Harbor, Clyde River, Lake Harbour, Cage Smith, and N.W.T. See Remarks.

Remarks:

Although Lyster (1940) does not discuss *Phoca virtulina* as a host of *Phocascaris nitsiki* in the text portion of his paper, he does list this host species in the remaining section of the paper.

Phocascaris osculatum

Hosts and Locality:

From Dailey and Brownell, 1972 - Found in the hooded seal (*Cystophora cristata*). Information regarding geographical location of host was not provided by authors.

Phocascaris phocae

Hosts and Locality:

From Dailey and Brownell, 1972 - Found in the

harp seal (*Phoca groenlandica*). Information regarding geographical location of host was not provided by authors.

From Delyamure, 1955 - Found in the harp seal (*Phoca groenlandica*) from various points in the White Sea.

From King, 1964 - Found in the harp seal (*Phoca groenlandica*). Information regarding geographical location of host was not provided by author.

Remarks:

Delyamure (1955) reviews the biology and ecology of *Phocacaris phocae*.

Physaloptera guiarti

Hosts and Locality:

From King, 1964 - Found in the Weddell seal (*Leptonychotes weddelli*). Information regarding geographical location of host was not provided by author.

Placentonema sp.

Hosts and Locality:

From Dailey and Brownell, 1972 - Found in the Dall porpoise (*Phocoenoides dalli*). Information regarding geographical location of host was not provided by authors.

From Johnston and Ridgway, 1969 - Found in the Dall porpoise (*Phocoenoides dalli*) from California.

From Margolis and Dailey, 1972 - Found in the Dall porpoise (*Phocoenoides dalli*) from California.

Placentonema gigantissima

Hosts and Locality:

From Dailey and Brownell, 1972 - Found in the sperm whale (*Physeter catodon*). Information regarding geographical location of host was not provided by authors.

From Delyamure, 1955 - Found in the sperm whale (*Physeter catodon*) from the Pacific Ocean (Kurile Islands region).

From Margolis and Dailey, 1972 - Found in the sperm whale (*Physeter catodon*) from California.

From Rice, 1963 - Found in the sperm whale (*Physeter catodon*) from California.

Porrocaecum sp.

Hosts and Locality:

From Dailey and Brownell, 1972 - Found in the California sea lion (*Zalophus californianus*). Information regarding geographical location of host was not provided by authors.

From Margolis and Dailey, 1972 - Found in the California sea lion (*Zalophus californianus*) from the San Diego Zoo. See Remarks.

From Scheffer and Slipp, 1944 - Found in the harbor seal (*Phoca vitulina*) from Washington.

From Scott and Fisher, 1958a - Found in the harbor porpoise (*Phocoena phocoena*) from the lower Bay of Fundy (near Passamaquoddy Bay).

Remarks:

Margolis and Dailey (1972) feel this species is undoubtedly a *Terranova*, probably *Terranova decipiens*.

Porrocaecum callotariae

Hosts and Locality:

From Dailey and Brownell, 1972 - Found in the northern fur seal (*Callorhinus ursinus*). Information regarding geographical location of host was not provided by authors.

From King, 1964 - Found in the northern fur seal (*Callorhinus ursinus*). Information regarding the geographical location of host was not provided by author.

Porrocaecum decipiens

Synonymy:

From Johnston, 1937c - *Ascaris decipiens* Krabbe 1878; *Ascaris bulbosa* Cobb 1888; *Ascaris simplex* Linstow 1888; *Ascaris osculate* Leidy 1891; *Ascaris rectangular* Linstow 1907; *Kathleena rectangular* Leiper and Atkinson 1914; *Contracaecum rectangularum* Baylis 1920; *Porrocaecum decipiens* Baylis 1920.

Hosts and Locality:

From Dailey and Brownell, 1972 - Found in the South American sea lion (*Otaria byronia*), the New Zealand sea lion (*Neophoca hookeri*), the Australian fur seal (*Arctocephalus doriferus*), the Kerguelen fur seal (*Arctocephalus tropicalis*), the northern fur seal (*Callorhinus ursinus*), the walrus (*Odobenus romarus*), the harbor seal (*Phoca vitulina*), the ringed seal (*Pusa hispida*), the bearded seal (*Erignathus barbatus*), the gray seal (*Halichoerus grypus*), the hooded seal (*Cystophora cristata*), the harp seal (*Phoca groenlandica*), the northern elephant seal (*Mirounga angustirostris*), the southern elephant seal (*Mirounga leonina*), the leopard seal (*Hydrurga leptonyx*), the Weddell seal (*Leptonychotes weddelli*), the Ross seal (*Ommatophoca rossi*), the Mediterranean monk seal (*Monachus monachus*), the Steller sea lion (*Eumetopias jubata*), the narwhal (*Monodon monoceros*), the white whale (*Delphinapterus leucas*), the little piked whale (*Balaenoptera acutorostrata*), the blue whale (*Balaenoptera musculus*), and in the harbor porpoise (*Phocoena phocoena*). Information regarding geographical location of hosts was not provided by authors.

From Johnston, 1937c - Found in the Weddell seal (*Leptonychotes weddelli*) from Commonwealth Bay (Antarctica) and in the elephant seal (*Mirounga leonina*) from Commonwealth Bay and Macquarie Island (Antarctica).

From King, 1964 - Found in the bearded seal (*Erignathus barbatus*), the gray seal (*Halichoerus grypus*), the harbor seal (*Phoca vitulina*), the ringed seal (*Pusa hispida*), the harp seal (*Phoca groenlandica*), the leopard seal (*Hydrurga leptonyx*), the Weddell seal (*Leptonychotes weddelli*), the Ross seal (*Ommatophoca rossi*), the Mediterranean monk seal (*Monachus monachus*), the hooded seal (*Cystophora cristata*), the southern elephant seal (*Mirounga leonia*), the northern elephant seal (*Mirounga angustirostris*), the northern fur seal (*Callorhinus ursinus*), the Kerguelen fur seal (*Arctocephalus tropicalis*), the walrus (*Odobenus rosmarus*), the California sea lion (*Zalophus californianus*), the Steller sea lion (*Eumetopias jubata*), and in the South American sea lion (*Otaria byronia*). Information regarding geographical location of hosts was not provided by author.

From Rauch, 1953 - Found in the sea otter (*Enhydra lutris*) from the Aleutian Islands, Alaska.

From Scott and Fisher, 1958a - Found in the harbor porpoise (*Phocoena phocoena*) from the Lower Bay of Fundy.

From Scott and Fisher, 1958b - Found in the harbor seal (*Phoca vitulina*), the harp seal (*Phoca groenlandica*), and in the gray seal (*Halichoerus grypus*) from the southern Canadian Atlantic mainland.

Porrocaecum sulcatum

Synonymy:

From Delyamure, 1955 - *Ascaris sulcata* Rudolphi, 1819.

Hosts and Locality:

From Dailey and Brownell, 1972 - Found in the South American fur seal (*Arctocephalus australis*). Information regarding geographical location of host was not provided by authors.

From Delyamure, 1955 - Found in the southern fur seal (*Arctocephalus australis*) from the south Atlantic (Brazil).

From King, 1964 - Found in the South American fur seal (*Arctocephalus australis*). Information regarding geographical location of host was not provided by author.

Pseudalius inflexus

Synonymy:

From Arnold and Gaskin, 1975 - *Strongylus inflexus* Rudolphi, 1809; *Strongylus inflexus major* Raspail, 1829; *Strongylus major* Raspail, 1829; *Pseudalius filum* Dujardin, 1845; *Prosthecosacter inflexus* Diesing, 1851; *Pseudalius inflexus* (Rudolphi) Schneider 1866.

From Baylis, 1932 - *Strongylus inflexus* Rudolphi, 1809; *Strongylus inflexus major* Raspail, 1829; *Strongylus major* Raspail, 1829; *Pseudalius filum* Dujardin, 1845; *Prosthecosacter inflexus* Diesing, 1851; "(?)" *Prosthecosacter convolutus* Cobbold, 1864; *Prosthecosacter convolutus* Cobbold, 1879; ("Not *Strnurus inflexus*" Dujardin, 1845.)

Hosts and Locality:

From Arnold and Gaskin, 1975 - Found in the harbor porpoise (*Phocoena phocoena*) from the Bay of Fundy in Canada and the North Sea (off the Netherlands).

From Baylis, 1932 - Found in the harbor porpoise (*Phocoena phocoena*). Information regarding geographical location of host was not provided by author.

From Dailey and Brownell, 1972 - Found in the harbor porpoise (*Phocoena phocoena*). Information regarding geographical location of host was not provided by authors.

Pseudoterranova kogiae

Synonymy:

From Delyamure, 1955 - *Porrocaecum kogiae* Johnston and Mawson, 1939.

Hosts and Locality:

From Dailey and Brownell, 1972 - Found in the pigmy sperm whale (*Kogia breviceps*). Information regarding the geographical locality of host was not provided by authors.

From Delyamure, 1955 - Found in the pigmy sperm whale (*Kogia breviceps*) from South Australia.

Skrjabinalius cryptocephalus

Hosts and Locality:

From Dailey and Brownell, 1972 - Found in the common dolphin (*Delphinus delphis*). Information regarding geographical location of host was not provided by authors.

From Delyamure, 1955 - Found in the common dolphin (*Delphinus delphis*) from the Black Sea.

Skrjabinaria heteromorpha

Hosts and Locality:

From King, 1964 - Found in the common seal (*Phoca vitulina*). Information regarding geographical location of host was not provided by author.

Skrjabinaria spirocauda

Synonymy:

From Delyamure, 1955 - *Filaria spirocauda* Leidy, 1858; *Skrjabinea spirocauda* Leidy, 1858 (after Freund, 1932).

Hosts and Locality:

From Dailey and Brownell, 1972 - Found in a captive (zoo) common seal (*Phoca vitulina*), and in the ringed seal (*Pusa hispida*). Information regarding geographical location of hosts was not provided by authors.

From Delyamure, 1955 - Found in the common seal (*Phoca vitulina*) and the ringed seal (*Pusa hispida*). Geographical distribution includes the North Sea (Heligoland Station) and the Moscow Zoo. See Remarks.

From Railliet, 1899 - Found in the common seal (*Phoca vitulina*) from the Gulf of Somme.

Remarks:

Although Delyamure (1955) does not specify which host was from the Moscow Zoo, Dailey and Brownell (1972) list *Phoca vitulina* as a host from a zoo.

Delyamure (1955) provides a brief review of the genus *Skrjabinaria*.

Skrjabinia spirocauda

Hosts and Locality:

From King, 1964 - Found in the ringed seal (*Pusa hispida*) and the California sea lion (*Zalophus californianus*). Information regarding geographical location of hosts was not provided by author.

Stenurus sp.

Hosts and Locality:

From Dailey and Brownell, 1972 - Found in the Dall porpoise (*Phocoenoides dalli*). Information regarding geographical location of host was not provided by authors.

From Norris and Prescott, 1961 - Found in the Dall porpoise (*Phocoenoides dalli*) from Southern California (four miles south of Pt. Fermin, Los Angeles).

Stenurus alatus

Synonymy:

From Delyamure, 1955 - *Torynurus alatus* Leuchart, 1848; *Prothecosacter alatus* (Leuckart, 1848) Diesing, 1851; *Strongylus (Pharurus) alatus* Leuckart, 1848; *Pseudalius alatus* Linstow, 1888; *Pharurus alatus* (Leuckart, 1848) Stiles and Hassall, 1905 in Dougherty, 1943.

Hosts and Locality:

From Dailey and Brownell, 1972 - Found in the narwhal (*Monodon monoceros*). Information regarding geographical location of host was not provided by authors.

From Delyamure, 1955 - Found in the narwhal (*Monodon monoceros*). Geographical distribution includes the North Sea (coast of Greenland).

Stenurus arcticus

Synonymy:

From Baylis, 1932 - *Strongylus pallasii*, v. Beneden, 1870 (*nomen nudum*); *Strongylus arcticus* Cobb, 1888; *Pseudalius arcticus*, v. Linstow, 1906.

Hosts and Locality:

From Baylis, 1932 - Found in the white whale (*Delphinapterus leucas*). Information regarding geographical location of host was not provided by author.

Stenurus arctomarinus

Hosts and Locality:

From Arnold and Gaskin, 1975 - Found in the white whale (*Delphinapterus leucas*) from the MacKenzie River Delta in Canada, and from Churchill, Manitoba, Canada.

From Dailey and Brownell, 1972 - Found in the white whale (*Delphinapterus leucas*). Information regarding geographical location of host was not provided by authors.

Stenurus auditivus

Hosts and Locality:

From Dailey and Brownell, 1972 - Found in the black finless porpoise or the common Chinese porpoise (*Neophocoena phocaenoides*). Information regarding geographical location of host was not provided by authors.

From Delyamure, 1955 - Found in the finless porpoise or common Chinese porpoise (*Neomeris phocaenoides*) from the Pacific Ocean.

Stenurus globicephalus

Hosts and Locality:

From Arnold and Gaskin, 1975 - Found in the North Atlantic pilot whale (*Globicephalus melaena*), and in the Risso dolphin (*Grampus griseus*) from Newfoundland; the Atlantic white-sided dolphin (*Lagenorhynchus acutus*) from Cape Cod, Massachusetts; and the short-fin pilot whale (*Globicephala macrorhyncha*) from Castries, St. Lucia, Lesser Antilles.

From Baylis, 1932 - Found in the North Atlantic pilot whale (*Globicephalus melaena*). Information regarding geographical location of host was not provided by author.

From Beverley-Burton, 1978 - Found in the Atlantic white-sided dolphin (*Lagenorhynchus acutus*) from Lingley Cove, Edmunds, Maine.

From Dailey and Brownell, 1972 - Found in the North Atlantic pilot whale (*Globicephalus melaena*). Information regarding geographical location of host was not provided by authors.

From Delyamure, 1955 - Found in the North Atlantic pilot whale (*Globicephalus melaena*) from the North Atlantic.

Stenurus minor

Synonymy:

From Arnold and Gaskin, 1975 - *Strongylus minor* Kuhn, 1829; *Stenurus inflexus* Dujardin, 1845; *Prosthecosacter minor* (Kuhn) Diesing, 1851; *Pseudalius minor* (Kuhn) Schneider, 1866; *Pseudalius minor* (Kuhn) Cobbold, 1879; *Stenurus minor* (Kuhn) Baylis and Daubney, 1925; *Stenurus Phocoenae* Dougherty, 1943; *Stenurus vegans* (Eschricht, 1841) Dougherty, 1943.

From Baylis, 1932 - *Strongylus minor* Kuhn, 1829; *Strnurus inflexus* Dujardin, 1845 (nec *Strongylus inflexus* Rudolphi, 1809); *Prosthecosacter minor* Diesing, 1851; *Prosthecosacter (Stenurus) minor* Diesing, 1861; *Pseudalius minor* Schneider, 1866; *Pharurus minor* Cobbold, 1879.

From Delyamure, 1955 - *Strongylus minor* Kuhn, 1829; *Stenurus inflexus* Dujardin, 1845 (nec *Strongylus inflexus* Rudolphi), 1808; *Prosthecosacter minor* (Kuhn, 1829) Diesing, 1851; *Prosthecosacter minor* (Kuhn, 1829) Diesing, 1861; *Pseudalius minor* (Kuhn, 1829) Cobbold, 1879; *Stenurus Phocoenae* Dougherty, 1943.

From Margolis and Dailey, 1972 - *Stenurus phocoenae* Dougherty, 1943; *Stenurus vegans* (Eschricht, 1841) Dougherty, 1943.

Hosts and Locality:

From Arnold and Gaskin, 1975 - Found in the harbor porpoise (*Phocoena phocoena*) from the Bay of Fundy in Canada, off Newfoundland and the North Sea off the Netherlands.

From Baylis, 1932 - Found in the harbor porpoise (*Phocoena phocoena*). Information regarding the geographical locality of host was not provided by author.

From Dailey and Brownell, 1972 - Found in the Risso dolphin (*Grampus griseus*), the white whale (*Delphinapterus leucas*), and in the harbor porpoise (*Phocoena phocoena*). Information regarding the geographical locality of hosts was not provided by authors.

From Delyamure, 1955 - Found in the finned porpoise (*Phocoena phocoena*), the Black Sea porpoise (*Phocoena phocoena relicta*), and in the white whale (*Delphinapterus leucas*). Geographical distribution includes the Arctic Ocean, North Atlantic, North Sea, Black Sea, Azov Sea, Asiatic coast of the Pacific Ocean, and USSR (Black Sea, Azov Sea and Pacific Ocean).

From Margolis and Dailey, 1972 - Found in the harbour porpoise (*Phocoena phocoena*) and the Dall porpoise (*Phocoenoides dalli*). Both host species were from California.

Stenurus ovatus

Synonymy:

From Baylis, 1932 - *Pseudalius ovatus* Linstow, 1910.

From Delyamure, 1955 - *Pseudalius ovatus* Linstow, 1910.

Hosts and Locality:

From Baylis, 1932 - Found in the bottlenosed dolphin (*Tursiops truncatus*). Information regarding the geographical locality of host was not provided by author.

From Dailey and Brownell, 1972 - Found in the bottlenosed dolphin (*Tursiops truncatus*). Information regarding the geographical locality of host was not provided by authors.

From Delyamure, 1955 - Found in the bottlenosed dolphin (*Tursiops truncatus*) from the Mediterranean Sea (Elba Island) and the Black Sea (Kerch Strait).

Stenurus pallasii

Synonymy:

From Delyamure, 1955 - *Strongylus arcticus* Cobb 1888; *Pseudalius arcticus* (Cobb, 1888) Linstow, 1900; *Stenurus arcticus* (Cobb, 1888) Baylis and Daubney, 1925.

Hosts and Locality:

From Dailey and Brownell, 1972 - Found in the

white whale (*Delphinapterus leucas*). Information regarding geographical location of host was not provided by authors.

From Delyamure, 1955 - Found in the white whale (*Delphinapterus leucas*) from the Arctic.

Strongylus [? *Stenurus*] *alatus*

Synonymy:

From Baylis, 1932 - *Prothecosacter alatus* Diesing, 1851; *Strongylus* (*Pharurus*) *alatus* Diesing, 1851; *Pseudalius alatus* Linstow, 1888; ("Not *Strongylus alatus*" Linstow, 1879).

Hosts and Locality:

From Baylis, 1932 - Found in the narwhal (*Monodon monoceros*). Information regarding geographical location of host was not provided by author.

Terranova decipiens

Synonymy:

From Margolis and Dailey, 1972 - *Ascaris decipiens* Krabbe, 1978; *Porrocaecum decipiens* (Krabbe, 1978) Baylis, 1920; *Phocanema decipiens* (Krabbe, 1978) Myers, 1959.

Hosts and Locality:

From Margolis and Dailey, 1972 - Found in the northern fur seal (*Callorhinus ursinus*), the sea otter (*Enhydra lutris*), the Steller sea lion (*Eumetopias jubatus*), the bearded seal (*Erignathus barbatus*), the harbour seal (*Phoca vitulina richardi*) and in the ringed seal (*Pusa hispida*). Hosts were from Alaska, British Columbia, and Washington.

Torynurus convolutus

Synonymy:

From Arnold and Gaskin, 1975 - *Strongylus convolutus* Kuhn, 1829; *Strongylus vegans* Eschricht 1841; *Prosthecosacter convolutus* (Kuhn) Diesing, 1851; *Pseudalius convolutus* Schneider, 1866; *Pseudalius bicostatus* von Linstow 1906; *Torynurus convolutes* (Kuhn)

Baylis and Daubney 1925; *Torynurus bicostatus* (von Linstow) Schmidt-Ries 1939; 1906; *Pharurus convolutes* (Kuhn) Dougherty 1943.

From Baylis, 1932 - *Strongylus convolutus* Kuhn, 1829; *Prosthecosacter convolutus* Diesing, 1851; *Prosthecosacta convolutus* Cobbold, 1864; *Pseudalius convolutus* Schneider, 1866; ? (sic) *Pseudalius bicostatus*, v. Linstow, 1906.

Hosts and Locality:

From Arnold and Gaskin, 1975 - Found in the common porpoise (*Phocoena phocoena*) from the Bay of Fundy, Canada; Vancouver Island and British Columbia, Canada; the North Sea off the Netherlands; and in the north east Atlantic Ocean.

From Baylis, 1932 - Found in the pilot whale (*Globicephala melaena*) and the common porpoise (*Phocoena phocoena*). Information regarding the geographical location of hosts was not provided by author.

Torynurus dalli

Synonymy:

From Arnold and Gaskin, 1975 - *Irukanema dalli* Yamaguti 1951; *Pharurus dalli* (Yamaguti) Yamaguti 1962; *Torynurus dalli* (Yamaguti) Delyamure 1972.

Hosts and Locality:

From Arnold and Gaskin, 1975 - Found in the Dall porpoise (*Phocoenoides dalli*) from Long Beach, California.

Trichinella spiralis

Hosts and Locality:

From Dailey and Brownell, 1972 - Found in the walrus (*Odobenus romarus*), the bearded seal (*Erignathus barbatus*), and in the ringed seal (*Pusa hispida*). Information regarding geographical location of hosts was not provided by authors.

From King, 1964 - Found in the bearded seal (*Erignathus barbatus*), the walrus (*Odobenus romarus*), and in the ringed seal (*Pusa hispida*). Information regarding the geographical location of hosts was not provided by author.

From Kuitunen, 1956 - Larvae found in the walrus (*Odobenus romarus*) from the Canadian Arctic (Southhampton Island and Cape Dorset). See Remarks.

From Margolis and Dailey, 1972 - Found in the walrus (*Odobenus romarus*) from Alaska.

From Rausch et al, 1956 - Found in unidentified seals (*Phoca sp.*) from Alaska (St. Lawrence Island) and the Arctic coast. Larval forms found in the bearded seal (*Erignathus barbatus*) and the white whale (*Delphinapterus leucas*) from Arctic Alaska. See Remarks.

From Roth, 1949 - Found in the bearded seal (*Erignathus barbatus*) from Thule (the extreme northern district of West Greenland).

Remarks:

Most of the "unidentified seals" examined by Rausch et al (1956) were comprised of two species; *Phoca hispida* and *Phoca vitulina*.

Kuitunen (1956) notes that "a Danish scientist" reported trichinosis in two walruses from the west coast of Greenland.

Uncinaria sp.

Hosts and Locality:

From Dailey and Brownell, 1972 - Found in the California sea lion (*Zalophus californianus*). Information regarding geographical location of host was not provided by authors.

From Dailey and Hill, 1970 - Found in the California sea lion (*Zalophus californianus*) from San Nicholas Island, California.

From Margolis and Dailey, 1972 - Found in the California sea lion (*Zalophus californianus*) from California.

Uncinaria hamiltoni

Synonymy:

From Delyamure, 1955 - *Dochmius* Dujardin, 1845; *Dochmoides* Cameron, 1924.

Hosts and Locality:

From Baylis, 1933 - Found in the Steller sea

lion (*Eumetopias jubata*) and the southern elephant seal (*Mirounga leonia*). Both hosts were from the Falkland Islands.

From Dailey and Brownell, 1972 - Found in the South American sea lion (*Otaria byronia*), the southern elephant seal (*Mirounga leonina*), and in the Steller sea lion (*Eumetopias jubata*). Information regarding geographical location of hosts was not provided by authors.

From Delyamure, 1955 - Found in the southern sea lion (*Otaria byronia*) and the southern elephant seal (*Mirounga leonia* [= *Macrorhynus leonia*]). Information regarding geographical location of hosts was not provided by author.

From King, 1964 - Found in the southern elephant seal (*Mirounga leonia*), the southern sea lion (*Otaria byronia*), and in the Steller sea lion (*Eumetopias jubata*). Information regarding geographical location of hosts was not provided by author.

From Hamilton, 1934 - Found in the South American sea lion (*Otaria byronia*) from the Falkland Islands.

From Margolis and Dailey, 1972 - See Remarks.

Remarks:

Margolis and Dailey (1972) note this parasite was possibly found in a Steller sea

lion (*Eumetopias jubata*) from Palo Alto (San Francisco Bay). Positive identification of the host was not made.

Uncinaria lucasi

Synonymy:

From Delyamure, 1955 - *Unicinaria sp.* Stiles and Hassall, 1899; ("?" sic *Unicinaria stemmacephala*; in Afans' ev, 1941).

Hosts and Locality:

From Dailey and Brownell, 1972 - Found in the northern fur seal (*Callorhinus ursinus*) and the ringed seal (*Pusa hispida*). Information regarding geographical location of hosts was not provided by authors.

From Delyamure, 1955 - Found in the northern fur seal (*Callorhinus ursinus*) from the Bering Sea (Pribilof Islands).

From King, 1964 - Found in the northern fur seal (*Callorhinus ursinus*). Information regarding geographical location of hosts was not provided by author.

From Margolis and Dailey, 1972 - Found in the northern fur seal (*Callorhinus ursinus*) and the Steller sea lion (*Eumetopias jubata*). Both host species were from Alaska.

Trematoda

Trematodes, commonly known as flukes, are less common in marine mammals but are common and diverse in sea turtles, where they can be found in almost any tissue including the vascular space, liver and gall bladder, free in the intestine, and in the urinary bladder. The larval forms of all trematodes require a mollusk to complete their indirect life cycle, however, most life cycles are unknown and in need of further study.

Brachycladiinae are billary and air sinus flukes of marine mammals that occasionally cause significant pathology and strandings, however they are also commonly encountered as incidental findings at necropsy. Two stomach flukes of cetaceans, *Braunia cordiformis* and *Pholeter gastrophilus* are common, and not generally associated with disease. Robust communities of trematodes are seen in sea turtles where species diversity is abundant and over fifty species can be found in a single host. Even significant numbers in the intestinal lumen are unlikely to cause disease, but Spirochid vascular flukes of sea turtles are often cited as pathogens similar to Schistosomiasis in humans.

Amphimerus lancea

Synonymy:

From Baylis, 1932 - *Distomum lancea* Diesing, 1850; *D. (Dicrocoelium) lancea* Stossich, 1892; *Opisthorchis lancea* Braun, 1901.

From Price, 1932 - *Distoma lancea* Diesing, 1850; *Opisthorchis lancea* (Diesing, 1850) Braun, 1901.

Hosts and Locality:

From Baylis, 1932 - Found in the dolphins *Sotalia tucuxii* (= *S. fluviatilis*) and *Orcaella brevirostris*. Information regarding the geographical location of hosts was not provided by author.

From Dailey and Brownell, 1972 - Found in the Irrawaddy River dolphin (*Orcaella brevirostris*) and the Amazon River dolphin or tookashee (*Sotalia fluviatilis*). Information regarding the geographical location of hosts was not provided by authors. See Remarks.

From Delyamure, 1955 - Found in the dolphins *Sotalia tucuxii* (= *S. fluviatilis*) and *Orcaella brevirostris* from the Pacific and Indian oceans (Brazil and India).

From Price, 1932 - Found in the Amazon River dolphin (*Sotalia fluviatilis*) from Brazil (Barra do Rio Negro), and in the Irrawaddy River dolphin (*Orcaella brevirostris*) from a northeastern province of India.

Remarks:

Dailey and Brownell (1972) list the Amazon River dolphin or tookashee (*Sotalia fluviatilis*) as a host of *Amphimerus lancea* and cite Baylis (1932) as a source reference. However, Baylis only lists the Irrawaddy River dolphin (*Orcaella brevirostris*) and the Amazon River dolphin (*Sotalia tucuxi*) as hosts of this parasite.

Braunina cordiformis

Hosts and Locality:

From Dailey and Brownell, 1972 - Found in the bottlenosed dolphin (*Tursiops truncatus*), the common dolphin (*Delphinus delphis*), and in the eastern Pacific spotted dolphin (*Stenella graffmani*). Information regarding the geographical location of hosts was not provided by authors.

From Delyamure, 1955 - Found in the bottle-nosed dolphin (*Tursiops truncatus*), the common dolphin (*Delphinus delphis*), and in the eastern Pacific spotted dolphin (*Stenella graffmani*). Geographical distribution includes the Adriatic Sea (Trieste, Lesina), Atlantic Ocean (Rio de Janeiro), California (Maryland State [sic], and Panama (Bay hova [sic]).

From Johnston and Ridgway, 1969 - Found in the bottlenosed dolphin (*Tursiops truncatus*). The host died in captivity, apparently from chocking on a fish, at the Naval Undersea Research and Development Center, Point Mugu, California.

From Margolis and Dailey, 1972 - Found in the bottlenosed dolphin (*Tursiops truncatus*) from California.

From Yamaguti, 1958 - Found in the common dolphin (*Delphinus delphis*) from the Adriatic Sea, the bottlenosed dolphin (*Tursiops truncatus*) from Florida; and in the eastern Pacific spotted dolphin (*Stenella graffmani*) from Panama.

Campula delphini

Synonymy:

From Baylis, 1932 - *Distomum delphini* Poirier, 1886; *Cladocoelium delphini* Stossich, 1892; *Brachycladium delphini* Looss, 1889.

From Delyamure, 1955 - *Distomum delphini* Poirier, 1886; *Cladocoelium delphini* (Poirier, 1886) Stossich, 1892; *Brachycladium delphini* (Poirier, 1886) Looss, 1889.

Hosts and Locality:

From Baylis, 1932 - Found in the common dolphin (*Delphinus delphis*). Information regarding the geographical location of host was not provided by author.

From Dailey and Brownell, 1972 - Found in the common dolphin (*Delphinus delphis*). Information regarding the geographical location of host was not provided by authors.

From Delyamure, 1955 - Found in the common dolphin (*Delphinus delphis*) from the Atlantic Ocean (Europe).

Campula folium

Hosts and Locality:

From Dailey and Brownell, 1972 - Found in the black finless porpoise or common Chinese porpoise (*Neophocoena phocaenoides*). Information regarding the geographical location of host was not provided by authors.

From Delyamure, 1955 - Found in the black finless porpoise or common Chinese porpoise (*Neomeris phocaenoides*) from the coast of Japan.

Campula gondo

Synonymy:

From Yamaguti, 1958 - *Odhneriella gondo* Yamaguti, 1942.

Hosts and Locality:

From Dailey and Brownell, 1972 - Found in short-finned pilot whale (*Globicephala macrorhyncha*). Information regarding the geographical location of host was not provided by authors.

From Yamaguti, 1958 - Found in the short-finned pilot whale (*Globicephala macrorhynchus*) from Japan.

Campula laevicaecum

Hosts and Locality:

From Dailey and Brownell, 1972 - Found in the long beaked dolphin (*Stenella longirostris*). Information regarding the geographical location of host was not provided by authors.

From Delyamure, 1955 - Found in the long beaked dolphin (*Stenella longirostris*) from Pacific Ocean (Japan).

Campula oblonga

Synonymy:

From Baylis, 1932 - *Distomum oblongum* Braun, 1891; *Distomum (Brachylaimus) oblongum* Stossich 1892; *Distomum tenuicolle* Olsson,

1893; *Opisthorchis oblongua* Kowalevsky, 1898; *Brachycladium oblongum* Looss, 1902.

From Delyamure, 1955 - *Distomum oblongus* (Colbold, 1858) Braun, 1892; *Distomum (Brachylaimus) oblongus* (Colbold, 1858) Stossich 1892; *Brachycladium oblongum* (Colbold, 1858) Looss, 1902; *Distomum tenuicolle* Rud. (after Olsson, 1893).

Hosts and Locality:

From Baylis, 1932 - Found in the harbor porpoise (*Phocoena phocoena*). Information regarding the geographical location of host was not provided by author.

From Ching and Robinson, 1959 - Found in the harbor porpoise (*Phocoena vomerina*) [= *Phocoena phocoena*] from Washington, and in the Dall porpoise (*Phocoenoides dalli*) from the Sea of Japan.

From Dailey and Brownell, 1972 - Found in the harbor porpoise (*Phocoena phocoena*). Information regarding the geographical location of host was not provided by authors.

From Delyamure, 1955 - Found in the finned porpoise (*Phocoena phocoena*) from the North Atlantic (Europe and North America).

From Margolis and Dailey, 1972 - Found in the harbor porpoise (*Phocoena phocoena*) from Washington.

Campula palliata

Synonymy:

From Baylis, 1932- *Distomum palliatum* Looss, 1885; *Cladocoelium palliatum* Stossich, 1892; *Brachycladium palliatum* Looss, 1889.

From Delyamure, 1955 - *Distomum palliata* Looss, 1885; *Brachycladium palliata* (Looss, 1885) Looss, 1889; *Cladocoelium palliata* (Looss, 1885) Stossich, 1892.

Hosts and Locality:

From Baylis, 1932- Found in the common dolphin (*Delphinus delphis*). Information regarding the geographical location of host was not provided by author.

From Dailey and Brownell, 1972 - Found in common dolphin (*Delphinus delphis*). Infor-

mation regarding the geographical location of host was not provided by authors.

From Yamaguti, 1958 - Found in the common dolphin (*Delphinus delphis*) from Europe.

Remarks:

The precise geographical location of this host/parasite could not be determined. Both Delyamure (1955) and Price (1932) list Europe as the geographical location of the parasite.

Campula rochebruni

Synonymy:

From Baylis, 1932 - *Distomum rochebruni* Poirier, 1886; *Cladocoelium rochebruni* Stossich, 1892; *Brachycladium rochebruni* Looss, 1899.

From Delyamure, 1955 - *Distomum rochebruni* Poirier, 1886; *Cladocoelium rochebruni* (Poirier, 1886) Stossich, 1892; *Brachycladium rochebruni* (Poirier, 1886) Looss, 1899.

Hosts and Locality:

From Baylis, 1932 - Found in the common dolphin (*Delphinus delphis*). Information regarding the geographical location of host was not provided by author.

From Dailey and Brownell, 1972 - Found in common dolphin (*Delphinus delphis*). Information regarding the geographical location of host was not provided by authors.

From Dailey and Perrin, 1973 - Found in the eastern Pacific spotted dolphin (*Stenella graffmani*) from the tropical Pacific (Lat. 12° 51' N, Long. 93° 18' W); and in the long beaked dolphin (*Stenella longirostris*) from the tropical Pacific (Lat. 12° 51' N, Long. 93° 18' W).

From Yamaguti, 1958 - Found in the common dolphin (*Delphinus delphis*) from Europe.

Cryptocotyle fusiforme

Hosts and Locality:

From Delyamure, 1955 - Found in the ringed seal (*Pusa hispida*), the commander fur seal (*Callorhinus ursinus ursinus*), and in the sea otter (*Enhydra lutris*). Geographical distribution includes the Commander Islands and the Hanaishiki Zoo in Japan.

From Goto and Ozaki, 1930 - Found in a ringed seal (*Pusa hispida*) that died in the Hanaishiki Zoological Gardens, Tokyo, Japan.

From Neiland, 1961 - Found in the northern fur seal (*Callorhinus ursinus*) from Valdez, Alaska.

From Rausch, 1953 - Found in the sea otter (*Enhydra lutris*) from Alaska.

Cryptocotyle jejuna

Hosts and Locality:

From Dailey and Brownell, 1972 - Found in the northern fur seal (*Callorhinus ursinus*). Information regarding the geographical location of host was not provided by authors.

From King, 1964 - Found in the northern fur seal (*Callorhinus ursinus*). Information regarding the geographical location of host was not provided by author.

From Margolis and Dailey, 1972 - Found in the northern fur seal (*Callorhinus ursinus*) from Alaska.

From Neiland, 1961 - Found in the northern fur seal (*Callorhinus ursinus*) from Valdez, Alaska.

Cryptocotyle lingua

Synonymy:

From Delyamure, 1955 - *Distomum lingua* Creplin 1825; *Tocotrema lingua* Looss, 1899; *Hallum lingua* Wigdor, 1912.

From Ransom, 1921 - *Dermocystis ctenolabri* Stafford, 1905; *Distomum lingua* Creplin, 1825; *Tocotrema lingua* (Creplin, 1825) Looss 1899; *Hallum caninum* Wigdor, 1918.

From Yamaguti, 1958 - *Hallum caninum* Wigdor, 1918.

Hosts and Locality:

From Delyamure, 1955 - Found in a northern elephant seal (*Mirounga angustirostris*)

that died at the New York Aquarium. Also found in the common seal (*Phoca vitulina*) and the Caspian seal (*Phoca caspica*). Geographical distribution includes the North Atlantic and the Caspian Sea.

From Dailey and Brownell, 1972 - Found in the harbor seal (*Phoca vitulina*), the gray seal (*Halichoerus grypus*), the northern elephant seal (*Mirounga angustirostris*), and in the Caspian seal (*Phoca caspica*). Information regarding the geographical location of hosts was not provided by authors.

From King, 1964 - Found in the harbor seal (*Phoca vitulina*), the gray seal (*Halichoerus grypus*), the northern elephant seal (*Mirounga angustirostris*), and in the Caspian seal (*Phoca caspica*). Information regarding the geographical location of hosts was not provided by author.

From Ransom, 1920 - Found in a captive harbor seal (*Phoca vitulina*) from the National Zoological Park in Washington D.C.

Remarks:

A brief historical account of this parasite is provided by Delyamure (1955).

Cyclorchis campula

Synonymy:

From Baylis, 1932 - *Distoma campula* Cobbold, 1876; *Campula oblonga* Cobbold, 1876, nec Cobbold, 1858; *Opisthorchis campula* Looss, 1899; *Metorchis campula* Looss, 1899.

From Delyamure, 1955 - *Distoma campula* Cobbold, 1876; *Metorchis campula* (Cobbold, 1876) Looss, 1899; *Opisthorchis campula* (Cobbold, 1876) Looss, 1899.

Hosts and Locality:

From Baylis, 1932 - Found in the Susu or Blind River dolphin (*Platanista gangetica*). Information regarding the geographical location of host was not provided by author.

From Dailey and Brownell, 1972 - Found in the Susu or Blind River dolphin (*Platanista gangetica*). Information regarding the geographical location of host was not provided by authors.

From Delyamure, 1955 - Found in the Susu or Blind River dolphin (*Platanista gangetica*) from Asia (India).

Delphinicola tenuis

Hosts and Locality:

From Dailey and Brownell, 1972 - Found in the long beaked dolphin (*Stenella longirostris*). Information regarding the geographical location of host was not provided by authors.

From Delyamure, 1955 - Found in the long beaked dolphin (*Prodelphinus longirostris*) [= *Stenella longirostris*] from the Pacific Ocean (Japan).

Distoma andersoni

Synonymy:

From Baylis, 1932 - *Distomum (Brachylaimus) andersoni* Stossich, 1892.

Hosts and Locality:

From Baylis, 1932 - Found in the Gangetic dolphin (*Platanista gangetica*). Information regarding the geographical location of host was not provided by author.

Distomum pallasii

Synonymy:

From Baylis, 1932 - *Dicrocoelium pallasii* Stossich, 1892.

Hosts and Locality:

From Baylis, 1932 - Found in the harbor porpoise (*Phocoena phocoena*). Information regarding the geographical location of host was not provided by author.

Distomum philocholum

Hosts and Locality:

From Baylis, 1932 - Found in the harbor porpoise (*Phocoena phocoena*). Information regarding the geographical location of host was not provided by author. See Remarks.

Remarks:

Baylis (1932) notes that Price (1932) considers the examined host was actually a common dolphin (*Delphinus delphis*) rather than a harbor porpoise (*Phocoena phocoena*).

Distomum validum

Synonymy:

From Baylis, 1932 - *D. (Brachylaimus) validum* Stossich, 1892.

Hosts and Locality:

From Baylis, 1932 - Found in the dolphin *Delphinus sp.* Information regarding the geographical location of host was not provided by author.

Echinochasmus andersoni

Synonymy:

See Remarks.

Hosts and Locality:

From Dailey and Brownell, 1972 - Found in the Susu or blind river dolphin (*Platanista gangetica*). Information regarding the geographical location of host was not provided by authors. See Remarks.

Remarks:

Dailey and Brownell (1972) list this parasite and host as a "new combination". It appears that Delyamure (1955) describes the same parasite as *Distoma andersoni* and Yamaguti (1958) describes it as *Brachyaema andersoni*. Both authors list the same host as Dailey and Brownell (1972). Baylis (1932) lists *Distomum (Brachylaimus) andersoni* as a synonym of *Distoma andersoni*. Delyamure (1955) gives a brief historical account of the parasite and considers *Brachyaema* to be synonymous with *Campula*. Yamaguti (1958) retains *Brachyaema*. Price (1932) considers this parasite belonging to *Echinostoma*. The original description made by Cobbold (1876) was based on what Delyamure considers to be a "poor drawing". This led Delyamure to conclude that the taxonomic position of this parasite is uncertain.

Echinostoma acanthoides

Synonymy:

From Delyamure, 1955 - *Distoma acanthoides* Rudolphi, 1819.

Hosts and Locality:

From Dailey and Brownell, 1972 - Found in the harbor seal (*Phoca vitulina*) and the gray seal (*Halichoerus grypus*). Information regarding the geographical location of hosts was not provided by authors.

From Delyamure, 1955 - Found in a common seal (*Phoca vitulina*) that died in the Berlin Zoo.

From King, 1964 - Found in the gray seal (*Halichoerus grypus*) and the common seal (*Phoca vitulina*). Information regarding the geographical location of hosts was not provided by author.

Remarks:

A brief historical account of this parasite is provided by Delyamure (1955).

Fasciola skrjabini

Synonymy:

From Delyamure, 1955 - *Fasciola hepatica* Stiles and Hassall 1898 nec *Fasciola hepatica* L. 1758.

Hosts and Locality:

From Dailey and Brownell, 1972 - Found in the short-finned pilot whale (*Globicephala macrorhyncha*), the little piked whale or minke whale (*Balaenoptera acutorostrata*), and in the killer whale (*Orcinus orca*). Information regarding the geographical location of hosts was not provided by authors.

From Delyamure, 1955 - Found in the killer whale (*Orcinus orca*) and the piked whale (*Balaenoptera acutorostrata*). Geographical distribution includes the North Atlantic (Europe).

Galactosumum erinaceum

Synonymy:

From Baylis, 1932 - *Distomum erinaceum*

Poireier, 1866; *Dicrocoelium erinaceum* Stossich, 1892; *Astiotrema erinacea* Stossich, 1904.

Hosts and Locality:

From Baylis, 1932 - Cysts found in the common dolphin (*Delphinus delphis*). Information regarding the geographical location of host was not provided by author.

From Dailey and Brownell, 1972 - Found in common dolphin (*Delphinus delphis*). Information regarding the geographical location of host was not provided by authors.

From Price, 1932 - Found in the common dolphin (*Delphinus delphis*) from Europe.

Remarks:

Price (1932) is "extremely doubtful" that the dolphin is a host to this parasite since all other members of the *Galactosumum* genera are parasites of birds. The original parasite specimen taken from the dolphin was described by Poirier (1886) and was found free in the intestines while still in the encysted form.

Hadwenius nipponicus

Synonymy:

See Remarks.

Hosts and Locality:

From Margolis and Dailey, 1972 - Found in the harbour porpoise (*Phocoena phocoena*) from Washington.

Remarks:

Both Skrjabin (1944) and Yamaguti (1958) consider *Hadwenius* to be synonymous with *Odhneriella*.

Hadwenius seymouri

Synonymy:

From Margolis and Dailey, 1972 - *Odhneriella seymouri* Price, 1932.

See Remarks.

Hosts and Locality:

From Baylis, 1932 - Found in the white whale (*Delphinapterus leucas*). Information regarding the geographical location of host was not provided by author.

From Margolis and Dailey, 1972 - Found in the white whale (*Delphinapterus leucas*) from Alaska.

Remarks:

Both Skrjabin (1944) and Yamaguti (1958) consider *Hadwenius* to be synonymous with *Odhneriella*.

Heterophyes heterophyes

Synonymy:

From Yamaguti, 1958 - *Heterophyes aegyptiaca* Cobbold, 1866; *Mesogonimus heterphyes* Railliet, 1890; *Coenogonimus heterphyes* Looss, 1900; *Cotylogonimus heterophyes* Lühe, 1900; *Heterophyes fraternus* Looss, 1884.

Hosts and Locality:

From Dailey and Brownell, 1972 - Found in the California sea lion (*Zalophus californianus*). Information regarding the geographical location of host was not provided by authors.

From King, 1964 - Found in a captive (zoo) California sea lion (*Zalophus californianus*). Information regarding the geographical location of host was not provided by author.

Remarks:

Yamaguti (1958) does not list *Z. californianus*, or any other marine mammal, as a host to this parasite.

Hunterotrema caballeroi

Hosts and Locality:

From Dailey and Brownell, 1972 - Found in the Bouta or Amazon River dolphin (*Inia geoffrensis*). Information regarding the geographical location of host was not provided by authors.

From Layne and Caldwell, 1964 - Found in the Amazon dolphin (*Inia geoffrensis*). The host was captured in the upper Amazon River (near Leticia, Columbia) but died in captivity in Florida.

Lecithodesmus sp.

Hosts and Locality:

From Dailey and Brownell, 1972 - Found in the Hawaiian spinner dolphin (*Stenella roseiventris*) and the humpback whale (*Megaptera novaengliae*). Information regarding the geographical location of hosts was not provided by authors.

From Margolis and Dailey, 1972 - Found in the sei whale (*Balaenoptera borealis*) and the humpback whale (*Megaptera novaengliae*) from California.

Lecithodesmus goliath

Synonymy:

From Baylis, 1932 - *Distomum goliath* van Beneden, 1858.

From Delyamure, 1955 - *Distomum goliath* van Beneden, 1858.

Hosts and Locality:

From Baylis, 1932, - Found in the bowhead whale (*Balaena mysticetus*), the sei whale (*Balaenoptera borealis*), and in the piked whale (*Balaenoptera acutorostrata*). Information regarding the geographical location of hosts was not provided by author.

From Dailey and Brownell, 1972 - Found in the Greenland right whale or bowhead whale (*Balaenoptera mysticetus*), the sei whale (*Balaenoptera borealis*), the fin whale (*Balaenoptera physalus*), and in the little piked whale or minke whale (*Balaenoptera acutorostrata*). Information regarding the geographical location of hosts was not provided by authors.

From Delyamure, 1955 - Found in the piked whale (*Balaenoptera acutorostrata*), the sei whale (*Balaenoptera borealis*), the fin whale (*Balaenoptera physalus*), and in the bowhead whale (*Balaena mysticetus*). Geographical distribution includes the Atlantic Ocean, the Arctic Ocean (Europe), and Russia (Sea of Okhotsk and Pacific Ocean).

From Margolis and Dailey, 1972 - Found in the fin whale (*Balaenoptera physalus*) from British Columbia.

From Margolis and Pike, 1955 - Found in the bowhead whale (*Balaenoptera mysticetus*), the piked whale (*Balaenoptera acutorostrata*), and in the sei whale (*Balaenoptera borealis*). All above hosts were from northwestern European seas. Also found in the fin whale (*Balaenoptera physalus*) from British Columbia.

Lecithodesmus nipponicus

Hosts and Locality:

From Dailey and Brownell, 1972 - Found in the long beaked dolphin (*Stenella longirostris*), the harbor porpoise (*Phocoena phocoena*), and in the short-finned pilot whale (*Globicephala macrorhynchus*). Information regarding the geographical location of hosts was not provided by authors.

From Yamaguti, 1958 - Found in the long beaked dolphin (*Stenella longirostris*) and the short-finned pilot whale (*Globicephala macrorhynchus*). Both hosts were from the coast of Japan.

Lecithodesmus spinosus

Hosts and Locality:

From Dailey and Brownell, 1972 - Found in the sei whale (*Balaenoptera borealis*). Information regarding the geographical location of host was not provided by authors.

From Margolis and Dailey, 1972 - Found in the sei whale (*Balaenoptera borealis*) from British Columbia.

From Margolis and Pike, 1955 - Found in the sei whale (*Balaenoptera borealis*) from British Columbia.

Leucasiella arctica

Hosts and Locality:

From Dailey and Brownell, 1972 - Found in the beluga or white whale (*Delphinapterus leucas*). Information regarding the geographical location of host was not provided by authors.

From Kleinenberg et al, 1964 - Found in the beluga whale (*Delphinapterus leucas*) from the Barents Sea (Novaya Zemlya settlement).

Leucasiella mironovi

Hosts and Locality:

From Dailey and Brownell, 1972 - Found in the beluga or white whale (*Delphinapterus leucas*). Information regarding the geographical location of host was not provided by authors.

From Kleinenberg et al, 1964 - Found in the beluga or white whale (*Delphinapterus leucas*) from the Pacific Ocean, LaPerouse Strait, Aniva Gulf.

From Tomilin, 1967 - Found in the white whale (*Delphinapterus leucas*) from the Sea of Okhotsk, Aniva Bay.

Mesorchis denticulatus

Hosts and Locality:

From King, 1964 - Found in the California sea lion (*Zalophus californianus*). Information regarding the geographical location of hosts was not provided by author.

Metorchis albidus

Synonymy:

From Delyamure, 1955 - *Distomum albidum* Braun, 1893; *Distoma (Dicrocoelium) albidum* Braun, 1893; *Opisthorchis albidum* (Braun, 1893) Railliet, 1896.

Hosts and Locality:

From Dailey and Brownell, 1972 - Found in the gray seal (*Halichoerus grypus*) and the hooded seal (*Cystophora cristata*). Information regarding the geographical location of hosts was not provided by authors.

From Delyamure, 1955 - Found in the gray seal (*Halichoerus grypus*) and the hooded seal (*Cystophora cristata*). Geographical distribution includes the Atlantic Ocean and Arctic Ocean (Europe).

From King, 1964 - Found in the gray seal (*Halichoerus grypus*) and the hooded seal (*Cystophora cristata*). Information regarding the geographical location of hosts was not provided by author.

Microphallus enhydrae

Hosts and Locality:

From Rausch and Locker, 1951- Found in the sea otter (*Enhydra lutris*) from Amchitka, Alutian Islands (Alaska).

Microphallus orientalis

Hosts and Locality:

From Dailey and Brownell, 1972 - Found in the walrus (*Odobenus rosmarus*) and the bearded seal (*Erignathus barbatus*). Information regarding the geographical location of hosts was not provided by authors.

From Yurakhno, 1968 - Found in the walrus (*Odobenus rosmarus romarus*), and the bearded seal (*Erignathus barbatus*) from the Bering Sea and Chukotski Sea.

Microphallus pirum

Synonymy:

From Dailey and Brownell. 1972 - *Microphallus enhydrae*.

From Margolis and Dailey, 1972 - *Microphallus enhydrae* Rausch and Locker, 1951.

Hosts and Locality:

From Dailey and Brownell, 1972 - Found in the sea otter (*Enhydra lutris*). Information regarding the geographical location of host was not provided by authors.

From Margolis and Dailey, 1972 - Found in the sea otter (*Enhydra lutris*) from Alaska.

From Rausch, 1953 - Found in the sea otter (*Enhydra lutris*) from Alaska.

Monostromum delphini

Synonymy:

From Baylis, 1932 - *Monostromum blainville* Cobbold, 1860; *Monostromulum delphini* Brandes, 1892; *Agamodistomum delphini* Price, 1932.

Hosts and Locality:

From Baylis, 1932 – Found in the whale "*Delphinus dalei* spec affin". See Remarks.

Remarks:

Baylis (1932) notes the likely host was either a bottled-nosed whale (*Hyperoodon rostratus*) or a Sowerby's whale (*Mesoplodon bidens*).

Nasitrema sp.

Hosts and Locality:

From Dailey and Brownell, 1972 - Found in the broad-beaked dolphin (*Peoponocephala electra*). Information regarding the geographical locality of hosts was not provided by authors. See Remarks.

Remarks:

Dailey and Brownell (1972) also list the bottlenosed dolphin (*Tursiops truncatus*) and the Pacific bottlenosed dolphin (*Tursiops gillii*) as hosts of *Nasitrema sp.* and cite Neiland et al (1970) as a source reference. However, no mention of these hosts could be found in the Neiland et al (1970) paper.

Nasitrema attenuata

Hosts and Locality:

From Dailey and Brownell, 1972 - Found in the false killer whale (*Pseudorca crassidens*). Information regarding the geographical location of host was not provided by authors.

From Margolis and Dailey, 1972 - Found in the false killer whale (*Pseudorca crassidens*) from Mexico.

From Neiland et al, 1970 - Found in the false killer whale (*Pseudorca crassidens*) from Mazatlan, Mexico (21° 51' N, 105° 56' W).

Nasitrema dalli

Hosts and Locality:

From Dailey and Brownell, 1972 - Found in the Dall porpoise (*Phocoenoides dalli*). Information regarding the geographical location of host was not provided by authors.

From Yamaguti, 1958 - Found in the Dall porpoise (*Phocoenoides dalli*) from the Sea of Japan.

Nasitrema delphini

Hosts and Locality:

From Dailey and Brownell, 1972 - Found in the common dolphin (*Delphinus delphis*). Information regarding the geographical location of host was not provided by authors.

From Margolis and Dailey, 1972 - Found in the common dolphin (*Delphinus delphis*) from California.

From Neiland et al, 1970 - Found in the common dolphin (*Delphinus delphis*) from California (26° 51' N, 114° 10' W).

Nasitrema globicephalae

Hosts and Locality:

From Dailey and Brownell, 1972 - Found in the Pacific white-sided dolphin (*Lagenorhynchus obliquidens*), the false killer whale (*Pseudorca crassidens*), the short-finned pilot whale (*Globicephala macrorhynchus*), and the northern right whale (*Lissodelphis borealis*). Information regarding the geographical location of hosts was not provided by authors.

From Margolis and Dailey, 1972 - Found in the short-finned pilot whale (*Globicephala macrorhynchus*), the Pacific white-sided dolphin (*Lagenorhynchus obliquidens*), the northern right whale (*Lissodelphis borealis*), and the false killer whale (*Pseudorca crassidens*). Hosts were from California.

From Neiland et al, 1970 - Found in the Pacific white-sided dolphin (*Lagenorhynchus obliquidens*) from California (30° 37' N, 118° 56' W); in the northern right whale (*Lissodelphis borealis*) from California (33° 37'N, 119°

22' W); in the false killer whale (*Pseudorca crassidens*) from California (21° 51' N, 105° 56' W); and in the short-finned pilot whale (*Globicephala macrorhynchus*) from two locations in California (32° 46' N, 118° 24' W and 22° 08' N, 107° 47' W).

Nasitrema gondo

Hosts and Locality:

From Dailey and Brownell, 1972 - Found in the short-finned pilot whale (*Globicephala macrorhyncha*). Information regarding the geographical location of host was not provided by authors.

From Yamaguti, 1958 - Found in the short-finned pilot whale (*Globicephala macrorhynchus*) from the Pacific coast (Japan).

Nasitrema lanceolata

Hosts and Locality:

From Dailey and Brownell, 1972 - Found in the short-finned pilot whale (*Globicephala macrorhyncha*). Information regarding the geographical location of host was not provided by authors.

From Margolis and Dailey, 1972 - Found in the short-finned pilot whale (*Globicephala macrorhyncha*) from California.

From Neiland et al, 1970 - Found in the short-finned pilot whale (*Globicephala macrorhynchus*) from California (near San Clemente Island (32° 71' N, 119° 15' W).

Nasitrema spathulatum

Hosts and Locality:

From Dailey and Brownell, 1972 - Found in the black finless porpoise or common Chinese porpoise (*Neophocoena phocaenoides*). Information regarding the geographical location of host was not provided by authors.

From Neiland et al, 1970 - Found in the black finless porpoise or common Chinese porpoise (*Neomeris phocaenoides*) from Batavia Bay (East Indies).

From Yamaguti, 1958 - Found in the black finless porpoise (*Neomeris phocaenoides*) from the Inland Sea of Japan.

Nasitrema stenosoma

Hosts and Locality:

From Dailey and Brownell, 1972 - Found in the eastern Pacific spotted dolphin (*Stenella graffmani*). Information regarding the geographical location of host was not provided by authors.

From Margolis and Dailey, 1972 - Found in the spotted dolphin (*Stenella dubia* [= *Stenella graffmani*]) from Mexico.

From Neiland et al, 1970 - Found in the eastern Pacific spotted dolphin (*Stenella graffmani*) from Mazatlan, Mexico (22° 58' N, 106° 21' W).

Nasitrema sunameri

Hosts and Locality:

From Yamaguti, 1958 - Found in the black finless porpoise or common Chinese porpoise (*Neomeris phocaenoides*) from the Inland Sea of Japan.

Odhneriella rossica

Hosts and Locality:

From Dailey and Brownell, 1972 - Found in the walrus (*Odobenus rosmarus*). Information regarding the geographical location of host was not provided by authors.

From Delyamure, 1955 - Found in the walrus (*Odobenus rosmarus*). Geographical distribution includes the Arctic Ocean, near Kalyuchinskii inlet (Chukchi Peninsula), and the White Sea (near Kanuchinskie Koshki).

From King, 1964 - Found in the walrus (*Odobenus rosmarus*). Information regarding the geographical location of host was not provided by author.

Odhneriella seymouri

Synonymy:

From Delyamure, 1955 - *Hadwenius seymouri* Price, 1932.

See Remarks.

Hosts and Locality:

From Dailey and Brownell, 1972 - Found in the beluga or white whale (*Delphinapterus leucas*). Information regarding the geographical location of host was not provided by authors.

From Delyamure, 1955 - Found in the beluga or white whale (*Delphinapterus leucas*) from Alaska and the Sea of Okhotsk.

From Kleinenberg et al, 1964 - Found in the beluga or white whale (*Delphinapterus leucas*) from the Bering Sea (Alaska), Okhotsk Sea, White Sea, and Barents Sea.

Remarks:

Yamaguti (1958) argues the correct name for this parasite is *Hadwenius seymouri*.

Ogmogaster antarcticum

Synonymy:

From Delyamure, 1955 - *Ogmogaster* Leiper and Atkinson, 1915 nec Creplin, 1829.

From Johnston, 1937a - *Ogmogaster plicatus*

Hosts and Locality:

From Dailey and Brownell, 1972 - Found in the crab-eating seal (*Lobodon carcinophagus*), the Weddell seal (*Leptonychotes weddelli*), the fin whale (*Balaenoptera physalus*), the blue whale (*Balaenoptera musculus*), and in the gray whale (*Eschrichtius gibbosus*). Information regarding the geographical location of hosts was not provided by authors.

From Delyamure, 1955 - Found in the Weddell seal (*Leptonychotes weddelli*), the crab-eating seal (*Lobodon carcinophagus*), the blue whale (*Balaenoptera musculus*), and in the fin whale (*Balaenoptera physalus*). Geographical distribution includes the Antarctic (King George IV Land and other points), and the Pacific Ocean (northern hemisphere).

From Johnston, 1937a - Found in the Weddell seal (*Leptonychotes weddelli*) from Antarctica (Commonwealth Bay and King George V Land).

From King, 1964 - Found in the crab-eating seal (*Lobodon carcinophagus*) and the Weddell seal (*Leptonychotes weddelli*). Information regarding the geographical location of hosts was not provided by author.

From Klumov, 1963 - Found in the fin whale (*Balaenoptera physalus*) from the Antarctic.

From Margolis and Dailey, 1972 - Found in the gray whale (*Eschrichtius gibbosus*) and the fin whale (*Balaenoptera physalus*) from British Columbia and California.

From Rausch and Fay, 1966 - Found in the fin whale (*Balaenoptera physalus*) from the north Pacific, and in the Weddell seal (*Leptonychotes weddelli*).

From Yamaguti, 1958 - Found in the Weddell seal (*Leptonychotes weddelli*) and the crab-eating seal (*Lobodon carcinophagus*). Both hosts were from Australia.

Ogmogaster pentalineatus

Synonymy:

From Rausch and Rice, 1970 - *Ogmogaster delyamurei*.

Hosts and Locality:

From Dailey and Brownell, 1972 - Found in the gray whale (*Eschrichtius gibbosus*). Information regarding the geographical location of host was not provided by authors.

From Margolis and Dailey, 1972 - Found in the gray whale (*Eschrichtius gibbosus*) from Alaska and California.

From Rausch and Fay, 1966 - Found in the gray whale (*Eschrichtius gibbosus*) from the Bering Sea (about Lat 63° 41′ N; Long 171° 50′ W of Point Kaghoopalik), west coast of St. Lawrence Island.

From Rausch and Rice, 1970 - Found in the gray whale (*Eschrichtius gibbosus*) from the Chukchi Sea.

Remarks:

This new species was proposed by Rausch and Fay (1966).

Ogmogaster plicatus

Synonymy:

From Baylis, 1932 - *Monostomum plicatum* (Creplin, 1829), Jägerskiöld, 1891.

From Dawes, 1946 - *Monostomum plicatum* Creplin 1829.

From Delyamure, 1955 - *Monostomum plicatum* Creplin. See Remarks.

From Johnston, 1937a - *Ogmogaster antarcticum*

Hosts and Locality:

From Baylis, 1932 - Found in the the piked whale (*Balaenoptera acutorostrata*), the sei whale (*Balaenoptera borealis*), the blue whale (*Balaenoptera musculus*), and in the fin whale (*Balaenoptera physalus*). Information regarding the geographical location of hosts was not provided by author.

From Dawes, 1946 - Found in the piked whale [lesser rorqual] (*Balaenoptera acutorostrata*), sei whale (*Balaenoptera borealis*), the fin whale [common rorqual] (*Balaenoptera physalus*), and in "some seals (*Leptonychotis weddelli* and *Lobodon carcinophagus*)" from Europe (Norway) and the Antarctic regions.

From Dailey and Brownell, 1972 - Found in the Greenland right whale (*Balaena mysticetus*), the sei whale (*Balaenoptera borealis*), the fin whale (*Balaenoptera physalus*), the blue whale (*Balaenoptera musculus*), and in the little piked whale or minke whale (*Balaenoptera acutorostrata*). Information regarding the geographical location of hosts was not provided by authors.

From Delyamure, 1955 - Found in the sei whale (*Balaenoptera borealis*), the blue whale (*Balaenoptera musculus*), the piked whale (*Balaenoptera acutorostrata*), and in the fin whale (*Balaenoptera physalus*). Geographical distribution includes the Atlantic Ocean (near the coast of Norway) and the Sea of Okhotsk (Kurile Islands region).

From Margolis and Dailey, 1972 - Found in the sei whale (*Balaenoptera borealis*) and the fin whale (*Balaenoptera physalus*). Geographical localities include British Columbia and California.

From Margolis and Pike, 1955 - Found in the sei whale (*Balaenoptera borealis*) and the fin whale (*Balaenoptera physalus*). Both hosts were from northern Norway.

From Price, 1932 - Found in the sei whale (*Balaenoptera borealis*), the blue whale (*Balaenoptera musculus*), the minke whale (*Balaenoptera acutorostrata*), the Weddell seal (*Leptonychotes weddelli*), and in the crab-eating seal (*Lobodon carcinophagus*). Geographical distribution includes Europe (Norway) and the Antarctic waters (Cape Evans region).

From Rausch and Fay, 1966 - Found in the fin whale (*Balaenoptera physalus*) and the sei whale (*Balaenoptera borealis*). "Possible" locality may include Rugen Island, Baltic Sea (Creplin's material). Definitely recorded off the northern coast of Norway. Geographical distribution includes the northern sector of the North Atlantic and north Pacific oceans, including the Sea of Okhotsk (Delyamure, 1955).

From Tomilin, 1967 - Found in the Greenland right whale (*Balaena mysticetus*). Information regarding the geographical location of host was not provided by author.

See Remarks.

Remarks:

The taxonomic history of this parasite is very involved and is reviewed by Rausch and Fay (1966). Price (1932) and Dawes (1946) both consider *O. plicatus* to be synonymous with *O. antarcticus*, and neither considered the blue whale (*Balaenoptera musculus*) to be a host of the parasite. Margolis and Pike (1955) doubt the minke whale (*Balaenoptera acutorostrata*) is a host to this parasite. Johnston (1931) regarded the *O. plicatus* specimens described by Price (1932) from pinnipeds (*Leptonychotis weddelli* and *Lobodon carcinophagus*) to be a distinct species and renamed them *Ogmogaster antarcticus*.

Ogmogaster trilineatus

Hosts and Locality:

From Margolis and Dailey, 1972 - Found in the fin whale (*Balaenoptera physalus*) from California.

From Rausch and Rice, 1970 - Found in the fin whale (*Balaenoptera physalus*) from the north Pacific Ocean off San Francisco, California, (Lat. 37° 33′ N; Long. 124° 06′ W).

Opisthorchis tenuicollis

Synonymy:

From Price, 1932 - *Distoma tenuicollis* Rudolphi, 1819; *Distoma viverrini* Poirier, 1866; *Opisthorchis viverrini* Stiles and Hassall, 1896; *Opisthorchis tenuicollis-felineus* Looss, 1899.

Hosts and Locality:

From Baylis, 1932 - Found in the harbor porpoise (*Phocoena phocoena*). Information regarding the geographical location of host was not provided by author.

From Dailey and Brownell, 1972 - Found in the bearded seal (*Erignathus barbatus*), the hooded seal (*Cystophora cristata*), the gray seal (*Halichoerus grypus*), and in the harbor porpoise (*Phocoena phocoena*). Information regarding the geographical location of hosts was not provided by authors.

From Delyamure, 1955 - Found in the bearded seal (*Erignathus barbatus*), the gray seal (*Halichoerus grypus*), the hooded seal (*Cystophora cristata*), and in the harbor porpoise (*Phocoena phocoena*). Geographical distribution includes the Atlantic Ocean and Arctic Oceans (Europe).

From King, 1964 - Found in the bearded seal (*Erignathus barbatus*), the hooded seal (*Cystophora cristata*), and in the gray seal (*Halichoerus grypus*). Information regarding the geographical location of hosts was not provided by author.

Remarks:

Both Price (1932) and Yamaguti (1958) note that when other hosts of this parasite are considered (cat, wolf, civet, dog, man), the distribution of this parasite extends to the United States and Asia. A brief account of this parasite is provided by Delyamure (1955).

Orthosplanchnus albamarinus

Hosts and Locality:

From Dailey and Brownell, 1972 - Found in the beluga or white whale (*Delphinapterus leucas*). Information regarding the geographical location of host was not provided by authors. See Remarks.

From Treshchev, 1968 - Found in the beluga or white whale (*Delphinapterus leucas*) from the White Sea.

Remarks:

In Dailey and Brownell (1972) list, "*Orthosplanchnus*" is erroneously spelt "*Orthosplanchus*".

Orthosplanchnus arcticus

Hosts and Locality:

From Cowen, 1967 - Found in the North Atlantic pilot whale (*Globicephala melaena*) from Newfoundland.

From Dailey and Brownell, 1972 - Found in the North Atlantic pilot whale (*Globicephala melaena*), the bearded seal (*Erignathus barbatus*), the harp seal (*Pagophilus groenlandica*), the ringed seal (*Pusa hispida*) and in the North Atlantic pilot whale (*Globicephala melaena*). Information regarding the geographical location of hosts was not provided by authors.

From Delyamure, 1955 - Found in the bearded seal (*Erignathus barbatus*), the ringed seal (*Pusa hispida*), and in the Greenland seal (*Pagophilus groenlandica*). Geographical distribution includes Europe (Spitzbergen, West Greenland), Canada, and Russia (Kara Sea and White Sea).

From Johnson et al, 1966 - Found in the bearded seal (*Erignathus barbatus*) from Alaska.

From King, 1964 - Found in the bearded seal (*Erignathus barbatus*), the harp seal (*Pagophilus groenlandica*), and in the ringed seal (*Pusa hispida*). Information regarding the geographical location of hosts was not provided by author.

From Margolis and Dailey, 1972 - Found in the bearded seal (*Erignathus barbatus*) from Alaska.

From Price, 1932 - Found in the bearded seal (*Erignathus barbatus*) and the ringed seal (*Pusa hispida*). Geographical distribution includes Europe, Greenland, Spitzbergen, and Canada.

From Yamaguti, 1958 - Found in the bearded seal (*Erignathus barbatus*) from Spitzbergen.

Orthosplanchnus elongatus

Hosts and Locality:

From Dailey and Brownell, 1972 - Found in the black finless porpoise or common Chinese porpoise (*Neophocoena phocaenoides*). Information regarding the geographical location of host was not provided by authors.

From Delyamure, 1955 - Found in the black finless porpoise (*Neomeris phocaenoides*) from Japan.

Orthosplanchnus fraterculus

Hosts and Locality:

From Dailey and Brownell, 1972 - Found in the walrus (*Odobenus rosmarus*), the sea otter (*Enhydra lutris*), and in the bearded seal (*Erignathus barbatus*). Information regarding the geographical location of hosts was not provided by authors.

From King, 1964 - Found in the bearded seal (*Erignathus barbatus*). Information regarding the geographical location of host was not provided by author.

From Margolis and Dailey, 1972 - Found in the sea otter (*Enhydra lutris*) and the bearded seal (*Erignathus barbatus*). Both hosts were from Alaska.

From Price, 1932 - Found in the walrus (*Odo-*

benus rosmarus) and the bearded seal (Erignathus barbatus). Both hosts were from Spitsbergen.

From Rausch, 1953 - Found in the sea otter (Enhydra lutris) from Alaska.

From Rausch and Locker, 1951. - Found in the sea otter (Enhydra lutris) from Alaska (Amchitka [Aleutian Islands], Point Barrow, and Wainwright), and from St. Lawrence Island, near Siberia.

Orthosplanchnus odobaeni

Hosts and Locality:

From Treshchev et al, 1969 - Found in the walrus (Odobenus rosmarus) from the Chukchi Sea (in the Enurmino area, Far-Eastern USSR).

Orthosplanchnus sudarikovi

Hosts and Locality:

From Dailey and Brownell, 1972 - Found in the beluga or white whale (Delphinapterus leucas). Information regarding the geographical location of host was not provided by authors.

From Treshchev, 1966 - Found in the beluga or white whale (Delphinapterus leucas). Information regarding the geographical location of host was not provided by author.

Oschmarinella laevicaecum

Hosts and Locality:

From Beverley-Burton, 1978 - Found in the Atlantic white-sided dolphin (Lagenorhynchus acutus) from Lingley Cove, Edmunds, Maine.

Oschmarinella sobolevi

Hosts and Locality:

From Dailey and Brownell, 1972 - Found in the giant bottlenosed whale (Berardius bairdi). Information regarding the geographical location of host was not provided by authors. See

Remarks.

From Delyamure, 1955 - Found in the bottlenosed whale (Hyperoodon ampullatus) from Russia, Sea of Okhotsk, and the Pacific Ocean (Kurile Islands region).

Remarks:

Dailey and Brownell (1972) cite Delyamure (1955) as a source reference for their claim that the giant bottlenosed whale (Berardius bairdi) is a host of Oschmarinella sobolevi. Delyamure lists the host as "Hyperoodon ampullatus [= H. rostratus]".

Phocitrema fusiforme

Hosts and Locality:

From Dailey and Brownell, 1972 - Found in the ringed seal (Phoca hispida). Information regarding the geographical location of host was not provided by authors. See Remarks.

From Goto and Ozaki, 1930 - Found in a ringed seal (Phoca hispida) that died in the Hanayashiki Zoological Garden, Tokyo.

From King, 1964 - Found in the northern fur seal (Callorhinus ursinus), the ringed seal (Phoca hispida), and in the harbor seal (Phoca vitulina). Information regarding the geographical location of hosts was not provided by author.

From Margolis and Dailey, 1972 - Found in the northern fur seal (Callorhinus ursinus), the sea otter (Enhydra lutris) and the harbor seal (Phoca vitulina richardi). See Remarks.

From Rausch, 1953 - Found in the sea otter (Enhydra lutris) from the Aleutian Island of Amchitka, Alaska.

From Rausch and Locker, 1951- Found in the sea otter (Enhydra lutris) from Amchitka, Alutian Islands (Alaska) and in the common seal (Phoca vitulina) from St. Lawrence Island (Alaska).

Remarks:

Dailey and Brownell (1972) and Margolis and Dailey (1972) list the northern fur seal (Callorhinus ursinus), the sea otter (Enhydra lutris) and the harbor seal (Phoca vitulina)

as hosts of *P. fusiforme* and cite Goto and Ozaki, 1930 as a source reference. However Goto and Ozaki only list a ringed seal (*Phoca hispida*) that died in the Hanayashiki Zoological Garden in Tokyo as a host of *P. fusiforme*. King (1964) does list the harbor seal (*Phoca vitulina*) as a host of *P. fusiforme*.

Pholeter gastrophilus

Synonymy:

From Baylis, 1932 - *Distomum gastrophilus* Kossack, 1910.

From Delyamure, 1955 - *Distomum gastrophilus* Kossack, 1910.

Hosts and Locality:

From Baylis, 1932 - Cysts found in the harbor porpoise (*Phocoena phocoena*). Information regarding the geographical location of host was not provided by author.

From Beverley-Burton, 1978 - Found in the Atlantic white-sided dolphin (*Lagenorhynchus acutus*) from Lingley Cove, Edmunds, Maine.

From Dailey and Brownell, 1972 - Found in the harbor porpoise (*Phocoena phocoena*). Information regarding the geographical location of host was not provided by authors.

From Delyamure, 1955 - Found in the common dolphin (*Delphinus delphis*) from Europe (Port Pillau, and Germany [now Baltusk USSR]).

Pricetrema zalophi

Synonymy:

From Delyamure, 1955 - *Apophallus zalophi* Price, 1932.

From Margolis and Dailey, 1972 - *Apophallus zalophi* Price, 1932.

Hosts and Locality:

From Dailey and Brownell, 1972 - Found in the California sea lion (*Zalophus californianus*), the sea otter (*Enhydra lutris*), and in the northern fur seal (*Callorhinus ursinus*). Information regarding the geographical location

of hosts was not provided by authors.

From Delyamure, 1955 - Found in the California sea lion (*Zalophus californianus*) from the Washington D.C. Zoo.

From King, 1964 - Found in the California sea lion (*Zalophus californianus*) and the northern fur seal (*Callorhinus ursinus*). Information regarding the geographical location of hosts was not provided by author.

From Margolis and Dailey, 1972 - Found in the northern fur seal (*Callorhinus ursinus*), the sea otter (*Enhydra lutris*), the Steller's sea lion (*Eumetopias jubatus*), and in the California sea lion (*Zalophus californianus*). Geographical distribution includes Alaska, California, and Washington D.C. (zoo).

From Neiland, 1961 - Found in the northern fur seal (*Callorhinus ursinus*) from Alaska (Pribilof Islands).

From Rausch, 1953 - Found in the sea otter (*Enhydra lutris*) from Alaska.

From Rausch and Locker, 1951 - Found in the sea otter (*Enhydra lutris*) from Amchitka, Alutian Islands (Alaska).

Pseudamphistomum truncatum

Synonymy:

From Price, 1932 - *Amphistoma truncatum* Rudolphi, 1819; *Distoma conus* Creplin, 1825 (nec Gurlt, 1831); *Distoma lancoelatum* Mehlis of Diesing, 1858; *Distoma campanulatum* Ercolani, 1875; *Distoma truncatum* Railliet, 1866; *Opisthorchis truncatus* Railliet, 1896; *Metorchis truncatus* Looss, 1899.

Hosts and Locality:

From Dailey and Brownell, 1972 - Found in the harbor seal (*Phoca vitulina*), the gray seal (*Halichoerus grypus*), the harp seal (*Pagophilus groenlandica*), the hooded seal (*Cystophora cristata*), and in the ringed seal (*Pusa hispida*). Information regarding the geographical location of hosts was not provided by authors.

From Delyamure, 1955 - Found in the gray seal (*Halichoerus grypus*), the hooded seal (*Cystophora cristata*), the common seal (*Phoca vit-*

ulina vitulina), the ringed seal (*Pusa hispida*), and in the harp seal (*Pagophilus groenlandica*). Geographical distribution includes various points in the Atlantic Ocean (European and Greenland coasts).

From King, 1964 - Found in the harbor seal (*Phoca vitulina*), the gray seal (*Halichoerus grypus*), the harp seal (*Pagophilus groenlandica*), the hooded seal (*Cystophora cristata*), and in the ringed seal (*Pusa hispida*). Information regarding the geographical location of hosts was not provided by author.

Remarks:

Both Delyamure (1955) and Yamaguti (1958) note this parasite is carried by a number of other hosts in Europe and Russia; including the dog, fox, mink, wolverine and man.

Pseudechinostomum advena

Synonymy:

From Yamaguti, 1958 - *Aequistoma adventa* Beaver, 1942. See Remarks.

Hosts and Locality:

From Dailey and Brownell, 1972 - Found in the Caspian seal (*Pusa caspica*). Information regarding the geographical location of host was not provided by authors.

From King, 1964 - Found in the Caspian seal (*Pusa caspica*). Information regarding the geographical location of host was not provided by author.

From Shchupakov, 1936 - Found in the Caspian seal (*Pusa caspica*) from the Caspian Sea (Chechen' Island).

Remarks:

Yamaguti (1958) considers *Aequistoma* to be the correct genera for this parasite.

Rossicotrema venustus

Synonymy:

From Delyamure, 1955 - *Cotyllophyllus venustus* Ransom, 1920; *Cotyllophyllus similis* Ransom, 1920; *Rossitrema similis* Wittenberg, 1929; *Apophallus venustus* Price, 1931; *Apo-*

phallus similis Price, 1931; *Apophallus donicum* (Skrjabin and Lindtrop, 1919) Price, 1932 nec *Rossicotrema donicum* Skrjabin and Lindtrop, 1919.

Hosts and Locality:

From Dailey and Brownell, 1972 - Found in the harbor seal (*Phoca vitulina*). Information regarding the geographical location of host was not provided by authors.

From Delyamure, 1955 - Found in the harbor seal (*Phoca vitulina*) from the North Atlantic and north Arctic Ocean (Alaska and Canada).

From King, 1964 - Found in the common seal (*Phoca vitulina*). Information regarding the geographical location of host was not provided by author.

Remarks:

Delyamure (1955) notes this parasite is also found in a number of other hosts, including dogs, cats and raccoons. Delyamure (1955) also provides a brief historical account of this parasite.

Schistosoma haematobium

Hosts and Locality:

From Dailey and Brownell, 1972 - Found in a captive (zoo) California sea lion (*Zalophus californianus*). Information regarding the geographical location of host was not provided by authors.

From King, 1964 - Found in a captive (zoo) California sea lion (*Zalophus californianus*). Information regarding the geographical location of host was not provided by author.

Schistosoma mansoni

Hosts and Locality:

From Dailey and Brownell, 1972 - Found in a captive (zoo) California sea lion (*Zalophus californianus*). Information regarding the geographical location of host was not provided by authors.

From King, 1964 - Found in a captive (zoo)

California sea lion (*Zalophus californianus*). Information regarding the geographical location of host was not provided by author.

Stephanoprora denticulata

Synonymy:

From Delyamure, 1955 - *Mesorchis denticulatus* Rudolphi, 1802; *Fasciola denticulta* Rudolphi, 1802; *Distoma denticulatum* Rudolphi 1809; *Echinostoma denticulatum* Cobbold, 1860.

Hosts and Locality:

From Dailey and Brownell, 1972 - Found in the California sea lion (*Zalophus californianus*). Information regarding the geographical location of host was not provided by authors.

From Margolis and Dailey, 1972 - Found in the California sea lion (*Zalophus californianus*) from a zoo in Washington D.C.

From Price, 1932 - Found in the California sea lion (*Zalophus californianus*) from the Washington Zoo.

Remarks:

In a brief historical account of *S. denticulate*, Delyamure (1955) notes that this parasite also has been found in a number of bird species and states an opinion that the correct genus for this parasite should be *Mesorchis*.

Stictodora haematobium

Synonymy:

From Yamaguti, 1958 - *Bilharzia magna* Cobbold, 1859; *Bilharzia capensis* Harley, 1864.

Hosts and Locality:

From King, 1964 - Found in a captive (zoo) California sea lion (*Zalophus californianus*). Information regarding the geographical location of host was not provided by author.

Remarks:

Yamaguti (1958) does not list *Zalophus californianus*, or any other marine mammal, as a host to this parasite.

Stictodora mansoni

Hosts and Locality:

From King, 1964 - Found in a captive (zoo) California sea lion (*Zalophus californianus*). Information regarding the geographical location of host was not provided by author.

Remarks:

Yamaguti (1958) does not list *Zalophus californianus*, or any other marine mammal, as a host to this parasite.

Stictodora ubelakeri

Hosts and Locality:

From Dailey, 1969 - Found in the California sea lion (*Zalophus californianus*) from Alamitos Bay, California.

From Dailey and Brownell, 1972 - Found in the California sea lion (*Zalophus californianus*). Information regarding the geographical location of host was not provided by authors.

From Margolis and Dailey, 1972 - Found in the California sea lion (*Zalophus californianus*) from California.

Synthesium tursionis

Synonymy:

From Baylis, 1932 - *Distomum tursionis* Marchi, 1873; *Distomum longissimum* Poirier, 1866; *Dicrocoelium longissimum* Stossich, 1892; *Dicrocoelium tursionis* Paroma, 1896; *Fasciolopis* (? sic) *tursionis* Nicoll, 1923.

From Delyamure, 1955 - *Distomum tursionis* Marchi, 1873; *Distomum longissimum* Poirier, 1866 nec *Distomum longissimum* Linstow, 1896; *Distomum (Dicrocoelium) tursionis* (Marchi, 1872) Paroma, 1896.

Hosts and Locality:

From Baylis, 1932 - Found in the bottlenosed dolphin (*Tursiops truncatus*). Information regarding the geographical location of host was not provided by author.

From Dailey and Brownell, 1972 - Found in the bottlenosed dolphin (*Tursiops truncatus*). Information regarding the geographical location of host was not provided by authors.

From Delyamure, 1955 - Found in the bottlenosed dolphin (*Tursiops truncatus*) from Europe.

Unidentified trematoda eggs

Hosts and Locality:

From Dailey and Brownell, 1972 - Found in the Bouta or Amazon River dolphin (*Inia geoffrensis*). Information regarding the geographical location of host was not provided by authors.

From Layne and Caldwell, 1964 - Found in the Amazon River dolphin or Boutu (*Sotalia fluviatilis*). The host was captured in the Amazon River (near Leticia) but died in captivity in Florida.

Zalophotrema curilensis

Hosts and Locality:

From Dailey and Brownell, 1972 - Found in the sperm whale (*Physeter catodon*). Information regarding the geographical location of host was not provided by authors.

From Delyamure, 1955 - Found in the sperm whale (*Physeter catodon*) from the Sea of Okhotsk (Kurile Islands region).

Zalophotrema hepaticum

Hosts and Locality:

From Brown et al, 1960 - Found in a bottlenosed dolphin (*Tursiops truncatus*) that died in captivity at the Marine Studios, St. Augustine, Florida.

From Dailey and Brownell, 1972 - Found in the California sea lion (*Zalophus californianus*), the northern elephant seal (*Mirounga angustirostris*), the harbor seal (*Phoca vitulina*) and in the bottlenosed dolphin (*Tursiops truncatus*). Information regarding the geographical location of hosts was not provided by authors. See Remarks.

From King, 1964 - Found in the harbor seal

(*Phoca vitulina*), the California sea lion (*Zalophus californianus*), the South American fur seal (*Arctocephalus australis*), and in the northern elephant seal (*Mirounga angustirostris*). Information regarding the geographical location of hosts was not provided by author.

From Margolis and Dailey, 1972 - Found in the California sea lion (*Zalophus californianus*) from California and Baja California (wild and captive animals), the New York Aquarium, the Washington D.C. Zoo and the Baltimore Zoo.

From Stunkard and Alvey, 1929 - Found in the California sea lion (*Zalophus californianus*). Geographical location of host was not provided by authors.

Remarks:

Dailey and Brownell (1972) also list the South American fur seal (*Arctocephalus australis*) as a host of *Z. hepaticum* and give Stunkard and Alvey (1929) as a source reference. However, no mention of *A. australis* could be found in the Stunkard and Alvey (1929) paper. However, King (1964) does list *Arctocephalus australis* as a host of *Z. hepaticum*

Zalophotrema lubimowi

Hosts and Locality:

From Dailey and Perrin, 1973 - Found in a captive South American sea lion (*Otaria byronia*) from the Moscow Zoo.

Zalophotrema pacificum

Hosts and Locality:

From Dailey and Perrin, 1973 - Found in the long beaked dolphin (*Stenella longirostris*) and the Eastern Pacific spotted dolphin (*Stenella graffmani*). Both hosts were from the eastern tropical Pacific Ocean (Lat. 12° 51' N, Long. 93° 18' W).

Remarks:

This new species was introduced by Dailey and Perrin (1973).

Host/ Parasite Listing

Pinnipedia

Arctocephalus australis (South American fur seal)

Acanthocephala:
Corynosoma semerme

Acarina:
Orthohalarchne megellanica

Cestoda:
Adenocephalus pacificus
Diphyllobothrium glaciale
Diphyllobothrium pacificum
Phyllobothrium delphini

Nematoda:
Anisakis similis
Contracaecum corderoi
Contracaecum osculatum
Contracaecum rectangulum
Porrocaecum sulcatum

Trematoda:
Zalophotrema hapaticum

Arctocephalus doriferus (Australian fur seal)

Acanthocephala:
Corynosoma sp.
Corynosoma australe

Cestoda:
Diphyllobothrium arctocephalinum

Nematoda:
Contracaecum osculatum
Porrocaecum decipiens

Arctocephalus forsteri (New Zealand fur seal)

Acanthocephala:
Corynosoma australe (erroneously reported)

Cestoda:
Adenocephalus pacificus
Diphyllobothrium arctocephalinum
(erroneously reported)

Nematoda:
Contracaecum osculatum
(erroneously reported)

Arctocephalus gazella (Kerguelen fur seal)

Nematoda:
Phocanema decipiens

Arctocephalus hookeri (Hooker's sea lion)

Nematoda:
Phocanema decipiens

Arctocephalus pusillus (South African fur seal)

Acanthocephala:
Corynosoma villosum

Acarina:
Orthohalarachne attenuate
Orthohalarachne diminuata

Anoplura:
Proechinopthirius zumpti

Cestoda:
Diphyllobothrium arctocephalinum
Phyllobothrium delphini

Nematoda:
Contracaecum osculatum

Arctocephalus tasmanicus (Tasmanian fur seal)

Acarina:
  Halarachne reflexa
  Orthohalarachne reflexa

Cestoda:
  Adenocephalus pacificus
  Diphyllobothrium arctocephali
  Diphyllobothrium arctocephalinum

Nematoda:
  Anisakis sp.

Arctocephalus tropicalis (Kerguelen fur seal)

Acanthocephala:
  Corynosoma strumosum

Cestoda:
  Diphyllobothrium sp.
  Phyllobothrium delphini

Nematoda:
  Contracaecum osculatum
  Porrocaecum decipiens

Callorhinus ursinus (northern fur seal)

Acanthocephala:
  Bolbosoma bobrovi
  Bolbosoma nipponicum
  Corynosoma semerme
  Corynosoma similis
  Corynosoma strumosum
  Corynosoma villosum

Acarina:
  Orthohalarchne attenuata
  Orthohalarchne diminuata

Anoplura:
  Antarctophthirius callorhini
  Proechinophthirius fluctus

Cestoda:
  Adenocephalus pacificus
  Adenocephalus septentrionalis
  Clestobothrium glaciale
  Diphyllobothrium glaciale
  Diphyllobothrium krooyi *
  Diphyllobothrium krotovi
  Diphyllobothrium macrocephalus
  Diphyllobothrium macrophallos

  Diphyllobothrium pacificus
  Diplogonoporus sp.
  Diplogonoporus tetrapterus

* May be a misspelling of
  Diphyllobothrium krotovi.

Nematoda:
  Contracaecum callotariae
  Contracaecum osculatum
  Dipetlonema spirocauda
  Porrocaecum callotariae
  Porrocaecum decipiens
  Terranova decipiens
  Uncinaria lucasi

Trematoda:
  Cryptocotyle fusiforme
  Cryptocotyle jejuna
  Phocitrema fusiforme
  Pricetrema zalophi

Callorhinus (sic) *ursinus alascanus* (Alaskan fur seal)

Cestoda:
  Diphyllobothrium krotovi

Callorhinus (sic) *ursinus curilensis* (Kurile fur seal)

Acanthocephala:
  Bolbosoma nipponicum

Cestoda:
  Diphyllobothrium krotovi
  Phyllobothrium hians

Callorhinus (sic) *ursinus cynocephalus* (northern fur seal)

Acarina:
  Orthohalarchne attenuata

Nematoda:
  Phocanema decipiens

Callorhinus (sic) *ursinus ursinus* (Commander fur seal)

Trematoda:
  Cryptocotyle fusiforme

Cystophora cristata (hooded seal)

Acanthocephala:
  Corynosoma bullosum
  Corynosoma semerme
  Corynosoma strumosum

Anoplura:
  Echinophthirius horridus

Cestoda:
  Diphyllobothrium elegans
  Diphyllobothrium latum
  Diphyllobothrium tetrapterus
  Diplogonoporus tetrapterus
  Pyramicocephalus phocarum

Nematoda:
  Contracaecum osculatum
  Dirofilaria immitis
  Filaria hebetata
  Phocanema decipiens
  Phocascaris ceptophora
  Phocascaris osculatum
  Porrocaecum decipiens

Trematoda:
  Metorchis albidus
  Opisthorchis tenuicollis
  Pseudamphistomum truncatum

Erignathus barbatus (bearded seal)

Acanthocephala:
  Corynosoma hadweni
  Corynosoma semerme
  Corynosoma strumosum
  Corynosoma validum

Anoplura:
  Echinophthirius horridus

Cestoda:
  Diphyllobothrium sp.
  Diphyllobothrium coniceps
  Diphyllobothrium cordatum
  Diphyllobothrium elegans
  Diphyllobothrium hians
  Diphyllobothrium lanceolatum
  Diphyllobothrium latum
  Diphyllobothrium macrocephalus
  Diphyllobothrium romeri
  Diphyllobothrium schistochilus
  Diphyllobothrium tetrapterus
  Diplogonoporus tetrapterus

Phyllobothrium hians
Polypocephalus tortus
Pyramicocephalus phocarum

Nematoda:
  Contracaecum osculatum
  Phocanema decipiens
  Porrocaecum decipiens
  Terranova decipiens
  Trichinella spiralis

Trematoda:
  Microphallus orientalis
  Opisthorchis tenuicollis
  Orthosplanchnus arcticus
  Orthosplanchnus fraterculus

Eumetopias jubata (Steller's sea lion)

Acanthocephala:
  Bolbosoma bobrovi
  Corynosoma sp.
  Corynosoma strumosum
  Corynosoma villosum

Acarina:
  Halarachne sp.
  Orthohalarchne attenuata
  Orthohalarchne diminuata
  Orthohalarchne zalophi

Anoplura:
  Antarctophthirius microchir
  Proechinophthirius fluctus

Cestoda:
  Abothrium gadi
  Adenocephalus pacificus
  Anophryocephalus ochotensis
  Diphyllobothrium elegans
  Diphyllobothrium krotovi
  Diphyllobothrium pacificus
  Diplogonoporus fasciatus
  Diplogonoporus tetrapterus
  Pyramicocephalus phocarum

Nematoda:
  Anisakis patagonica
  Anisakis similis
  Anisakis simplex
  Anisakis tridentata
  Contracaecum osculatum
  Parafilaroides sp.
  Parafilaroides nanus

Parafilaroides prolificus
Porrocaecum decipiens
Terranova decipiens
Uncinaria hamiltoni
Uncinaria lucasi

Trematoda:
Pricetrema zalophi

Gypsophoca dorifera (seal)

Acanthocephala:
Corynosoma clavatum

Gypsophoca tasmanica (Tasmanian fur seal)

Nematoda:
Anisakis sp.
Contracaecum gypsophocae

Halichoerus grypus (gray seal)

Acanthocephala:
Corynosoma falcatum
Corynosoma hadweni
Corynosoma magdaleni
Corynosoma reductum
Corynosoma semerme
Corynosoma strumosum

Acarina:
Halarachne halichoeri

Anoplura:
Echinophthirius horridus

Cestoda:
Ligula sp.
Schistocephalus solidus

Nematoda:
Anisakis similis
Contracaecum osculatum
Dioctophyme renale
Phocanema decipiens
Porrocaecum decipiens

Trematoda:
Cryptocotyle lingua

Echinostoma acanthoides
Metorchis albidus
Opisthorchis tenuicollis
Pseudamphistomum truncatum

Hydrurga leptonyx (leopard seal)

Acanthocephala:
Corynosoma sp.
Corynosoma antarcticum
Corynosoma australe
Corynosoma clavatum
Corynosoma hadweni
Corynosoma hamanni

Anoplura:
Antarctophthirius ogmorhini

Cestoda:
Diphyllobothrium archeri
Diphyllobothrium lashleyi
Diphyllobothrium quadratum
Diphyllobothrium scoticum
Diphyllobothrium scotti
Diphyllobothrium tectum
Diphyllobothrium ventropapillatum
Diphyllobothrium wilsoni
Phyllobothrium delphini

Nematoda:
Anisakis similis
Contracaecum ogmorhini
Contracaecum osculatum
Contracaecum radiatum
Contracaecum rectangulum
Contracaecum stenocephalum
Parafilaroides hydrurgae
Phocanema decipiens
Phocascaris hydrurgae
Porrocaecum decipiens

Leptonychotes weddelli (Weddell seal)

Acanthocephala:
Corynosoma antarcticum
Corynosoma hadweni
Corynosoma hamanni
Corynosoma sipho

Acarina:
  Halarachne sp.
  Lorryia leptonychotes
  Raphignathus johnstoni

Anoplura:
  Antarctophthirius ogmorhini

Cestoda:
  Diphyllobothrium archeri
  Diphyllobothrium lashleyi
  Diphyllobothrium mobile
  Diphyllobothrium perfoliatum
  Diphyllobothrium quadratum
  Diphyllobothrium rufum
  Diphyllobothrium scoticum
  Diphyllobothrium scotti
  Diphyllobothrium tectum
  Diphyllobothrium wilsoni
  Glandicephalus perfoliatus
  Glandicephalus perfoliatus var. *rufus*
  Phyllobothrium sp.
  Phyllobothrium delphini

Nematoda:
  Ascaris osculata
  Ascaris radiata
  Ascaris rectangula
  Contracaecum osculatum
  Contracaecum radiatum
  Contracaecum rectangulum
  Contracaecum stenocephalum
  Phocanema decipiens
  Physaloptera guiarti
  Porrocaecum decipiens

Trematoda:
  Ogmogaster antarcticum
  Ogmogaster plicatus

Lobodon carcinophagus (crab-eating seal)

Acanthocephala:
  Corynosoma antarcticum
  Corynosoma bullosum
  Corynosoma hadweni
  Corynosoma hamanni

Anoplura:
  Antarctophthirius lobodontis

Cestoda:
  Baylissia baylisi

Diphyllobothrium sp.

Nematoda:
  Contracaecum osculatum
  Contracaecum radiatum
  Contracaecum rectangulum

Trematoda:
  Ogmogaster antarcticum
  Ogmogaster plicatus

Mirounga angustirostris (northern elephant seal)

Acanthocephala:
  Corynosoma sp.

Acarina:
  Halarachne miroungae
  Orthohalarchne zalophi

Nematoda:
  Anisakis similis
  Contracaecum osculatum
  Porrocaecum decipiens

Trematoda:
  Cryptocotyle lingua
  Zalophotrema hepaticum

Mirounga leonia (southern elephant seal)

Acanthocephala:
  Corynosoma bullosum

Acarina:
  Halarachne sp.

Anoplura:
  Lepidophthirus macrorhini

Cestoda:
  Baylisiella tecta
  Diphyllobothrium lashleyi
  Diphyllobothrium scoticum
  Diphyllobothrium tectum
  Phyllobothrium sp.

Nematoda:
  Anisakis patagonica
  Anisakis similis
  Contracaecum osculatum
  Contracaecum radiatum
  Contracaecum rectangulum
  Filaria sp.

~~~~~~

Phocanema decipiens
Porrocaecum decipiens
Uncinaria hamiltoni

Monachus monachus (Mediterranean monk seal)

Cestoda:
Bothriocephalus sp.
Cysticercus cellulosae
Diphyllobothrium coniceps
Diphyllobothrium elegans
Diphyllobothrium hians
Diphyllobothrium lanceolatum
Diphyllobothrium latum
Diphyllobothrium tetrapterus
Diplogonoporus tetrapterus

Nematoda:
Anisakis pegreffii
Contracaecum osculatum
Porrocaecum decipiens

Monachus schauinslandi (Hawaiian monk seal)

Acanthocephala:
Corynosoma sp.
Corynosoma rauschi

Cestoda:
Diphyllobothrium cameroni
Diphyllobothrium hians
Phyllobothrium hians

Nematoda:
Contracaecum turgidum
Crassicauda sp.

Monachus tropicalis (Caribbean sea monk)

Acarina:
Halarachne americana

Neophoca cinerea (Australian sea lion)

Acanthocephala:
Corynosoma australe

Anoplura:
Antarctophthirius microchir

Cestoda:
Adenocephalus pacificus
Diphyllobothrium arctocephalinum

Nematoda:
Contracaecum osculatum

Neophoca hookeri [= Phocarctos hookeri] (New Zealand sea lion)

Acanthocephala:
Corynosoma semerme

Anoplura:
Antarctophthirius microchir

Nematoda:
Porrocaecum decipiens

Odobenus divergens (Pacific walrus)

Acanthocephala:
Corynosoma validum

Odobenus rosmarus (walrus)

Acanthocephala:
Corynosoma clavatum
Corynosoma semerme
Corynosoma strumosum
Corynosoma validum

Acarina:
Dermacentor rosmari
Orthohalarchne rosmari

Anoplura:
Antarctophthirius trichechi
Haematopinus trichechi

Cestoda:
Diphyllobothrium coniceps
Diphyllobothrium cordatum
Diphyllobothrium latum
Diphyllobothrium macrocephalus
Diphyllobothrium romeri
Diphyllobothrium schistochilus

Nematoda:
Anisakis alata
Anisakis bicolor
Anisakis rosmari
Contracaecum osculatum

Porrocaecum decipiens
Trichinella spiralis

Trematoda:
Microphallus orientalis
Odhneriella rossica
Orthosplanchnus fraterculus
Orthosplanchnus odobaeni

Odobenus rosmarus divergens (walrus)

Acanthocephala:
Corynosoma validum

Odobenus rosmarus rosmarus (walrus)

Trematoda:
Microphallus orientalis

Ommatophoca rossi (Ross seal)

Acanthocephala:
Corynosoma hadweni
Corynosoma hamanni

Anoplura:
Antarctophthirius mawsoni

Cestoda:
Diphyllobothrium antarcticus
Diphyllobothrium archeri
Diphyllobothrium mobile
Diphyllobothrium scotti
Diphyllobothrium wilsoni
Glandicephalus antarcticus

Nematoda:
Contracaecum osculatum
Contracaecum radiatum
Porrocaecum decipiens

Otaria byronia (South American sea lion)

Acanthocephala:
Corynosoma australe
Corynosoma hadweni
Corynosoma hamanni
Corynosoma semerme
Corynosoma strumosum

Acarina:
Orthohalarchne megellanica

Anoplura:
Antarctophthirius microchir

Cestoda:
Diphyllobothrium pacificus
Diphyllobothrium scoticum
Phyllobothrium sp.
Phyllobothrium delphini

Nematoda:
Anisakis patagonica
Anisakis similis
Contracaecum osculatum
Contracaecum rectangulum
Porrocaecum decipiens
Uncinaria hamiltoni

Trematoda:
Zalophotrema lubimowi

Otaria forster (seal)

Acanthocephala:
Corynosoma sp.

Otaria hookeri (Hooker's sea lion)

Acanthocephala:
Corynosoma australe

Pagophilus groenlandicus (harp seal)

Acanthocephala:
Corynosoma strumosum

Cestoda:
Diphyllobothrium cordatum
Diphyllobothrium lanceolatum
Diphyllobothrium sp.
Diphyllobothrium schistochilus

Nematoda:
Contracaecum sp.

Trematoda:
Orthosplanchnus articus
Pseudamphistomum truncatum

Pagophoca groenlandicus (Greenland seal)

Acanthocephala:
    Corynosoma strumosum

Cestoda:
    Diphyllobothrium coniceps

Nematoda:
    Contracaecum osculatum

Trematoda:
    Orthosplanchnus arcticus

Phoca sp. (seal)

Acanthocephala:
    Corynosoma hadweni
    Corynosoma strumosum
    Corynosoma validum
    Corynosoma wegeneri

Cestoda:
    Pyramicocephalus phocarum

Nematoda:
    Anisakis similis
    Trichinella spiralis

Phoca barbatus (bearded seal)

Cestoda:
    Diphyllobothrium lanceolatum
    Phyllobothrium hians

Phoca caspica (Caspian seal)

Acanthocephala:
    Corynosoma strumosum

Trematoda:
    Cryptocotyle lingua

Phoca groenlandica (Greenland harp seal)

Anoplura:
    Echinophthirius horridus

Cestoda:
    Diphyllobothrium coniceps
    Diphyllobothrium cordatum

Diphyllobothrium macrocephalus
Diphyllobothrium romeri
Diphyllobothrium schistochilus

Nematoda:
    Contracaecum osculatum
    Otostrongylus andreewaae
    Phocanema decipiens
    Phocascaris phocae
    Porrocaecum decipiens

Phoca hispida (ringed seal)

Anoplura:
    Echinophthirius horridus

Acanthocephala:
    Bolbosoma nipponicum
    Corynosoma sp.
    Corynosoma hadweni
    Corynosoma reductum
    Corynosoma semerme
    Corynosoma strumosum
    Corynosoma wegeneri

Cestoda:
    Anophryocephalus anophrys
    Diphyllobothrium fasciatus
    Diphyllobothrium hians
    Diphyllobothrium lanceolatum
    Diphyllobothrium latum
    Diphyllobothrium tetrapterus
    Diplogonporus fasciatus
    Diplogonoporus tetrapterus
    Phyllobothrium hians
    Polypocephalus tortus
    Pyramicocephalus phocarum
    Schistocephalus solidus
    Trigonocotyle skrjabini

Nematoda:
    Ascaris dehiscens
    Contracaecum osculatum
    Halocercus gymnurus
    Otostrongylus andreewaae
    Otostrongylus circumlitus
    Phocascaris netsiki

Trematoda:
    Phocitrema fusiforme

Phoca hispida ochotensis (Okhotsk ringed seal)

Acanthocephala:
 Bolbosoma nipponicum
 Corynosoma semerme
 Corynosoma strumosum

Cestoda:
 Diphyllobothrium lanceolatum
 Pyramicocephalus phocarum
 Trigonocotyle skrjabini

Nematoda:
 Contracaecum osculatum
 Otostrongylus andreewaae

Phoca hispida pomororum (White Sea ringed seal)

Nematoda:
 Otostrongylus andreewaae

Phoca hispida soperi (ringed seal)

Nematoda:
 Phocanema decipiens

Phoca monachus

Cestoda:
 Phyllobothrium hians

Phoca sibirica (Baikal seal)

Nematoda:
 Contracaecum osculatum

Phoca vitulina (common or harbor seal)

Acanthocephala:
 Corynosoma sp.
 Corynosoma falcatum
 Corynosom magdaleni
 Corynosoma semerme
 Corynosoma strumosum

Acarina:
 Halarachne sp.
 Halarachne miroungae

Anoplura:
 Echinophthiriidae sp.

Cestoda:
 Bothriocephalus sp.
 Diphyllobothrium coniceps
 Diphyllobothrium cordatum
 Diphyllobothrium elegans
 Diphyllobothrium hians
 Diphyllobothrium latum
 Diphyllobothrium osmeri
 Diphyllobothrium polycalceolum
 Diphyllobothrium schistochilus
 Diphyllobothrium tetrapterus
 Diplogonoporus tetrapterus
 Phyllobothrium hians
 Schistocephalus solidus
 Tetrabothrium albertini

Nematoda:
 Anisakis similis
 Contracaecum osculatum
 Dirofilaria immitis
 Dirofilaria spirocauda
 Halocercus gymnurus
 Otostrongylus circumlitus
 Parafilaroides gymnurus
 Phocanema decipiens
 Phocascaris netsiki
 Porrocaecum sp.
 Porrocaecum decipiens
 Skrjabinaria heteromorpha
 Skrjabinaria spirocauda

Trematoda:
 Cryptocotyle lingua
 Echinostoma acanthoides
 Phocitrema fusiforme
 Pseudamphistomum truncatum
 Rossicotrema venustus
 Zalophotrema hepaticum

Phoca vitulina concolor (Atlantic harbor seal)

Acanthocephala:
 Corynosoma magdaleni

Nematoda:
 Dipetlonema spirocauda

Phoca vitulina geronimensis (harbor seal)

Nematoda:
Dipetalonema spirocauda

Phoca vitulina largha (harbor seal)

Acanthocephala:
Corynosoma strumosum

Phoca vitulina richardii (harbour seal)

Acanthocephala:
Corynosoma falcatum
Corynosoma semerme
Corynosoma strumosum
Corynosoma wegeneri

Acarina:
Halarachne sp.
Halarachne halichoeri
Halarachne miroungae

Anoplura:
Antarctophthirius microchir
Echinophthirius horridus

Cestoda:
Diphyllobothrium alascense
Diphyllobothrium lanceolatum
Diphyllobothrium osmeri

Nematoda:
Contracaecum osculatum
Dipetalonema spirocauda
Terranova decipiens

Trematoda:
Phocitrema fusiforme

Phoca vitulina vitulina (harbor seal)

Nematoda:
Otostrongylus circumlitus

Trematoda:
Pseudamphistomum truncatum

Phocarctos hookeri [= *Neophoca hookeri*] (New Zealand sea lion)

Anoplura:
Antarctophthirius microchir

Pusa caspica (Caspian seal)

Acanthocephala:
Corynosoma strumosum

Nematoda:
Anisakis schupakovi
Eustrongylides excisus

Trematoda:
Pseudechinostomum advena

Pusa hispida (ringed seal)

Acanthocephala:
Bolbosoma nipponicum
Corynosoma reductum
Corynosoma semerme
Corynosoma strumosum
Corynosoma wegeneri

Anoplura:
Echinophthirius horridus

Nematoda:
Anisakis rosmari
Ascaris dehiscens
Contracaecum sp.
Contracaecum osculatum
Dipetalonema spirocauda
Halocercus gymnurus
Otostrongylus andreewaae
Otostrongylus circumlitus
Parafilaroides articus
Phocanema sp.
Phocanema decipiens
Phocascaris netsiki
Porrocaecum decipiens
Skrjabinaria spirocauda
Skrjabinia spirocauda
Terranova decipiens
Trichinella spiralis
Uncinaria lucasi

Trematoda:
Cryptocotyle fusiforme
Orthosplanchnus arcticus
Pseudamphistomum truncatum

Pusa hispida ochotensis (Okhotsk ringed seal)

Nematoda:
Otostrongylus circumlitus

Pusa hispida pomororum (Pomor ringed seal)

Nematoda:
Otostrongylus circumlitus

Pusa sibirica (Baikal seal)

Anoplura:
Echinophthirius horridus

Nematoda:
Contracaecum osculatum baicalensis

Zalophus californianus (California sea lion)

Acanthocephala:
Corynosoma obtuscens
Corynosoma osmeri
Corynosoma strumosum

Acarina:
Demodex sp.
Orthohalarchne attenuata
Orthohalarchne diminuata
Orthohalarchne zalophi

Anoplura:
Antarctophthirius microchir

Cestoda:
Adenocephalus pacificum
Diphyllobothrium krotovi
Diphyllobothrium pacificus

Nematoda:
Anisakis sp.
Anisakis similis
Contracaecum osculatum
Dipetalonema odendhali
Dirofilaria immitis
Dujardinia sp.
Halocercus sp.
Parafilaroides decorus
Phocanema decipiens
Porrocaecum sp.

Porrocaecum decipiens
Skrjabinia spirocauda
Uncinaria sp.

Trematoda:
Heterophyes heterophyes
Mesorchis denticulatus
Pricetrema zalophi
Schistosoma haematobium
Schistosoma mansoni
Stephanoprora denticulata
Stictodora haematobium
Stictodora mansoni
Stictodora ubelakeri
Zalophotrema hepaticum

Cetacea

Balaena antarctica

Cestoda:
Priapocephalus grandis

Balaena australis (southern right whale)

Nematoda:
Odontobius ceti

Balaena mysticetus (Greenland right whale or bowhead whale)

Acanthocephala:
Bolbosoma balaenae
Bolbosoma porrigens

Cestoda:
Phyllobothrium delphini
Phyllobothrium physeteris

Trematoda:
Lecithodesmus goliath
Ogmogaster plicatus

Balaenoptera acutorostrata (piked whale)

Acanthocephala:
Bolbosoma balaenae

Bolbosoma brevicolle
Bolbosoma nipponicum
Bolbosoma porrigens
Bolbosoma turbinella

Nematoda:
Anisakis simplex
Crassicauda crassicauda
Porrocaecum decipiens

Trematoda:
Fasciola skrjabini
Lecithodesmus goliath
Ogmogaster plicatus

Balaenoptera borealis (sei whale)

Acanthocephala:
Bolbosoma sp.
Bolbosoma balaenae
Bolbosoma brevicolle
Bolbosoma nipponicum
Bolbosoma porrigens
Bolbosoma turbinella

Cestoda:
Diphyllobothrium sp.
Diplogonoporus balaenoptera
Priapocephalus grandis
Priapocephalus minor
Tetrabothrium sp.
Tetrabothrium arsenyevi
Tetrabothrius affinis
Tetrabothrius wilsoni

Nematoda:
Anisakis sp.
Anisakis simplex
Crassicauda sp.
Crassicauda crassicauda
Crassicauda delamureana

Trematoda:
Lecithodesmus sp.
Lecithodesmus goliath
Lecithodesmus spinosus
Ogmogaster plicatus

Balaenoptera musculus (blue whale)

Acanthocephala:
Bolbosoma sp.
Bolbosoma balaenae

Bolbosoma brevicolle
Bolbosoma hamiltoni
Bolbosoma nipponicum
Bolbosoma porrigens
Bolbosoma turbinella

Cestoda:
Diplogonoporus balaenoptera
Priapocephalus grandis
Tetrabothrius affinis
Tetrabothrius schaeferi
Tetrabothrius wilsoni

Nematoda:
Anisakis simplex
Crassicauda crassicauda
Odontobius ceti
Porrocaecum decipiens

Trematoda:
Ogmogaster antarcticum
Ogmogaster plicatus

Balaenoptera mysticetus (Greenland right whale or bowhead whale)

Acanthocephala:
Bolbosoma balaenae
Bolbosoma porrigens

Nematoda:
Crassicauda crassicauda

Trematoda:
Lecithodesmus goliath

Balaenoptera physalus (fin whale)

Acanthocephala:
Bolbosoma sp.
Bolbosoma balaenae
Bolbosoma brevicolle
Bolbosoma hamiltoni
Bolbosoma nipponicum
Bolbosoma turbinella

Cestoda:
Diplogonoporus balaenoptera
Phyllobothrium delphini
Priapocephalus grandis
Priapocephalus minor
Tetrabothrium ruudi

Tetrabothrius affinis
Tetrabothrius wilsoni

Nematoda:
Anisakis sp.
Anisakis simplex
Contracaecum sp.
Crassicauda sp.
Crassicauda boopis
Crassicauda crassicauda
Crassicauda pacifica
Odontobius ceti

Trematoda:
Lecithodesmus goliath
Ogmogaster antarcticum
Ogmogaster plicatus
Ogmogaster trilineatus

Balaenoptera rostrata (piked whale)

Acanthocephala:
Bolbosoma nipponicum

Balaenoptera velifera (whale)*

Acanthocephala:
Bolbosoma sp.

* In listing this host/parasite relationship, Baylis (1932) questions whether *Balaenoptera velifera* is synonymous with the fin whale (*Balaenoptera physalus*).

Berardius bairdi (giant bottlenosed dolphin)

Cestoda:
Diphyllobothrium sp.
Phyllobothrium delphini
Trigonocotyle sp.

Nematoda:
Anisakis sp.
Anisakis simplex
Anisakis skrjabini
Crassicauda giliakiana
Delamurella hyperoodoni

Trematoda:
Oschmarinella sobolevi

Delphinapterus leucas (beluga or white whale)

Acanthocephala:
Corynosoma cameroni
Corynosoma hadweni
Corynosoma semerme
Corynosoma similis
Corynosoma strumosum
Corynosoma wegeneri

Cestoda:
Diphyllobothrium lanceolatum

Nematoda:
Anisakis sp.
Anisakis kükenthalii
Anisakis simplex
Crassicauda giliakiana
Otophocaenurus oserskoi
Pharurus oserkaiae
Pharurus pallasii
Porrocaecum decipiens
Stenurus arcticus
Stenurus arctomarinus
Stenurus minor
Stenurus pallasii
Trichinella spiralis

Trematoda:
Hadwenius seymouri
Leucasiella arctica
Leucasiella mironovi
Odhneriella seymouri
Orthosplanchnus albamarinus
Orthosplanchnus sudarikovi

Delphinus sp. (dolphin)

Cestoda:
Monorygma grimaldii
Strobilocephalus triangularis

Nematoda:
Anisakis dussumierii
Anisakis simplex

Trematoda:
Distomum validum

Delphinus dalei *

Trematoda:
 Monostromum delphini

 * Baylis (1932) notes "it appears" the likely
 host was either a bottled-nosed whale
 (*Hyperoodon rostratus*) or a Sowerby's whale
 (*Mesoplodon bidens*).

Delphinus delphis (common dolphin)

Acanthocephala:
 Bolbosoma aurantiacum
 Bolbosoma pellucidum
 Bolbosoma vasculosum
 Corynosoma sp.
 Corynosoma cetaceum

Cestoda:
 Diphyllobothrium stemmacephalum
 Monorygma delphini
 Monorygma grimaldii
 Phyllobothrium delphini
 Tetrabothrius forsteri

Nematoda:
 Anisakis simplex
 Anisakis typica
 Echinocephalus uncinatus
 Halocercus delphini
 Halocercus kleinenbergi
 Skrjabinalius cryptocephalus

Trematoda:
 Braunina cordiformis
 Campula delphini
 Campula palliata
 Campula rochebruni
 Galactosumum erinaceum
 Nasitrema delphini
 Pholeter gastrophilus

Delphinus dussumieri [= *Prodelphinus longirostris*] [=
Delphinus longirostris]

Cestoda:
 Diphyllobothrium fuhrmanni
 Diphyllobothrium stemmacephalum

Delphinus forsteri

Acanthocephala:
 Echinorhynchus sp.

Delphinus longirostris (spotted dolphin)

Acanthocephala:
 Corynosoma sp.

Cestoda:
 Diphyllobothrium stemmacephalum

Eschrichtius gibbosus (gray whale)

Acanthocephala:
 Corynosoma sp.

Cestoda:
 Priapocephalus sp.
 Priapocephalus eschrichtii
 Pseudophyllidae sp.
 Tetrabothrium sp.

Trematoda:
 Ogmogaster antarcticum
 Ogmogaster pentalineatus

Eubalaena glacialis (black right whale)

Acanthocephala:
 Bolbosoma brevicolle
 Bolbosoma turbinella

Cestoda:
 Priapocephalus grandis

Eubalaena glacialis sieboldi (true right whale)

Acanthocephala:
 Bolbosoma turbinella

Globicephala edwardi (pilot whale)

Cestoda:
 Trigonocotyle globicephalae
 Trigonocotyle lintoni

Globicephala macrorhyncha (short-fin pilot whale)

Cestoda:
Anophryocephala sp.
Monorygma sp.
Phyllobothrium sp.

Nematoda:
Anisakis sp.
Pharurus convolutus
Stenurus globicephalus

Trematoda:
Campula gondo
Fasciola skrjabini
Lecithodesmus nipponicus
Nasitrema globicephalae
Nasitrema gondo
Nasitrema lanceolata

Globicephala melaena (North Atlantic pilot whale)

Acanthocephala:
Bolbosoma capitatum

Cestoda:
Diphyllobothrium sp.
Monorygma grimaldii
Phyllobothrium delphini
Plicobothrium globicephalae
Trigonocotyle globicephalae
Trigonocotyle lintoni
Trigonocotyle monticellii

Nematoda:
Anisakis simplex
Pharurus convolutus
Stenurus globicephalus
Torynurus convolutus

Trematoda:
Orthosplanchnus arcticus

Globicephala melas (pilot whale)

Acanthocephala:
Bolbosoma capitatum

Cestoda:
Phyllobothrium delphini

Nematoda:
Anisakis typica

Globicephala svineval (pilot whale)

Acanthocephala:
Bolbosoma capitatum

Globicephalus ventricosus (pilot whale)

Nematoda:
Anisakis physeteris

Grampus griseus (Risso dolphin)

Cestoda:
Phyllobothrium delphini
Scolex delphini

Nematoda:
Crassicauda grampicola
Stenurus globicephalus
Stenurus minor

Hyperoodon ampullatus (northern bottlenosed whale)

Acanthocephala:
Bolbosoma turbinella
Bolbosoma balaenae

Cestoda:
Strobilocephalus triangularis
Trigonocotyle sp.

Nematoda:
Anisakis physeteris
Anisakis simplex
Anisakis skrjabini
Crassicauda giliakiana
Delamurella hyperoodoni

Trematoda:
Oschmarinella sobolevi

Hyperoodon planiforns (southern botlenosed whale)

Nematoda:
Crassicauda bennetti

Hyperoodon rostratus (bottled-nosed dolphin)

Acanthocephala:
Bolbosoma turbinella

Cestoda:
Strobilocephalus triangularis

Nematoda:
Anisakis simplex

Inia geoffrensis (Amazon River dolphin or Bouta)

Nematoda:
Anisakis insignis
Halocercus sp.

Trematoda:
Hunterotrema caballeroi
Unidentified trematode eggs

Kogia breviceps (pygmy sperm whale)

Cestoda:
Monorygma grimaldii
Phyllobothrium delphini

Nematoda:
Anisakis physeteris
Anisakis simplex
Crassicauda duguyi
Crassicauda magna
Phocanema sp.
Pseudoterranova kogiae

Kogia simus (dwarf sperm whale)

Cestoda:
Phyllobothrium sp.

Lagenorhynchus acutus (Atlantic white-sided dolphin)

Acanthocephala:
Bolbosoma sp.

Cestoda:
Monorygma chamissonii
Monorygma grimaldii
Phyllobothrium sp.
*Strobilocephalus triangularis**
Tetrabothrius forsteri

 * Reported incidences of *Strobilocephalus triangularis* being a parasite of the Atlantic white-sided dolphin (*Lagenorhynchus acutus*) appear to have originated based on

erroneous information published in 1932 (Baer, 1932). In a later paper Baer corrects this mistake (Baer 1954).

Nematoda:
Anisakis sp.
Stenurus globicephala

Trematoda:
Oschmarinella laevicaecum
Pholeter gastrophilus

Lagenorhynchus albirostris (white beaked dolphin)

Nematoda:
Anisakis simplex
Halocercus lagenorhynchus
Phocanema sp.

Lagenorhynchus australis (dolphin)

Cestoda:
Trigonocotyle prudhoei

Lagenorhynchus obliquidens (Pacific white sided or striped dolphin)

Cestoda:
Phyllobothrium sp.
Phyllobothrium delphini

Nematoda:
Contracaecum sp.

Trematoda:
Nasitrema globicephalae

Lagenorhynchus obscurus (dusky or piebald dolphin)

Cestoda:
Phyllobothrium sp.

Nematoda:
Anisakis simplex
Anisakis typica

Lissodelphis borealis (northern right whale dolphin)

Cestoda:
Phyllobothrium sp.

Trematoda:
   Nasitrema globicephalae

Megaptera nodosa (humpback whale)

Acanthocephala:
   Bolbosoma porrigens
   Bolbosoma turbinella
   Corynosoma sp.

Nematoda:
   Anisakis sp.
   Crassicauda boopis
   Odontobius ceti

Megaptera novaengliae (humpback whale)

Acanthocephala:
   Bolbosoma sp.
   Bolbosoma balaenae
   Bolbosoma turbinella
   Corynosoma sp.

Cestoda:
   Diplogonoporus balaenoptera

Nematoda:
   Anisakis sp.
   Crassicauda sp.
   Crassicauda boopis
   Crassicauda crassicauda

Trematoda:
   Lecithodesmus sp.

Mesoplodon bidens (Sowerby beaked whale)

Acanthocephala:
   Bolbosoma aurantiacum
   Bolbosoma pellucidum
   Bolbosoma vasculosum

Cestoda:
   Phyllobothrium delphini
   Phyllobothrium inchoatum
   Strobilocephalus triangularis
   Tetrabothrius forsteri

Nematoda:
   Anisakis simplex

Mesoplodon mirus (True's beaked whale)

Nematoda:
   Crassicauda anthonyi

Monodon monoceros (narwhal)

Nematoda:
   Anisakis simplex
   Pharurus alatus
   Porrocaecum decipiens
   Stenurus alatus
   Strongylus [? *Stenurus sic*] *alatus*

Neomeris phocaenoides (black finless or common Chinese porpoise)

Cestoda:
   Diphyllobothrium fuhrmanni

Nematoda:
   Crassicauda fuelleborni
   Stenurus auditivus

Trematoda:
   Campula folium
   Nasitrema spathulatum
   Nasitrema sunameri
   Orthosplanchnus elongatus

Neophocoena phocoenoides (black finless or common Chinese porpoise)

Cestoda:
   Diphyllobothrium fuhrmanni

Nematoda:
   Crassicauda fuelleborni
   Halocercus pingi
   Stenurus auditivus

Trematoda:
   Campula folium
   Nasitrema spathulatum
   Orthosplanchnus elongatus

Orcaella brevirostris (Irrawaddy River dolphin)

Trematoda:
Amphimerus lancea

Orcinus orca (killer whale)

Acanthocephala:
Bolbosoma physeteris

Cestoda:
Phyllobothrium sp.
Trigonocotyle spasskyi

Nematoda:
Anisakis sp.
Anisakis simplex

Trematoda:
Fasciola skriabini

Peoponocephalus electra (broad-beaked dolphin)

Cestoda:
Monorygma sp.

Nematoda:
Halocercus sp.

Trematoda:
Nasitrema sp.

Phocoena sp. (porpoise)

Nematoda:
Pharurus convolutus

Phocoena phocoena (finned or harbor porpoise)

Acanthocephala:
Corynosoma alaskensis
Corynosoma semerme
Corynosoma strumosum

Cestoda:
Diphyllobothrium lanceolatum
Diphyllobothrium latum
Diphyllobothrium stemmacephalum
Pyramicocephalus phocarum

Nematoda:
Anisakis simplex
Anisakis typica

Halocercus inflexocaudatus
Halocercus invaginatus
Halocercus ponticus
Halocercus taurica
Pharurus convolutes
Pharurus inflexus
Porrocaecum sp.
Porrocaecum decipiens
Pseudalius inflexus
Stenurus minor
Torynurus convolutus

Trematoda:
Campula oblonga
Distomum pallasii
Distomum philocholum
Hadwenius nipponicus
Lecithodesmus nipponicus
Opisthorchis tenuicollis
Pholeter gastrophilus

Phocoena phocoena relicta (Black Sea porpoise)

Nematoda:
Stenurus minor

Phocoena vomerina (harbor porpoise)

Trematoda:
Campula oblonga

Phocoenoides dalli (Dall porpoise)

Cestoda:
Phyllobothrium sp.

Nematoda:
Anisakis sp.
Anisakis simplex
Anisakis typical
Halocercus sp.
Halocercus kirbyi
Placentonema sp.
Stenurus sp.
Stenurus minor
Torynurus dalli

Trematoda:
Campula oblonga
Nasitrema dalli

Physeter catodon (sperm whale)

Acanthocephala:
   Bolbosoma brevicolle
   Bolbosoma capitatum
   Bolbosoma physeteris
   Corynosoma curilensis

Cestoda:
   Diplogonoporus sp.
   Hexagonoporus physeteris
   Phyllobothrium sp.
   Phyllobothrium delphini
   Phyllobothrium physeteris
   Priapocephalus grandis
   Tetrabothrium curilensis
   Tetrabothrius affinis
   Tetrabothrius wilsoni
   Tetraphyllidean sp.
   Trigonocotyle sp.

Nematoda:
   Anisakis sp.
   Anisakis catodontis
   Anisakis ivanizkii
   Anisakis physeteris
   Anisakis simplex
   Anisakis skrjabini
   Placentonema gigantissima

Trematoda:
   Zalophotrema curilensis

_____

Platanista gangetica (Susu or blind river dolphin)

Nematoda:
   Anisakis simplex
   Ascaris delphini
   Ascaris lobulata
   Contracaecum lobulatum

Trematoda:
   Cyclorchis campula
   Distoma andersoni
   Echinochasmus andersoni

_____

Pontoporia blainvillei (La Plata or Franciscana dolphin)

Acanthocephala:
   Corynosoma sp.

Nematoda:
   Contracaecum sp.

_____

Prodelphinus sp. (dolphin)

Nematoda:
   Anisakis typica

_____

Prodelphinus longirostris (long-beaked dolphin)

Trematoda:
   Delphinicola tenuis

_____

Pseudorca crassidens (false killer whale)

Acanthocephala:
   Bolbosoma capitatum

Nematoda:
   Anisakis simplex

Trematoda:
   Nasitrema attenuata
   Nasitrema globicephalae

_____

Sotalia fluviaitlis (Amazon River dolphin)

Trematoda:
   Amphimerus lancea
   Unidentified trematoda eggs

_____

Sotalia guianensis (Guiana dolphin)

Nematoda:
   Halocercus brasiliensis

_____

Sotalia tucuxii (Amazon River dolphin)

Trematoda:
   Amphimerus lancea

_____

Sousa chinensis (Chinese white-sided dolphin)

Nematoda:

Anisakis alexandri

Stenella attenuata (narrow-snouted dolphin)

Cestoda:

Monorygma sp.
Phyllobothrium sp.

Stenella caeruleoalba (striped or blue white dolphin)

Cestoda:

Monorygma sp.
Phyllobothrium sp.

Nematoda:

Anisakis sp.
Anisakis typica

Stenella graffmani (Eastern Pacific spotted dolphin)

Acanthocephala:

Bolbosoma balaenae
Bolbosoma vasculosum

Cestoda:

Monorygma sp.
Monorygma grimaldii
Phyllobothrium sp.
Phyllobothrium delphini
Strobilocephalus sp.
Strobilocephalus triangularis
Tetrabothrius forsteri

Nematoda:

Anisakis simplex
Crassicauda sp.
Mastigonema stenella

Trematoda:

Braunina cordiformis
Campula rochebruni
Nasitrema stenosoma
Zalophotrema pacificus

Stenella longirostris (long beaked dolphin)

Acanthocephala:

Bolbosoma balaenae
Bolbosoma vasculosum

Cestoda:

Diphyllobothrium fuhrmanni
Monorygma sp.
Phyllobothrium sp.
Phyllobothrium delphini
Tetrabothrius forsteri

Nematoda:

Anisakis simplex
Mastigonema stenella

Trematoda:

Campula laevicaecum
Campula rochebruni
Delphinicola tenuis
Lecithodesmus nipponicus
Zalophotrema pacificus

Stenella roseiventris (Hawaiian spinner dolphin)

Cestoda:

Monorygma sp.
Phyllobothrium sp.

Trematoda:

Lecithodesmus sp.

Steno bredanensis (rough-toothed dolphin)

Acanthocephala:

Bolbosoma capitatum

Cestoda:

Stobilocephalus triangularis
Tetrabothrius fosteri
Trigonocotyle prudhoei

Nematoda:

Anisakis sp.

Steno frontatus (dolphin)

Cestoda:

Tetrabothrius forsteri

Carnivora

Steno rostratus (dolphin)

Acanthocephala:
Bolbosoma capitatum

Cestoda:
Tetrabothrius forsteri

Turisops gillii (Pacific bottlenosed dolphin)

Trematoda:
Nasitrema sp.

Turisops truncatus (bottlenosed dolphin)

Acanthocephala:
Corynosoma cetaceum

Cestoda:
Diphyllobothrium sp.
Monorygma delphini
Monorygma grimaldii
Phyllobothrium sp.
Phyllobothrium delphini

Nematoda:
Anisakis simplex
Anisakis typica
Crassicauda crassicauda
Halocercus lagenorhynchus
Stenurus ovatus

Trematoda:
Braunina cordiformis
Nasitrema sp.
Synthesium tursionis
Zalophotrema hepaticum

Ziphius cavirostris (goose-beaked or Cuvier whale)

Cestoda:
Phyllobothrium sp.

Nematoda:
Anisakis sp.
Crassicauda boopis
Crassicauda crassicauda

Enhydra lutris (sea otter)

Acanthocephala:
Corynosoma sp.
Corynosoma enhydri
Corynosoma macrosomum
Corynosoma strumosum
Corynosoma villosum

Acarina:
Halarachne miroungae

Anoplura:
Echinophthirius fluctus

Cestoda:
Diplogonoporus tetrapterus
Pyramicocephalus phocarum

Nematoda:
Porrocaecum decipiens
Terranova decipiens

Trematoda:
Cryptocotyle fusiforme
Microphallus enhydrae
Microphallus pirum
Orthosplanchnus fraterculus
Phocitrema fusiforme
Pricetrema zalophi

Enhydra lutris neris (sea otter)

Nematoda:
Phocanema decipiens

Bibliography

Anderson RC. 1959. The taxonomy of *Dipetalinema spirocauda* (Leidy, 1858) n. comb. (= *Skrajabinaria spirocauda*) and *Dirofilaria roemeri* (Linstow, 1905) n. comb. (= *Dipetalonema roemerii*). Can J Zool 37:481-493.

Arnold PW, Gaskin DE. 1975. Lungworms (Metastrongyloidea: Pseudaliidae) of harbor porpoise *Phocoena phocoena* (L. 1758). Can J Zool 53:713-735.

Ass MY. 1935. Ektoparazity baikal'skogo tyulenya (Ectoparasites of the Tyuleni Seal). Trudy Baikal'skoi Limnologicheskoi Stantsii. 6:10-45.

Babero BB, Thomas LJ. 1960. A record of *Pharurus oserkaiae* (Skrjabin, 1942) in an Alaskan whale.

Baer JG. 1969. *Diphyllobothrium pacificum*, a tapeworm from sea lions endemic in man along the coastal area of Peru. J Fish Res Bd Can 26:717-723.

Baer JG, Miranda H, Fernandez W, Medina J. 1967. Human Diphyllobothriasis in Peru. Z. Parasitenk. 28:277-289.

Ball GH. 1930. An Acanthocephalan, *Corynosoma strumosum* from the California harbor seal. Univ. Calif. Publ. Zool. 33:301-305.

Barabash-Nikiforov I. 1935. The sea otters of the Commander Islands. Jour. of Mammal. 16(4): 255-261.

Baylis HA. 1916a. Some ascarids in the British Museum (Natrual History). Parasitology 8(3): 360-378.

Baylis HA. 1916b. On *Crassicauda crassicauda* (Crepl.). Nematode and its hosts. Ann. Mag. Nat. Hist. 8(17):144-148.

Baylis HA. 1920a. On the classification of *Ascaridae*. I. The systematic value of certain characters of the alimentary canal. Parasitology 12(3):253-264.

Baylis HA. 1920b. Observations on the genus *Crassicauda*. Ann. Mag. Nat. Hist. 9(5):410-419.

Baylis HA. 1929. Parasitic Nematoda and Acanthocephala collected in 1925-1927. Discovery Reports 1:541-559.

Baylis HA. 1932. A list of worms parasitic in Cetacea. Discovery Report 6:395-418.

Baylis HA. 1933. A new species of nematode genus *Uncinaria* from a sea lion with some observations on related species. Parasitology 25:308-316.

Baylis HA, in (sic) Hamilton JE. 1934. The southern sea lion *Otaria byronia* (De Blainville). Discovery Reports 8:306.

Benson SB, Groody TC. 1942. Notes on the Dall porpoise (*Phocoenoides dalli*). Jour. of Mammal. 23(1):41-51.

Beverley-Burton B. 1978. Helminths of the alimentary track from a stranded herd of the Atlantic white-sided dolphin, *Lagenorhynchus acutus*. J Fish Res Bd Can 35:1356-1359.

Brown DH, McIntyre RW, Delli Quardi CA, Schroeder RJ. 1960. Health problems of captive dolphins and seals. J Am Vet Med Assoc 137:534-538.

Caballero y CE, Peregrina DI. 1938. Nematodos de los maniferos de México. An. Inst. Biol. Univ. Nac. México 9:289-306.

Chabaud AG. 1963. Description de *Crassicauda anthonyi* n. sp., nematode parasite renal de *Mesoplodon mirus* True. Bulletin du Museum National D' Histoire Naturelle 34(5):397-403.

Ching HL, Robinson ES. 1959. Two campulid trematodes from a new host, the harbor porpoise. J Parasitol 45:181.

Clark R. 1956. Sperm whales of the Azores. Discovery Reports. 28:239-298.

Codero EH. 1933. Sur quelques Acanthocephales de l'Amerique Meridonale, I. Am. Parasitol 1:271-279.

Cowan DF. 1966. Pathology of the pilot whale. Arch Pathol 82:178-189.

Cowan DF. 1967. Helminth parasites of the pilot whale *Globicephala melaena* (Traill 1809). J Parasitol 53:166-167

Dailey MD. 1969. *Stictodora ubelakeri* a new species of heterophyid trematode from the California sea lion (*Zalophus californianus*). Bulletin of the Southern California Academy of Sciences 68(2):82-85.

Dailey MD. 1970. The transmission of *Parafilaroides decorus* (Nematode: *Metastrongyloidae*) in the California sea lion (*Zalophus californianus*). Proc. Helminthol. Soc. Wash. 37:215-222.

Dailey MD. 1975. The distribution and intraspecific variation of helminth parasites in pinnipeds. Rapport et Proces-Verbaux des Reunions-Conseil International pour l'Exploration de la Mer, 169: 338-352.

Dailey MD, Brownell RL Jr. 1972. A checklist of marine mammal parasites. *In*: Mammals of the Sea, Biology and Medicine, ed. Ridgway SH. Charles C. Thomas, Springfield, IL, pp. 528-589.

Dailey MD, Hill BL. 1970. A survey of metazoan parasites infesting the California (*Zalophus californianus*) and Steller (*Eumetopias jubatus*) sea lion. Bull. S. California Acad. Sci. 69:126-132.

Dailey MD, Perrin WF. 1973. Helminth parasites of the genus *Stenella* in the Easter tropical Pacific, with descriptions of two new species: *Mastigonema stenella* gen. et *sp*. n. (Nematoda: *Spiruroidea*) and *Zalophotrema pacificum sp*. n. (Trematoda: *Digenea*). Fishery Bulletin 71: 455-471.

Davey JT. 1971. A revision of the genus *Anisakis* Dujardin, 1845 (Nematoda: *Ascaridata*). J Helminthol 45:51-72.

Dawes B. 1946. The Trematoda with special reference to British and other European forms. Cambridge University Press. 644 pp.

Delyamure SL. 1955. Helminthofauna of Marine Mammals (Ecology and Phylogeny). Academy of Sciences USSR, pp. 1-522. (Translated by Israel Program for Scientific Translation, 1968 for the US Department of Interior and National Science Foundation). National Technical Informational Services, US Department of Commerce, Springfield, VA.

Delyamure SL. Kleinenberg SE, 1958. New data on the helminthfauna of the porpoise *Delphinapterus leucas*. Byull. Mosk. Obshcn. Ispytat. Prerody. Otd. Biol. 63:25-32.

Doetschman WH. 1941. The occurrence of mites in pinnipeds, including a new species from the California sea lion, *Zalophus califorianus*. J. Parasitol, 27(supp #37):23.

Doetschman WH.1944a. A new species of endoparasitic mite of the family *Halarachnidae* (Acarina). T Am Micros Soc 63:68-72.

Doetschman WH.1944b. Notes on Anoplura infesting marine carnivores. J Parasitol 30:200.

Dougherty EC. 1949a. A list of the *Trichostrongylid* lungworms (phylum Nematoda) and a key to the six genera. Parasitology 39(3,4):218-221.

Dougherty EC. 1949b. The Phylogeny of the Nematode Family *Metastrongylidae* Leiper (1909): a correlation of the host and symbiotic evolution. Parasitology 39 (3,4):222-234.

Dougherty EC, Herman CM. 1947. New species of the Genus *Parafilaroides* Dougherty, 1946 (Nematoda: *Melastrongylidae*) from Sea Lions, with a list of the Lungworms of the Pinnipedia. P Helm Soc Wash 14(2):77-87.

Drummond FH. 1937. Lady Julia Percy Island: Report of the Expedition of the McCoy Society for Field Investigation and Research. Proc Roy Soc Victoria 49 (16) Cestoda: 401-406.

Edmonds SJ. 1957. Acanthocephala. B.A.N.Z. Antarctic Res. Exped. 1929-1931. Reports Ser. B. (Zoology and Botany) 6(5):91-98.

Edmonds SJ. 1955. Acanthocephala collected by the Australian National Antarctic Research Expedition on Heard Island and Macquarie Island during 1948-1950. T Roy Soc South Aust 78:141-144.

Eguchi S. 1934. On the secondary intermediate host of *Diphyllobothrium latum* in Japan, with special reference to fishes of the genus *Oncorhynchus*. Proc. 5th Pacific Sci. Cong. (Canada, 1933), 5:4145-4149.

Enderlein G. 1906. Laussetudien 5. Schuppen sla sekundare Atmungsor, soure uber eine neue antarktische Echinophthiriiden-Gattung. 12. Beitrag zur Kenntris der antarkischen Fauna. Zool. Anz, 29:659-665.

Ferris GF. 1916. Anoplura from sea lions of the Pacific Ocean. Entomol News 27:366-370.

Ferris GF. 1942. Observations on some ectoparasites mites (Arachida: Acarina: *Dermanyssidae.* Microentomology 7:77-83.

Finnegan S. 1934. On a new species of mite of the family *Halarachnidae* from the southern sea lion. Discovery Reports 8:319-327.

Fisher WK. 1952. The status of the harbour seal in British Columbia, with particular reference to the Skeena River. Fish Res. Bd. Can. Bull. 93:1-58 pp.

Fukui T, Morisita T. 1939. Contributions to the knowledge of two species of Acanthocephala. Vol. Jubilare pro Prof. S. Yoshida. 1:137-139.

Golvan YJ. 1959. Acanthocèphales du genre *Coryonsoma* Lühe, 1904 Parasites de mammifères de' Alaska et de Midway. Ann. Parasitology Hum Comp 34:288-321.

Goto S, Ozaki Y. 1930. Brief notes on new trematodes. Jpn J Zool 3(1):73-82.

Gower WC. 1939. Host-parasite catalogue of the helminths of ducks. Am Midl Nat 22:580-628.

Guiart J. 1935. Cestodes parasites provenant des campagnes scientifiques de S.A.S. le Prince Albert ler de Monaco (1886-1913). Res. Camp. Sci. Monaco. 91:1-100.

Hamilton J. 1934. The southern sea lion *Otaria byronia* (de Blainville). Discovery Reports 8: 269-318.

Harada J. 1931. Das Nervensystem von *Bolbosoma turbinella*. Jpn J Zool 3:161-199.

Hilliard DK. 1960. Studies on the helminth fauna of Alaska XXXVIII. The taxonomic significance of eggs and coracidia of some diphyllobothriid cestodes. J Parasitol 46:703-716.

Holloway HL, Bier JW. 1967. Notes on the host specificity of *Corynosoma hamanni* L. Bull. Wildlife Disease Assoc 3:76-78.

Jellison WL. 1952. Anoplura from mammals of the Pribilof Islands. J Parasitol 38:274-275.

Jellison WL, Neiland KA. 1965. Parasites of Alaskan vertebrates. Host-parasite index. Norman, Okla., University of Oklahoma Research Institute, Proj. 1508, 73 pp.

Johnson ML, Fiscus CH, Ostenson BT, Barbour ML. 1966. Marine mammals. In: NJ Wilimovsky (Ed.): Environment of the Cape Thompson Region, Alaska, U.S. Atomic Energy Commission, Washington, 33:877-924.

Johnston DG, Ridgway SH. 1969. Parasitism in some marine mammals. J. Am. Vet. Med. Assoc., 155:1064-1072.

Johnston TH. 1937a. Report on the Trematodes of the Australasian Antarctica Expedition 1911-1914. Scientific Reports C (Zoology and Botany), Vol. X, Part 1, pp. 1-29.

Johnston TH. 1937b. Report on the Cestodes of the Australasian Antarctica Expedition 1911-1914. Scientific Reports C (Zoology and Botany) Vol. X, No. 4, pp. 1-74.

Johnston TH. 1937c. Report on the Parasitic Nematodes of the Australasian Antarctic Expedition 1911-1914. Scientific Reports C (Zoology and Botany) Vol. X, No. 5, pp. 1-31.

Johnston TH. 1937d. Report on Acarina of the Australasian Antarctic Expedition 1911-1914. Scientific Reports C (Zoology and Botany) Vol. X, No. 6, pp. 1-24.

Johnston TH. 1937e. Entozoa from the Australian hair seal. Proc. Linn. Soc. New South Wales 62:9-16.

Johnston TH, Best EW. 1937. Acanthocephala of the Australasian Antarctica Expedition. Scient. Rep. - Australasian Antarctica Expedition, Scientific Reports C (Zoology and Botany) Vol. X. Part 2, pp. 1-20.

Johnston TH, Best EW. 1942. Australian Acanthocephala No. 3. T Roy Soc South Aust 66:250-254.

Johnston TH, Deland E. 1929. Australian Acanthocephala, No. 1, Census of recorded hosts and
parasites. Royal Soc. Of South Australia, Trans-
actions and Proceedings 53:146-154.

Johnston TH, Edmonds SJ. 1953. Acanthocephala
from Auckland and Campbell Islands. Records
of the Dominion Museum, 2(2):55-61.

Johnston TH, Mawson PM. 1941. Nematodes from
Australian marine mammals. Rec. S. Aust., Mus.
6:429-434.

Johnston TH, Mawson PM. 1945. Parasitic nematodes. Rep. B.A.N.Z. Antarctic Research Exped.
1929-1931, Reports-Ser. B. 5:73-159.

Joyeux C, Baer JG. 1936. Cestodes. Faune Fr., 30,
Cestodes. P. Lechevalier, Paris, 613 pp.

Kagei N, Oshima T, Kobayashi A, Kumada M,
Koyama T, Komiya Y, Takemura A, Takemura
A. 1967. Survey of *Anisakis* spp. (*Anisakinae*,
Nematoda) on marine mammals in the coast of
Japan. Japan. Journal of Parasitology 16:427-435.

Kenyon KW. 1962. Notes on phocid seals at the Little Diomede Island, Alaska. J Wildlife Manage
26:380-387.

Kenyon KW. 1969. The sea otter in the eastern Pacific Ocean. North American Fauna 68. Washington, D.C. 352 pp.

Kenyon KW, Yunker CE, Newell IM. 1965. Nasal
mites (Halarachnidae) in the sea otter. J Parasitol 51:960.

Keyes MC. 1965. Pathology of the northern fur seal.
J Am Vet Med Assoc, 147:1090-1095.

King JE. 1964. Seals of the World. London, British
Museum of Natural History, 154 pp.

King JE. 1983. Seals of the World. 2nd Edition. London, British Museum of Natural History. Com-
stock Publishing Associates/Cornell Univ. Press.

Kleinenberg SE, Yablokov AV, Belkovich BM, Tara-
sevich MN. 1964. Beluga (*Delphinapterus leucas*):
Investigation of the species. Moscow: Akademii
Nauk SSSR. (Translation from original Russian
by Israel Program for Scientific Translations, Jerusalem, 1969.)

Klumov SK. 1963. Food and helminth fauna of
whalebone whales (*Mystacoceti*) in the main
whaling regions of the world oceans. Trudy In-
stituta Okeanologii, 71, 94-194 [transl. by Th.
Pidhayny, Fisheries Research Board of Canada,
Translation Series No. 589, 1965].

Kreis HA. 1938. Beiträge zur Kenntnis Parasitischer
Nematoden. 6. Parasitische Nematoden aus dem
Zoologischen Garten in Basel. Centralbl. Bakt.,
Parasitenkunde Infekt. I Abt., Org. Bd. 141, Heft.
5/6:279-304.

Kruidenier FJ. 1954. A seal host of the acanthocephalan Corynosoma: correction (rn). J Parasitol
40:363.

Kuitunen E. 1956. Walrus meat as a source of trich-
nosis in Eskimos. C J Public Health 45:30.

Kurochkin YV. 1975. Parasites of the Caspian seal
Pusa caspica. Rapports et Procès verbaux du Co-
seill international pour l'Exploration de la Mer
169:363-365.

Layne JN, Caldwell DK. 1964. Behavior of the Amazon dolphin, *Inia geoffrensis* (Blainville), in captivity. Zoologica-NY 49:81-108.

Leidy J. 1890. Notices of Entozoa. Proc. Acad. Nat.
Sci. Philia. 42:410-418.

Leiper RT, Atkinson EL. 1914. Helminths of the British Antarctic Expedition 1910-1913. Proc. Zool.
Soc. London, 1:222-226.

Leiper RT, Atkinson EL. 1915. Parasitic Worms with
a Note on a Free-living Nematode. Brit. Mus.
Nat. Hist., Brit. Antarctic (Terra Nova) Expedition, 1910, Nat. Hist. Rep. Zool. 2(3):19-60.

Linstow O. 1892. Helminthen von Sud-Georgien.
Jahrb. Der Hamburgischen Wiss. Ges. 9, 2,
ss.1-19.

Linstow O. 1906. Nematodes of the Scottish National Antarctic Expedition, 1902-1904. Proc.
Roy Soc. Edinburgh 26 (6) 464-472. [Communi-
cated by W.S. Bruce in 1906; issued separately
on January 4, 1907].

Linstow O. 1907. *Ascaris lobulata*, Schneider, ein Par-
asit des Darms von *Platanista gangetice*. Journ.
and Proc. Asiat. Soc. Bengal, Bd. 3, ss. 37-38.

Linton E. 1905. Notes on Cestode cysts; *Taenia
chamissonii*, new species from a porpoise. Proc.
U.S. Nat. Mus., 28:819-822.

Lyster LL. 1940. Parasites of some Canadian sea mammals. Canad. Jour. Research, 18:395-409.

Margolis L. 1954. List of parasites recorded from sea mammals caught off the coast of North America. J. Fish. Res. Bd. Canada 11:267-283.

Margolis L. 1956. Parasitic helminths and arthropods from Pinnipedia of the Canadian Pacific Coast. J. Fish. Res. Bd. Canada, 13:489-505.

Margolis L, Dailey MD. 1972. Revised annotated list of parasites from sea mammals caught off the west coast of North America. NOAA technical report NMFS, SSRF-647:1-23.

Margolis L, Pike GC. 1955. Some helminth parasites of Canadian pacific whales. J. Fish Res. Bd. Canada, 12:97-120.

Markowski S. 1952a. The cestodes of seals from the Antarctic. Brit. Bull Nat. Hist. 1:125-150.

Markowski S. 1952b. The cestodes of pinnipeds in the Arctic and other regions. J Helminthol 26:171-214.

Markowski S. 1955. Cestodes of whales and dolphins from the Discovery collection. Discovery Reports. 27:377-395.

Martin WE, Haun CK, Barrows HS, Cravioto H. 1970. Nematode damage to brain of striped dolphin *Lagenorynchus obliquidens*. T Am Microsc Soc 89(2) 200-205.

Matthews LH. 1937. The humpback whale, *Megaptera nodosa*. Discovery Reports 17:7-92.

Mawson PM. 1953. Parasitic nematode collected by the Australian National Antarctic Research Expedition: Heard Island and Macquarie Island, 1948-1951. Parasitology 43:291-297.

McEwin BW. 1957. Cestodes from Mammals, B.A.N.Z Antarctic Research Expedition, Reports Series B (Zoology and Botany). Volume VI, Part 4: pp. 75 - 90.

Meyer A. 1933. Acanthocephala. Bronn's Klass. U. Ordn. D. Tierreichs. V.4, abt.2, Buch 2, Lief. 2, 333-582. Akedemische Verlagsgesellschaft, Leipzig.

Migaki G, Van Dyke D, Hubbard RC. 1971. Some histopathological lesions caused by helminths in marine mammals. Jour. Wildlife Diseases 7:281-289.

Montreuil P. 1958. *Corynosoma magdaleni sp. nov.* (Acanthocephala) a parasite of the grey seal in eastern Canada. Can J Zool 36:205-215.

Murav'eva SI, Treskchev VV. 1970. Novaya tsestoda - *Priapocephalus eschrichtii sp. n.* (Cestode, Tetrabothriidae) - parazit serogo kita iz Chukotsogo Morya [New cestoda - *Priapocephalus eschrichtii sp. n.* (Tetrabothriidae) - a parasite of the gray whale (*Eschrichtius gibbosus* Erzleben, 1777) from the Chuhotsk Sea]. Vestnik Zool., Akad. Nauk. Ukr. SSR, 1970: 84-86.

Murray MD, Nicholls DG. 1965. Studies on the ectoparasites of seals and penguins 1. The ecology of the louse, *Lepidophthirus lacrorhini*, Enderlein on the southern elephant seal, *Mirounga leonina* (L.). Aust J Zoolog 13:437-454.

Murray MD, Smith MSR, Soucek Z. 1965. Studies on the ectoparasites of seals and penguins, II. The ecology of the louse *Antarctophthrius ogmorhini* Enderlein on the Weddell seal, *Leptonychotes weddelli* Lesson. Aust J Zoolog 13:761-771.

Myers BJ. 1957. Ascaroid parasites of harp seals (*Phoca groenlandica erxleben*) from the Magdalen Islands, Quebec. Can J Zool 35:291-292.

Myers BJ. 1959. *Phocanema*, a new genus for the anisakid nematode of seals. Can J Zool 37:459–465.

Neiland KA. 1961. Suspected role of parasites in non-rookery mortality of fur seals (*Callorhinus ursinus*). J Parasitol 47:732.

Neiland KA. 1962. Alaskan species of acanthocephalan genus *Corynosoma* Luehe, 1904. J Parasitol 48:69-75.

Neiland KA, Rice DW, Holden BL. 1970. Helminths of marine mammals, Part 1. The genus *Nasitrema*, air sinus flukes of delphinid Cetacean. J Parasitol 56:305-316.

Newell IM. 1947. Studies on the morphology and systematics of the family *Halarachnidae* Oudemans, 1906 (Acari, Parasitoidea). B Bingham OceÃnogr C 10(4):235-266.

Nikol BB, Holloway HL Jr. 1968. Morphology of the presoma of *Corynosoma hamanni* (Arctocephala: Polymorphidae). J Morphol 124:217-226.

Norris KS, Prescott JH. 1961. Observations on Pacific cetaceans of California and Mexican waters. Univ. Calif. Pub. Zool. 63:291-370.

Nybelin O. 1931. Saügetier-und and Vogelcestoden von Juan Fernandez. The Natural History of Juan Fernandez and Easter Island. Uppsala 3-4:493-524.

Oudemans AC. 1916. Acarologische aanteekeningen LX. Ent. Ber. Amst., 4:308-316.

Oudemans AC. 1926. Halarachne-Studien. Arch. Naturgesch., Abt. A. 91(7):48-108.

Perry ML. 1967. A new species of *Dipetalonema* from the California sea lion and a report of Microfilariae from a Steller sea lion (Nematoda: *Filaroidea*). J Parasitol 53:1076-1981.

Price EW. 1932. The trematode parasites of marine mammals. Proc. U.S. Nat. Mus., 81 (13):1-68.

Prudhoe S. 1969. Cestodes from fish, birds and whales. Reports B.A.N.Z. Antarctic Research Expedition, Series B 8:171-193.

Railliet A. 1899. Sur quelques parasites rencontres a l'autopsie d'une Phoque (*Phoca vitulina* L.) Comp. Rend. Soc. Biol. (Paris) 51:128-130.

Railliet A, Henry ACL. 1907. Nemathelminthes Parasites. Expid. Antarctique Francaise (1903-1905), Vers S. 11-15:1-14.

Rand RW. 1959. The Cape fur seal (*Arctocephalus pusillus*). Distribution, abundance, and feeding habits off the southwestern coast of the Cape Province. South African Division of Sea Fisheries Investigation Report 34:1-75.

Ransom BH. 1921. Synopsis of the trematode family *Heterophyidae* with descriptions of a new genus and five new species. Proc. U.S. Nat. Mus. Washington, 57:527-573.

Rausch R. 1953. Studies on the helminth fauna of Alaska. XIII. Disease in the sea otter, with special reference to helminth parasites. Ecology 34:584-604.

Rausch RL 1964. Studies on the helminth fauna of Alaska. XLI. Observations on cestodes of the genus *Diplogonoporus* Lönnberg 1892 (*Diphyllobothrium*). Can J Zoology 42:1049-1069.

Rausch RL. 1969. Diphyllobothriid cestodes from the Hawaiian monk seal, *Monachus schauinslandi* Matschie, from Midway Atoll. J. Fish Res. Bd. Canada, 26:947-956.

Rausch RL, Babero BB, Rausch RV, Schiller EL. 1956. Studies on the helminth fauna of Alaska. XXVII. The occurrence of larvae of *Trichinella spiralis* in Alaskan mammals. J Parasitol 42:259-271.

Rausch RL, Fay FH. 1966. Studies on the helminth fauna of Alaska XLIV. Revision of *Ogmogaster* Jaggerskïod, 1891, with a description of *O. pentalineatus sp.* n. (Trematoda: *Notocotylidae*). J Parasitol 52:26-38.

Rausch RL, Hilliard DK. 1970. Studies on the helminth fauna of Alaska. XLIX. The occurrence of *Diphyllobothrium latum* in Alaska with notes in other species. Can J Zool 48:1201-1219.

Rausch RL, Locker B. 1951. Studies of the helminth fauna of Alaska II. On some helminthes parasitic in the sea otter (*Enhydra lutris*) L. P Helm Soc Wash 18:77-81.

Rausch RL, Margolis L. 1969. *Plicobothrium globicephalae* gen. et *sp.* nov. (Ceastoda: *Diphyllobothriidae*) from the pilot whale, *Globicephalae melaena* Traill, in Newfoundland Waters. Can J Zoolog 47:745-750.

Rausch RL, Rice DW. 1970. *Ogmogaster trilineatus sp.* n. (Trematoda: *Notocotylidae*) from the fin whale, *Balaenoptera physalus* L. P Helm Soc Wash 37:196-200.

Rees G. 1953. A record of some parasites worms from whales in the Ross Sea area. Parasitology 43:27-34.

Rennie J. 1905-1906. "Scotia" collection . On *Echinorhynchus antarcticus* n. *sp.* and its allies. Proc. Roy. Soc. Edinburgh, 26:437-446.

Rennie J, Reid A. 1912. The Cestoda of the Scottish Antarctic Expedition (Scotia). Trans. Roy. Soc. Edinburgh, 48:441-453.

Rice DW. 1963. Progress report on biological studies of the larger Cetacean in the waters off California. Norsk Hvalfangst Tid. 7:181-187.

Rice DW, Scheffer VB. 1968. A list of the marine mammals of the world. U.S. Fish and Wildlife Serv., Special Scientific Rept. 579:1-16.

Rice DW, Wolman AA. 1971. The Life History and Ecology of the Gray Whale (*Eschrichtius robustus*). American Society of Mammalogists, Special Publication No. 3, 142 pp.

Roth H. 1949. Trichinosis in Arctic Animals. Nature 163:805-806.

Scheffer VB, Slipp JW. 1944. The Harbor Seal in Washington State. Am Midl Nat 32:373-416.

Schiller EL. 1954. Studies on the helminth fauna of Alaska, XVII. Notes on the intermediate stages of some helminth parasites of the sea otter. Biol Bull 106:107-121.

Schmidt-Ries H. 1939. Die bisher bei Kleinen Tümmler (*Phocaena phocaena* L.) festgestellten Parasiten. Z. Bakt. Abt. I Orig., 145:89-106.

Scott DM, Fisher HD. 1958a. Incidence of a parasitic ascarid, *Porrocaecum decipiens*, in the common porpoise, *Phocoena phocoena*, from the lower Bay of Fundy. Jour. Fish. Res. Board. Canada. 15:1-4.

Scott DM, Fisher HD. 1958b. Incidence of the ascarid *Porrocaecum decipiens* in the stomachs of three species of seals along the southern Canadian Atlantic mainland. Jour. Fish. Res. Bd. Canada, 15:495-516.

Shchupakov I. 1936. Parazitofauna kaspiiskogo tyulenya. K voprosu o parazitofauna reliktov. (The Parasitofauna of the Caspian Seal. The Problem of the Parasitofauna of Relict Animals). Uchenye Zapiski Leningradskogo Gosudarstvennogo Universiteta, Seriya Biologicheskaya, No. 7(3):134-143.

Skrjabin KI. 1944. On trematodes of the genus *Odhneriella* Skrjabin 1915, parasitic of sea mammals. Comptes Rend. (Doklady) Acad. USSR 44:302-303.

Southwell T, Walker AJ. 1936. Notes on a larval Cestode from a fur seal. Ann. Trop. Med. Parasitology 30:91-100.

Spaul EA. 1926. *Crassicauda bennetti, sp.* n., a new nematode parasite from the bottled-nosed whale (*Hyperoodon*). Ann. Mag. Nat. Hist. 9 (17): 581-585.

Stiles CW, Hassall A. 1899. VII. Internal parasites of the fur seal. *In*: The Fur Seals and Fur Seal Islands of the North Pacific Ocean (David Starr Jordan Report 1899), part 3, pp. 99-177. U.S. Treasury Department. Washington, DC.

Stunkard HW. 1948. Pseudophyllidean cestodes from Alaskan pinnipeds. J Parasitol 34:211-228.

Stunkard HW, Alvey CH. 1929. A new liver fluke, *Zalophotrema hepaticum*, from the California sea lion, *Zalophus californianus*. J Parasitol 16:106-107.

Stunkard HW, Schoenborn HW. 1936. Notes on the structure, distribution and synonyms of *Diphyllobothrium lanceolatum*. Amer Mus Novit 880:1-9.

Taylor AER, Brown DH, Heyneman D, McIntyre RW. 1961. Biology of the filarioid nematode *Dipetalonema spirocauda* (Leidy, 1858) from the heart of captive harbor seals and sea lions, together with pathology of the hosts. J Parasitol 47:971-976.

Tomilin AG. 1967. Mammals of the U.S.S.R. and adjacent countries (1957). Jerusalem, Israel Program for Scientific Translations 9:1-717.

Treshchev VV. 1966. A new trematode *Orthosplanchus sudarikovi* nov. *sp.*(Campuldae) from the beluga. In Russian. Mat. K. Konf. Vsesoyoir. Obva Gel'minthol. 3 Izat. Akad. Nauk. USSR, Moscow.

Treshchev VV. 1968. The new campulid *Orthosplanchnus albamarinus sp.* n. (Trematoda, Campuldae) - parasite of the white whale. Zool. Zhur. 47:937-940. (In Russian, English summary).

Treshchev VV, Serdyukov AM, Yurakhno MV. 1969. *Orthosplanchnus odobaeni* n.*sp.* (Trematoda, Campulidae) from the Pacific walrus. Nauchnye Doklady Vysshei Shkoly, Biologicheskie Nauki (8):7-9.

Tubb JA. 1937. Lady Julia Percy Island: Report of the Expedition of the McCoy Society for Field Investigation and Research. Proc Roy Soc Victoria 49 (19) Arachnida: 412-419.

Van Cleave HJ. 1953. Acanthocephala of North American mammals. Illinois Biol. Monogr. 23:1-179.

Van Thiel PH. 1966. The final hosts of the herringworm *Anisakis marina*. Trop. Geogr. Med., 18:310-328.

Wardle RA, McLeod JA, Stewart IE. 1947. Lühe's *"Diphyllobothrium"* (Cestoda). J Parasitol 33:319-330.

Weber NA. 1950. A survey of the insects and related arthropods of Arctic Alaska. Part I. T Am Entomol Soc 76 (3):147-206.

Williams HH. 1968. The taxonomy, ecology, and hosts specificity of some *Phyllobothriidae* (Cestoda: *Tetraphyllidea*), a critical revision of *Phyllobothrium* Beneden, 1849 and comments on some allied genera. Phil. Trans. Royal. Soc. London, Series B, Biol. Sci., 253:231-307.

Wilson TM, Stockdale PH. 1970. The harp seal, *Pagophilus groenlandicus* (Erxleben, 1777) XI. Contracaecum *sp.* infestation in a harp seal. J Wild Diseases 6:152-154.

Wormersley H. 1937. Acarina found in the Weddell seal from Commonwealth Bay and King George V. Land. Report on Acarina of the Australasian Antarctic Expedition 1911-1914. Scientific Reports C (Zoology and Botany) Vol. X Part 6.

Wulker G. 1930. Ueber Nematoden aus Nordseetieren. II - Zool. Anz. Leipzig 88:1-16.

Yamaguti S. 1939. Studies on the helminth fauna of Japan, Part 29, Acanthocephala II. Japan. Jour. Zool. 8(3):317-351.

Yamaguti S. 1958. Systema Helminthum, Vol. I. The Digenetic Trematodes of Vertebrates, Part I. Interscience, Inc., New York.

Yamaguti S. 1959. Systema Helminthium, Vol. II. The Cestoda of Vertebrates. Interscience, New York-London, 1-860.

Yamaguti S. 1961. Systema Helminthum, Vol. III. The Nematodes of Vertebrates. Interscience, New York.

Yamaguti S. 1963. Systema Helminthum Vol. V Acanthocephala. Interscience, New York - London, 1-423.

Young MR. 1939. Helminth Parasites of Australia. Imperial Bureau of Agricultural Parasitology (Helminthology). 145 pp.

Yurakhno MV. 1968. *Microphallus orientalis* n. *sp.* (Trematoda: *Microphallidae*), a parasite of the Pacific walrus and bearded seal. Zool Zh 77:630-631.

About the Author

John R. Felix is currently the Deputy Director of the Municipal Services Division at the Massachusetts Department of Environmental Protection. He also is a part-time lecturer at Northeastern University's Department of Marine and Environmental Sciences. Mr. Felix received his undergraduate degree in Fisheries Biology from the University of Massachusetts (Amherst), a M.S. degree in Biology from San Diego State University, and a M.P.A. degree from the Kennedy School at Harvard University. His current interests include assessing tools used for environmental protection, and climate change adaptation.

Nebraska
UNIVERSITY OF
Lincoln®

www.ingramcontent.com/pod-product-compliance
Lightning Source LLC
Chambersburg PA
CBHW080333270326
41927CB00014B/3208

* 9 7 8 1 6 0 9 6 2 0 4 2 4 *